Bonus study and revision support available **free,** online

online resource centre
www.oxfordtextbooks.co.uk/orc/concentrate/

Take your learning further:

➤ Multiple-choice questions

➤ Revision technique advice

➤ An interactive glossary

➤ Outline exam answers

➤ Flashcards of key cases

. . . and much more

New to this edition

- Fully updated in light of recent developments in the law including the *Family Justice Review*, *The Hague Convention 1996*, and the *Children and Families Bill*
- Includes recent case law on same sex marriage, adoption, and international parent-child abduction
- New problem question on Adoption to help aid learning
- Updated diagram on International Child Abduction to help explain the routes available to affect a return
- New '*Looking for Extra Marks*' features to help students prepare for their Family Law exam

Acknowledgements

We would like to thank the team at OUP and everyone else involved in the production of this book. However, particular thanks go to John Heenan for his advice and support, without which this book would not have been completed on time.

Family Law
Concentrate

2nd edition

Susan Heenan

Principal Lecturer in Law,
University of the West of England

Anna Heenan

Solicitor, Gregg Latchams LLP

OXFORD
UNIVERSITY PRESS

OXFORD

Great Clarendon Street, Oxford, OX2 6DP,
United Kingdom

Oxford University press is a department of the University of Oxford.
It furthers the University's objective of excellence in research, scholarship,
and education by publishing worldwide. Oxford is a registered trade mark of
Oxford University press in the UK and in certain other countries

© Oxford University Press 2013

The moral rights of the authors have been asserted

First Edition published in 2012

All rights reserved. No part of this publication may be reproduced, stored in
a retrieval system, or transmitted, in any form or by any means, without the
prior permission in writing of Oxford University press, or as expressly permitted
by law, by licence or under terms agreed with the appropriate reprographics
rights organization. Enquiries concerning reproduction outside the scope of the
above should be sent to the Rights Department, Oxford University Press, at the
address above

You must not circulate this work in any other form
and you must impose this same condition on any acquirer

Public sector information reproduced under Open Government Licence v1.0
(http://www.nationalarchives.gov.uk/doc/open-government-licence/open-government-licence.htm)

Crown Copyright material reproduced with the permission of the
Controller, HMSO (under the terms of the Click Use licence)

Published in the United States of America by Oxford University Press
198 Madison Avenue, New York, NY 10016, United States of America

British Library Cataloguing in Publication Data

Library of Congress Control Number: 2013936558

Printed in Great Britain by
Ashford Colour Press Ltd, Gosport, Hampshire

Links to third party websites are provided by Oxford in good faith and
for information only. Oxford disclaims any responsibility for the materials
contained in any third party website referenced in this work.

QR Code images are used throughout this book. QR Code is a registered trademark of
DENSO WAVE INCORPORATED. You can scan the code with your mobile device to launch the
relevant webpage from the Online Resource Centre. If your mobile device does not have a
QR Code reader try this website for advice www.mobile-barcodes.com/qr-code-software.

Coventry University College

Contents

Table of cases		vi
Table of legislation		ix
1	Family relationships, marriage, civil partnership, cohabitation	1
2	Nullity	18
3	Divorce, dissolution, and judicial separation	36
4	Domestic violence	54
5	Financial provision on divorce or dissolution	77
6	The Children Act—the private law	101
7	The Children Act—the public law	123
8	Adoption	142
9	International parent–child abduction	162
Exam essentials		A1
Outline answers		A3
Glossary		A8
Index		A11

Table of cases

A and B v Essex County Council [2002] EWHC 2709 (Fam) . . . 151

A County Council v M & F [2011] EWHC 1804 . . . 139

A Local Authority v Y, Z and Others [2006] 2 FLR 41 . . . 155

A v A (Maintenance Pending Suit: Provision for Legal Fees) [2001] 1 FLR 377 . . . 79

A v A (Minors) (Shared Residence Order) [1994] 1 FLR 669 . . . 112

A v T (Abduction: Consent) (2012) . . . 171

AR (Relocation), Re [2010] EWHC 1346 (Fam); [2010] 2 FLR 1577 . . . 112

Ash v Ash [1972] Fam 135 . . . 40, A4

(Axon) v Secretary of State for Health [2006] EWHC Admin 37 . . . 104, 120

B and L v UK [2006] 1 FLR 35 . . . 22

B v B [1999] 2 FCR 251 . . . 64, 73

B v B (Financial Provision: Welfare of Child and Conduct) [2002] 1 FLR 555 . . . 89

Banks v Banks [1999] 1 FLR 726 . . . 59

Barder v Barder (Calouri Intervening) [1988] AC 20 . . . 94, 97

Baxter v Baxter [1948] AC 274 . . . 26

Bellinger v Bellinger [2003] UKHL 21 . . . 3, 24, 33

Bergin v Bergin [1983] 1 All ER 905 . . . 40

Bradley v Bradley [1973] 3 All ER 750 . . . 41

Brierley v Brierley [1918] P 257 . . . 105

Buffery v Buffery [1988] 2 FLR 365 . . . 38

Burden and Burden v UK [2007] 1 FCR 69 . . . 5

C v C [1942] NZLR 356 . . . 28

C v C (non-molestation order: jurisdiction) [1998] Fam 70 . . . 59, 73

C v Solihull MBC [1993] 1 FLR 290 . . . 116

Cannon v Cannon [2004] EWCA Civ 1330 . . . 170

Chalmers v Johns [1999] 2 FCR 110 . . . 64, 73

Chechi v Bashier [1992] 2 FLR 489 . . . 74

Chios Property Investment Ltd v Lopez [1987] 20 HLR 120 . . . 8

Cleary v Cleary [1974] 1 All ER 498 . . . 39, 51

CO v CO [2004] 1 FLR 1095 . . . 91, A5

Corbett v Corbett [1971] P83, 105–6 . . . 3, 24, 33

Crabb v Arun District Council [1976] Ch 79 . . . 12, A3

Crake v Supplementary Benefits Commission [1982] 1 All ER 498 . . . 60

CW v NT and another [2011] EWHC 33 . . . 120

CW v SG [2013] EWCA 854 (Fam) . . . 110

D (Abduction: Child's Objections), Re [2011] EWCA Civ 1294 . . . 172, 178

D v A [1845] 1 Rob Ecl 279 . . . 26

D v D (Nullity) [1979] Fam 70 . . . 32

Da Silva v Portugal [2001] 1 FCR 653 ECHR . . . 117, A6

Dennis v Dennis [1995] 2 All ER 51 . . . 39

E (Children), Re [2011] UKSC 27 . . . 172, 177, A7

Eves v Eves [1975] 1 WLR 1338 . . . 11

Fitzpatrick v Sterling Housing Association Ltd [2000] 1 FCR 21 . . . 8

Ford v Ford (1987) 17 Fam Law 232 . . . 26

Fuller (Otherwise Penfold) v Fuller [1973] 2 All ER 650 . . . 42, 51

G v G [1924] AC 349 . . . 27

G v G [1964] 1 All ER 129 . . . 41

G v G [2000] 2 FLR 533 . . . 60, 74

G v G (Occupation Order: Conduct) [2000] 2 FLR 36 . . . 59

Gereis v Yagoub [1997] 1 FLR 854 . . . 23

Gillick v West Norfolk & Wisbech Area Health Authority [1986] 1 AC 112 . . . 104, 120

Glenister v Glenister [1945] 1 All ER 513 . . . 41

Goodrich v Goodrich [1971] 2 All ER 1340 . . . 39

Goodwin v UK [2002] 2 FLR 487 . . . 24, 33

Table of cases

H (Care Plan: Human Rights), Re [2011] EWCA Civ 1009 . . . 125

H v H (Financial Relief: Attempted Murder as Conduct) [2006] Fam Law 26 . . . 92

Hirani v Hirani (1983) 4 FLR 232 . . . 28, 33, A3

Hollens v Hollens (1971) 115 SJ 237 . . . 43, 51

Horner v Horner [1982] 2 All ER 495 . . . 59, 74

Horton v Horton [1947] 2 All ER 871 . . . 27, A3

Hudson v Leigh [2009] EWHC 1306 (Fam) . . . 20, 23

Humberside County Council v B [1993] FLR 357 . . . 63

Hussain v Hussain [1982] Fam 32 . . . 4

Hyde v Hyde (1866) LR 1 P&D 130 . . . 1, 2

Hyman v Hyman [1929] AC 601 . . . 88

Imerman v Tchenguiz [2010] EWCA Civ 908 . . . 97

In the Estate of Park (deceased) [1953] 2 All ER 1411 . . . 29

In the matter of G (a child) [2008] EWCA Civ 1468 . . . 111

Islington LBC v Alas & others [2012] EWHC 865 . . . 139

James v Thomas [2007] EWCA Civ 1212 . . . 15

Joseph v Joseph [1953] 2 ALL ER 710 . . . 42

K v K (Periodical Payment: Cohabitation) [2006] 2 FLR 468 . . . 80

K v L [2010] EWHC 1234 . . . 89, 92, A5

Kaur v Singh [1972] 1 All ER 292 . . . 27, 33, A3

Kernott v Jones [2011] UKSC 53 . . . 11, 12, 15

Krystman v Krystman [1973] 1 WLR 927 . . . 91

Lancashire County Council v B [2000] 1 FLR 583 . . . 134

Langdon v Horton [1951] 1 KB 666 . . . 7, 8

Lau v DPP [2000] All ER (D) 244 . . . 71

Le Brocq v Le Brocq [1964] 1 WLR 1085 . . . 41

Leeds Teaching Hospital v A [2003] EWHC 259 . . . 121

Livingstone-Stallard v Livingstone-Stallard [1974] 2 All ER 766 . . . 40, 52, A4

Lloyds Bank PLC v Rosset [1991] AC 107 . . . 11

Mabon v Mabon and Others [2005] EWCA Civ 634 . . . 104

McCartney v Mills McCartney [2008] EWHC 401 . . . 91

Martin v Martin [1978] Fam 12 . . . 81

Mason v Mason [1972] Fam 302 . . . 43

Mehta v Mehta [1945] 2 All ER 690 . . . 28

Mendoza v Ghaidan [2004] AC 27 . . . 8

Mercredi v Chaffe [2011] EWCA Civ 272 . . . 169

Mesher v Mesher [1980] 1 All ER 126 . . . 81

Miller v Miller; McFarlane v McFarlane [2006] 3 All ER 1, HL (two joined appeals) . . . 78, 86, 89, 92, 97, A3, A5

MK v CK [2011] EWCA Civ 793 . . . 175, 176

Mouncer v Mouncer [1972] 1 WLR 321 . . . 43, 52

N (Children) [2006] EWCA Civ 872 . . . 117, A6

Nachimson v Nachimson [1930] P 217 . . . 3

Neulinger and Shuruk v Switzerland (2011) application No 41615/07 . . . 172

O'Neill v O'Neill [1975] 3 All ER 289 . . . 40

Oxfordshire County Council v X and Others [2010] EWCA Civ 581 . . . 159

P, C and S v United Kingdom [2002] 2 FLR 631 . . . 125

P-J (Children) [2009] EWCA Civ 588 . . . 171, A7

Pankhania v Chandegra [2012] EWCA Civ . . . 11

Parlour v Parlour [2004] EWCA (Civ) 872 . . . 80

Payne v Payne [2001] EWCA Civ 166 . . . 175, 176

Perry v Perry [1963] 3 All ER 766 . . . 41

Pheasant v Pheasant [1972] Fam 202 . . . 40

Potter v Potter (1975) 5 Fam Law 161 . . . 27, A3

Practice Direction: Residence and Contact Orders: Domestic Violence and Harm [2009] 2 FLR 1400 . . . 58, 113

R (a Child) [2011] EWHC 1715 . . . 139

R v D [1984] 2 All ER 449 . . . 166

R v Registrar General, ex p Smith [1991] 1 FLR 255 CA . . . 157

Table of cases

****

Radmacher (formerly Granatino) v Granatino [2010] UKSC 42 . . . 87–8, 98

Rahman (1985) Times 5/6/85 . . . 166

Re AJ (A Child) [2007] EWCA Civ 55 . . . 155, 160

Re B (A Child) [2009] UKSC 5 . . . 117, 120

Re B (Adoption: Setting aside) [1995] 2 FLR 1 . . . 157

Re B (Care Proceedings: Standard of Proof) [2008] UKHL 35 . . . 138

Re B (Change of Surname) [1996] 1 FLR 791 . . . 114

Re C (A Minor) (Leave to seek Section 8 Order) [1994] 1 FLR 2 . . . 119

Re D (A Minor: Mother's Hostility) [1993] 2 FLR 1 . . . 113

Re D (Care or Supervision Order) (2000) Fam Law 600 . . . 134, A6

Re D (Children) [2010] EWCA Civ 50 . . . 175

Re E (Children) [2011] UKSC 27 . . . 172, 177

Re F (Child Abduction: Risk of Return) [1995] 2 FLR 31 . . . 172

Re F (Minors) (Denial of Contact) [1993] 2 FLR 677 . . . 113

Re G (A Child) (Domestic Violence: Direct Contact) [2001] 2 FCR 134 . . . 109

Re G (Children) (Residence: Same Sex Partner) [2006] UKHL 43 . . . 117

Re H: Re G (Adoption: Consultation of Unmarried Fathers) [2001] 1 FLR 646 . . . 152, 153

Re H; Re S (Abduction: Custody Rights) [1991] 2 AC 476 . . . 164, 171

Re H (Abduction: Acquiescence) [1998] AC 72 . . . 178, A7

Re H (Children) (Abduction) [2003] EWCA Civ 355 . . . 172

Re H (Minors) (Parental Responsibility) (No 3) [1991] 1 FLR 214 . . . 109

Re H (Minors) (Sexual Abuse: Standard of Proof) [1996] AC 563 (HL) . . . 134, 138, A6

Re J (Abduction: Wrongful Removal) [2000] 1 FLR 78 . . . 74

Re L (1998) 2 FLR 810 . . . 104, 121

Re L (Abduction: Pending Criminal Proceedings) [1999] 1 FLR 433 . . . 170

Re L (Care: Threshold Criteria) [2007] 1 FLR 2050 . . . 134, A6

Re L (Contact: Transsexual Applicant) [1995] 2 FLR 438 . . . 112

Re L, V, M & H [2001] Fam 260 . . . 113, 121

Re M (A Minor) (Care Order: Threshold Conditions) [1994] 2 FLR 557 . . . 134, 139

Re M (Abduction: Zimbabwe) [2007] UKHL 55 . . . 170, 178, A7

Re M-J (A Child) [2007] EWCA Civ 56 . . . 155, 160

Re N (Minors) (Abduction) [1991] 1 FLR 413 . . . 170

Re O (A Minor) (Care Order: Education: Procedure) [1992] 4 All ER 905 . . . 139

Re P (A Child) [2008] EWCA Civ 535 . . . 148, 159

Re P (A Child) (Adoption Order: Leave to Oppose Making of Adoption Order) [2007] EWCA Civ 616 . . . 159

Re P (Surrogacy: Residence) 2008 1 FLR 177 . . . 120

Re P (Terminating Parental Responsibility) [1995] 1 FLR 1048 . . . 110

Re R (Adoption: Contact) [2005] EWCA Civ 1128 . . . 159

Re R (Care: Rehabilitation in Context of Domestic Violence) [2006] EWCA Civ 1638 . . . 134

Re S (A Child) (Adoption Order or Special Guardianship Order) [2007] EWCA Civ 54 . . . 155, 160

Re S (A Minor) (Custody) [1991] 2 FLR 388 . . . 117

Re S (Abduction: Custody Rights) [2002] EWCA Civ 908 . . . 172

Re S (Change of Surname) [1999] 1 FLR 672 . . . 114

Re S (Minors) [2010] EWCA Civ 421 . . . 124

Re S (Minors) (Acquiesence) [1994] 1 FLR 819 CA . . . 171

Re W (Adoption Order: Set Aside and Leave to Oppose) [2010] EWCA Civ 1535 . . . 157

Re Y [2004] 2 FLR 330 . . . 175, 176

Redpath v Redpath [1950] 1 All ER 600 . . . 39

S (Children), Re [2012] UKSC 10 . . . 177, A7

S v S [1955] 2 WLR 246 . . . 26

Santos v Santos [1972] Fam 247 . . . 42, 52

Schalk v Austria (2011) application
no. 30141/04 . . . 4

Scott v UK [2000] 1 FLR 958, ECtHR . . . 145

Singh v Singh [1971] 2 WLR 963 . . . 27, 28, 34

Stack v Dowden [2007] UKHL 17 . . . 10, 11,
12, 15, A3

Sullivan v Sullivan (1812) 2 Hag Con 238 . . . 29

Suter v Suter and Jones [1987] 2 FLR 232 . . . 89

Szechter v Szechter [1971] 2 WLR
170 . . . 28, 33, A3

T v T [2010] EWCA Civ 1366 . . . 112

Thurlow v Thurlow [1975] 2 All ER 979 . . . 40

Vaughan v Vaughan [1973] 3 All ER 449 . . . 59, 75

Vervaeke v Smith [1983] 1 AC 145 . . . 21

Wachtel v Wachtel (No. 1) [1973] Fam 72 . . . 40,
92, A4

Watson v Lucas [1980] 1 WLR 1493 . . . 8

Wayling v Jones [1996] 2 FCR 41 . . . 16

Webster v Norfolk County Council & Others
[2009] EWCA 59 . . . 157, 160

White v White [2001] 1 All ER 1 . . . 78, 86, 89, 98

Wilkinson and Kitzinger v Lord Chancellor
[2006] EWHC 2022 (Fam) . . . 5, 16

X Council v B and Others (Emergency
Protection Orders) [2004] EWHC 2015
(Fam) . . . 139

X v Latvia (2012) application no. 30141/04 . . . 172

Table of legislation

UK legislation

Administration of Estates Act 1925
s 46 . . . 14

Adoption of Children Act 1926 . . . 144

Adoption and Children Act 2002 . . . 142, 143,
144, 155, 161, A1, A2
s 1 . . . 159
s 1(3) . . . 147
s 1(4) . . . 143, 149, 150, A7
s 1(4)(a) . . . 153
s 1(4)(b), (c) . . . 150
s 1(5) . . . 151, 158
s 1(6) . . . 143
s 2 . . . 146
s 2(1) . . . 147
s 19 . . . 143, 148
s 21 . . . 143, 149
s 25 . . . 148

s 42 . . . 143, 152
s 45 . . . 151
s 46(6) . . . 153
s 47 . . . 159
s 47(7) . . . 159
s 49 . . . 145
s 49(4)–(5) . . . 152
s 50 . . . 145
s 51 . . . 145
s 51(3) . . . 146
s 52 . . . 143, 149, 152, A7
s 52(1) . . . 143
s 52(3) . . . 153
s 67 . . . 143, 153
s 71 . . . 153
s 79 . . . 143, 157
s 80 . . . 143, 158
s 109 . . . 148

Table of legislation

✳✳✳✳✳✳✳✳✳✳✳✳

Borders Act 2007
  s 2 . . . 167

Child Abduction Act 1984 . . . 165–6
  s 1(1) . . . 165, 174
  s 1(2) . . . 162, 165
  s 1(3)–(4) . . . 165
  s 1(5) . . . 165, 166
  s 1(6) . . . 166
Child Abduction and Custody Act 1985 . . . 162
Child Maintenance and Other Payments Act 2008
  Sch 4 . . . 94
Child Support Act 1991 . . . 77, 80, 94–5, 96, A3
  s 1(1) . . . 95
  s 1(3) . . . 95
  s 3(1) . . . 94
  s 3(2)–(4) . . . 95
  s 8 . . . 96
  s 54 . . . 95
  Sch 1
    para 7 . . . 95
Children Act 1975 . . . 146
  s 37 . . . 146
Children Act 1989 . . . 44, 63, 64, 77, 89, 96, 101,
  103, 141, 155, 164, 176, A1, A2
  Part II . . . 165
  Part III (ss 17–30A) . . . 123, 125, 126
  Part IV (ss 31–42) . . . 123, 125, 126
  Part V (ss 43–52) . . . 123, 125, 126
  s 1 . . . 101
  s 1(1) . . . 115, 133, 136, A5, A6
  s 1(2) . . . 102, 115, 133, 136, A5, A6
  s 1(2A) . . . 115
  s 1(3) . . . 102, 116, 133, 136, 149, 150, A6
  s 1(3)(a) . . . 104, 117
  s 1(3)(b)–(c) . . . 117, 150
  s 1(3)(d)–(f) . . . 117
  s 1(3)(g) . . . 118
  s 1(5) . . . 102, 116, 133, 136, A5, A6
  s 2(1) . . . 102, 108
  s 2(2)(a) . . . 102, 108
  s 2(8) . . . 109

s 3 . . . 106
s 3(4) . . . 107
s 3(5) . . . 109
s 4 . . . 108
s 4(1)(a) . . . 102
s 4(1)(b) . . . 102, 108
s 4(1)(c) . . . 108, 109
s 4A . . . 108
s 4ZA . . . 108, 109
s 5 . . . 118
s 7 . . . 119
s 8 . . . 101, 102, 103, 104, 109, 111–15, 115,
  143, 154, 162, 167
s 8(1) . . . 111, A5
s 9(5) . . . 114
s 9(6) . . . 103
s 10 . . . 118
s 10(8) . . . 102, 119, A5
s 10(9) . . . 102, 119
s 11 . . . 116
s 11(4) . . . 111
s 11(5)(b) . . . 112
s 11(7) . . . 111
ss 11C–11G . . . 113
s 12(1) . . . 102, 109, 111
s 12(1A) . . . 109
s 12(2) . . . 108, 110, 111
s 13 . . . 114
s 14A . . . 111, 118, 143, 154
s 14B . . . 143
s 14B(1) . . . 155
s 14B(2) . . . 154
s 14C . . . 143
s 14C(1)–(4) . . . 154
ss 14D–14F . . . 143
s 16 . . . 102
s 16(1) . . . 115
s 16(4A) . . . 115
ss 17–30A . . . 123, 125, 126
s 17 . . . 124
s 17(1) . . . 126
s 17(10) . . . 126

s 20 . . . 124

s 20(1) . . . 127

ss 31–42 . . . 123, 125, 126

s 31(2) . . . 123, 132, 134, 136, 149, A6

s 31(5) . . . 135

s 31(9) . . . 117, 134, A6

s 31A . . . 132

s 33 . . . 109, 136

s 33(3)(a) . . . 108

s 34 . . . 132

s 34(6A) . . . 132

s 35 . . . 136

s 37 . . . 128

s 38 . . . 136

s 38A . . . 130

ss 43–52 . . . 123, 125, 126

s 43 . . . 131, 136, A6

s 44 . . . 129, 137

s 44A . . . 130

s 46 . . . 128, 137

s 47 . . . 124, 127, 137

s 47(1) . . . 127–8

s 47(1)(b) . . . 129

s 50 . . . 137

s 91 . . . 103

s 100 . . . 138

s 105 . . . 103

Sch 1 . . . 10, A3

   para 2 . . . 96

Children Act 2004 . . . 124

s 58 . . . 110

Children and Adoption Act 2006 . . . 144

Children (Scotland) Act 1995 . . . 106

Civil Partnership Act 2004 . . . 1, 5, 6, 18, 37, 39, 53, 77, 96, A8

s 3(1) . . . 6

s 6(1) . . . 6

s 6A . . . 6

s 41(1) . . . A4

s 44(1) . . . 37, 38, A4

s 44(5) . . . A4

s 44(5)(a)–(d) . . . 37

s 47 . . . 43

s 49 . . . 19, 20, 24, 25

s 50 . . . 19, 20, 31

s 51 . . . 19, 20, 32

Sch 5

   Part 5 . . . 79, 85

   Part 8 . . . 79

Crime and Security Act 2010

ss 24–33 . . . 72

Domestic Violence, Crime and Victims Act 2004 . . . 61

s 12 . . . 71

Education Act 1996

s 548 . . . 110

Equality Act 2010 . . . 23

Family Law Act 1996 . . . 9, 36, 47–8, 49, 54, 57

Part IV . . . 58, 61

s 1 . . . 47

s 30 . . . 9

s 30(2) . . . 9

s 33 . . . 9, 62, 63, 64, 65, 68, A4

s 33(3)–(4) . . . 69

s 33(6) . . . 64, 65, 68

s 33(7) . . . 63, 65

s 33(10) . . . 66

s 35 . . . 62, 63, 64, 66, 67, 68

s 35(3)–(5) . . . 69

s 35(6) . . . 64, 68

s 36 . . . 62, 63, 64, 66, 67, 68, A4

s 36(3)–(5) . . . 69

s 36(6) . . . 64, 68, A4

s 37 . . . 62, 63, 64, 67, 68

s 37(3) . . . 69

s 37(4) . . . 64, 68

s 38 . . . 62, 63, 64, 67, 68

s 38(3) . . . 69

s 38(4) . . . 64, 68

s 40 . . . 64

s 42 . . . 55, 58

Table of legislation

✳✳✳✳✳✳✳✳✳✳✳✳

s 42(2)(a) ... 59

s 42(2)(b) ... 55, 59

s 42(5) ... 55, 61

s 42(7) ... 55, 61

s 42A ... 55, 62, 70

s 43 ... 55, 59

s 43(2) ... 61

s 44 ... 60

s 45 ... 69

s 46(1)–(3) ... 70

s 46(3A) ... 70

s 46(4) ... 70

s 47(2)(b) ... 69

s 47(8) ... 62

s 62 ... A9

s 62(1) ... 60

s 62(2) ... 61

s 62(3) ... 55, 59

s 63 ... 55

s 63(1) ... 60, 63

s 63A ... 2, 72

Family Law Reform Act 1987

s 1 ... 102

Forced Marriage (Civil Protection) Act 2007 ... 2, 57, 72

Gender Recognition Act 2004 ... 24, 25, 26, 30, 31, 33

s 1 ... 3

s 2 ... 4

s 3 ... 4

Human Fertilisation and Embryology Act 1990 ... 106

Human Fertilisation and Embryology Act 2008 ... 106

s 33 ... 104

ss 35–37 ... 105

s 41(1) ... 105

ss 42–44 ... 106

s 54 ... 104

Human Rights Act 1998 ... 3, 8, 125, 160

Inheritance (Provision for Family and Dependants) Act 1975 ... 14

s 1(1)(ba) ... 14

s 1(1)(e) ... 14

Legal Aid, Sentencing and Punishment of Offenders Act 2012

s 49 ... 79

Lord Hardwicke's Act *see* Marriage Act 1753

Marriage Act 1753 ... 7

Marriage Act 1949 ... 6

Marriage (Prohibited Degrees of Relationship) Act 1986 ... 22

Matrimonial Causes Act 1973 ... 18, 19, 20, 37, 53, 77, 96

s 1(1) ... 37, 38

s 1(2) ... 38

s 1(2)(a) ... 37, 38, 39

s 1(2)(b) ... 37, 39, 40, 52

s 1(2)(c) ... 37, 39, 41–2

s 1(2)(d) ... 37, 39, 42, 52

s 1(2)(e) ... 37, 39, 43

s 2(1)–(2) ... 39

s 2(3) ... 40

s 2(4) ... 41

s 2(5) ... 42, 43

s 2(6) ... 42

s 2(7) ... 43

s 3 ... 38

s 5 ... 43, 44

s 10(2)–(3) ... 44

s 10A ... 44

s 10A(3)(a) ... 44

s 11 ... 19, 21

s 11(a) ... 21

s 11(a)(i) ... 21, 22

s 11(a)(ii)–(iii) ... 23

s 11(b) ... 22, 24

s 11(c) ... 3, 5, 22, 24

s 11(d) ... 5, 22, 24

s 12 ... 19, 25–6, 28

s 12(a) . . . 26–7, A3

s 12(b) . . . 27, A3

s 12(c) . . . 27, 32, A3

s 12(d) . . . 29, 32

s 12(e) . . . 30, 32

s 12(f) . . . 30, 32, A3

s 12(g) . . . 30, 32

s 12(h) . . . 30–1, 32

s 13 . . . 19, 31

s 13(1) . . . A3

s 13(1)(a), (b) . . . 31

s 13(2) . . . 32

s 13(3) . . . 32, A3

s 17 . . . 50

s 19 . . . 24

s 21A(1) . . . 82, 83

s 22 . . . 79

s 23 . . . 78, 79, 80, 82

s 23(1)(a)–(b) . . . 80, 83

s 23(1)(c) . . . 80

s 23(3)(c) . . . 80, 83

s 24 . . . 78, 81–2, 82

s 24(1)(a)–(b) . . . 81, 83

s 24(1)(c) . . . 82, 84

s 24A . . . 82

s 25 . . . 77, 78, 79, 85, 87, 92, A3

s 25(1) . . . 85, 87

s 25(2) . . . 78, 85, 96

s 25(2)(a) . . . 89

s 25(2)(b) . . . 90

s 25(2)(c) . . . 91

s 25(2)(d)–(e) . . . 91

s 25(2)(f)–(h) . . . 92

s 25(3)–(4) . . . 96

s 25A(1) . . . 92

s 25B(4) . . . 82, 83

s 28(1)(a)–(b) . . . 84

s 31 . . . 93

s 31(2) . . . 93

s 31(2)(b)–(d) . . . 84

s 31(2)(dd) . . . 84

s 31(2)(e) . . . 84

s 31(7) . . . 94

s 41 . . . 44, 45, 111

Mental Health Act 1983 . . . 25, 29

Nullity of Marriage Act 1971 . . . 19, 26

Offences Against the Person Act 1861 . . .
57, A4

s 57 . . . 4, 24

Police and Criminal Evidence Act 1984 . . . 62

Police and Security Act 2010

ss 24–33 . . . 57

Protection of Freedoms Act 2012 . . . 70

s 111 . . . 71

s 112 . . . 71

Protection from Harassment Act 1997 . . . 54,
57, 70–1, A4

s 2 . . . 71

s 2A . . . 71

s 2A(3) . . . 71

s 3 . . . 72

s 4 . . . 71

s 4A . . . 71

s 7(2) . . . 71

s 7(3)(a) . . . 71

Public Order Act 1986 . . . 57, 72

Rent Acts . . . 8

School Standards and Framework Act 1998

s 131 . . . 110

Bills before Parliament

Children and Families Bill 2013 . . . 25, 47, 49,
111, 115, 132, 133, 136

Clause 1 . . . 158

Clause 2 . . . 151

Clause 6 . . . 151

Clause 7 . . . 132

Clause 8 . . . 153

Crime and Courts Bill 2013

Sch 10 . . . 137

Table of legislation

****

Marriage (Same Sex Couples) Bill . . . 4

European legislation

Brussels II (Regulation 2201/2003) . . . 163, 168, 173, 174

European Convention on Recognition and Enforcement of Decisions concerning Custody of Children (Luxembourg Convention) 1980 . . . 168

International conventions

European Convention on Human Rights . . . 104, 133, 162, 163, 177
  Art 8 . . . 3, 8, 33, 120, 125, 133, 141, 145, 152, 153, 172, 177
  Art 12 . . . 3, 4, 22, 23, 33
  Art 14 . . . 8

Hague Convention on the Civil Aspects of International Child Abduction 1980 . . . 162, 163, 168–70, 173, 174, 176, 177, 179, A7
  Art 1 . . . 168
  Art 12 . . . 162, 170, 173, A7
  Art 13 . . . 162, 170, 172, 178, A7
  Art 13a . . . 170, A7
  Art 13b . . . 171, 172, 174, 177, A7

Hague Convention on Jurisdiction, Applicable Law, Recognition, Enforcement and Co-operation in Respect of Parental Responsibility and Measures for the Protection of Children (HC 1996) . . . 162, 163, 169, 172–4, 176

UN Convention on the Rights of the Child . . . 179
  Art 3.1 . . . 177
  Art 9 . . . 113
  Art 12 . . . 104, 117
Universal Declaration of Human Rights
  Art 16 . . . 2

UK secondary legislation

Family Procedure Rules 2010 (SI 2010/2955) . . . 79, 116
  r 2.3 . . . 79
Family Proceedings Rules 1991 (SI 1991/1247) . . . 79

Marriage Act 1949 (Remedial) Order 2007 (SI 2007/438) . . . 22

Registration of Births (Parents Not Married and Not Acting Together) Regulations (2009 draft) . . . 108

#1

Family relationships, marriage, civil partnership, cohabitation

Key facts

- Many attempts have been made to define 'a family' but the range of couples and larger groups, with or without children, who may be included or excluded, makes it difficult to find a widely acceptable definition.

- Marriage was defined in **Hyde v Hyde** (1866) as 'the voluntary union for life of one man and one woman to the exclusion of all others'.

- A civil partnership is a relationship between two people of the same sex which is formed when they register as civil partners of each other under the **Civil Partnership Act 2004**.

- There is no such thing as a 'common law marriage' and those living together acquire virtually no rights in relation to each other, regardless of the length of their **cohabitation**.

- Formalities have to be complied with both to form and to end marriage and civil partnership; no formalities govern the start and end of cohabitation.

- Parties to a marriage or civil partnership can acquire rights over property during the relationship by their contributions, other than money, towards the relationship.

- Cohabitees generally only acquire rights over things to which they contribute financially. They may be able to claim rights over property on the basis of trusts law or proprietary estoppel.

- There are often calls to reform the law in relation to cohabitants. Joint ownership of property is an issue of particular concern.

Introduction

The concept of a 'family' has become increasingly diverse. Today most people would think of the family as including single parent households (with a male or female parent), unmarried couples (heterosexual and homosexual) with or without children, and possibly polygamous families and extended or multi-generation groups. You can find statistics on the make up of British families at www.ons.gov.uk/ons/rel/mro/news-release/number-of-cohabiting-couples-doubles-since-1996/familiesandhouseholdsnr011112.html

The diversity of families today is reflected in the diversity of rights and responsibilities that attach to different types of family unit. In particular, there are big differences between those who marry or enter into a civil partnership as opposed to those who cohabit without entering into these types of union. However, you should note that many of these differences concern the relationship between the parties rather than between each of them and their children.

What is marriage?

In *Hyde v Hyde* (1866), Lord Penzance defined marriage as 'the voluntary union for life of one man and one woman to the exclusion of all others'. Even at the time of this judgment **divorce** was available, though this judgment could be taken to mean that the parties contemplate the union being for life at the time they enter into it.

Voluntary

Marriage must be freely entered into by both parties without pressure from others. This is reinforced by **Article 16 of the Universal Declaration of Human Rights** which states that: 'marriage shall be entered into only with free and full consent of the intending spouses'.

Note the difference between an **arranged marriage** and a **forced marriage**. Broadly, a forced marriage takes place where both parties have failed to give valid consent and there is **duress** involved. In contrast, arranged marriages, in which families select the future spouse, involve valid consent by both parties.

The **Forced Marriage (Civil Protection) Act 2007** inserted s 63A into the **Family Law Act 1996**, which gives family courts power to make Forced Marriage Protection Orders (injunctions) to protect a person from being forced into a marriage or from any attempt to be forced into a marriage; or a person who *has been* forced into a marriage.

An order can forbid families from:

- taking a person abroad for marriage
- taking their passport away
- intimidating someone into agreeing to marry.

It can also require family members to reveal the whereabouts of a person who is being forced into marriage. The police can apply for a Forced Marriage Protection Order, a breach of which can be punished by two years' imprisonment.

In June 2012, following a public consultation, the Government announced plans to make forced marriage a criminal offence. You can read the Government's comments and find statistics on forced marriage here: www.number10.gov.uk/news/forced-marriage-to-become-criminal-offence/. It is also intended that breach of a Forced Marriage Protection Order will become a criminal offence.

✅ Looking for extra marks?

In 'Criminalising Forced Marriage through Stand-Alone Legislation: Will it Work?' [2012] Fam Law 534–542 Nasreen Pearce and Dr Aisha K Gill argue that criminalisation of forced marriage is a distraction which may deter victims from reporting forced marriage. They consider that money could be better spent to protect victims in other ways.

For life

A marriage can be ended by decree of **nullity** (see Chapter 2, 'Introduction', p 18) or divorce (see Chapter 3, 'Introduction' p 37) as well as by the death of a party.

A marriage may be valid if the parties intended that it would be for life when they married, even if they married under a regime which allows the marriage to be ended by non-judicial means.

Nachimson v Nachimson [1930] P217

A couple married in Moscow in 1924 under the then Soviet law, which allowed a marriage to be terminated by one party giving notice to the other. The man had done this in 1929. The English courts had to determine whether the marriage had been valid. At first instance, it was declared that the fact it could be terminated at will by notice meant that it was not 'for life', and so it was not a valid marriage. The Appeal Court accepted that the parties had intended marriage to be for life when they entered into it, and reversed the decision.

One man and one woman

Corbett v Corbett (1971) decided that a person's sexual identity was fixed at birth, despite a later sex change operation (gender reassignment surgery).

However, following the **Human Rights Act**, in *Bellinger v Bellinger* (2003), a male to female transsexual married Mr Bellinger. She sought a declaration that the parties were respectively male and female so their marriage was not void by **s 11(c) of the Matrimonial Causes Act 1973**. The court felt bound to follow *Corbett*, but declared that the failure of the 1973 Act to recognise gender reassignment was not compatible with **Articles 8 and 12 of ECHR**.

The decision in *Bellinger* led to the **Gender Recognition Act 2004**. **Section 1** of that Act allows a transsexual to apply to the Gender Recognition Panel for a Gender Recognition Certificate allowing registration of their reassigned gender.

What is marriage?

✳✳✳✳✳✳✳✳✳✳

Section 2 requires the Panel to be satisfied that:

Section 2

- the person suffers or has suffered from gender dysphoria (they feel that their gender identity differs from their anatomical sex)
- they have lived in their acquired gender for two years before the application
- they intend to live in their acquired gender for the rest of their life
- they satisfy the evidential requirements under **s 3**

The Panel does not have to be satisfied that the applicant has had (or will have) gender reassignment surgery, if it would be inappropriate for them to do so.

Article 12 of the European Convention on Human Rights sets out a right to marry. In *Schalk v Austria* **(2011)** a gay couple argued that the fact they couldn't marry (they were able to enter into a civil partnership) breached their **Article 12** rights. The European Court of Human Rights disagreed, saying that it was up to the contracting state whether to allow same-sex marriage.

✅ *Looking for extra marks?*

The Marriage (Same Sex Couples) Bill received its second reading in February 2013. It will allow same sex couples to enter into a civil marriage and current civil partners to convert their partnership into a marriage. Transsexuals will be able to have their acquired gender legally recognised without having to divorce their current spouse.

Religious organisations will not be forced to conduct same sex marriages but can opt in to do so.

To the exclusion of all others

If a person marries while they are still legally married to someone else, they commit the offence of bigamy under **s 57 Offences Against the Person Act 1861**.

It may be a defence to a charge of bigamy if there is a reasonable belief that their first spouse is dead. However, the second marriage would still be void.

Hence, **polygamous marriages** are forbidden and a polygamous marriage lawfully entered into abroad by someone who is domiciled in the UK will be void. However, if the marriage is only potentially polygamous (because each party has, as yet, only one spouse), it will be recognised as valid here.

....

Hussain v Hussain [1982] Fam 32

An English-domiciled man and a Pakistan-domiciled woman celebrated a Muslim marriage in Pakistan in 1979. Pakistani law permitted the husband, though not the wife, to take a second spouse. In 1981, while both were living in England, the wife petitioned for judicial separation. The husband then asserted that the marriage was polygamous and therefore void under **s 11(d) of the Matrimonial Causes Act 1973**. It was held that the issue was whether the marriage was consistent with English law. The husband, by English law, could not marry as he was still lawfully married. The wife, by Pakistani law, could not marry while she remained married to her husband. Accordingly, the marriage could never become polygamous and was, in fact, monogamous and valid in English law.

What is a civil partnership?

The **Civil Partnership Act 2004** defines a **civil partnership** as a relationship between two people of the same sex which is formed when they register as civil partners of each other under the **Civil Partnership Act 2004**.

Entering into a civil partnership confers similar rights and advantages on civil partners as a marriage confers on a heterosexual couple. However, largely for political reasons, the Act stopped short of calling their relationship a marriage.

This difference was challenged in the following case:

Wilkinson and Kitzinger v Lord Chancellor [2006] EWHC 2022 (Fam)

A British lesbian couple lawfully married in Canada, then challenged the failure to recognise their relationship as a marriage in this country, asserting that it was discriminatory, because a heterosexual marriage abroad would have been recognised as such. It was decided that **s 11(c) Matrimonial Causes Act 1973**—'a marriage is void if the parties are not respectively male and female'—together with public policy considerations and the terms of the 2004 Act itself meant that their action failed.

A challenge from a different direction was launched in:

Burden and Burden v UK [2007] 1 FCR 69

Two elderly sisters asserted that it was discriminatory that the survivor of them would have to pay inheritance tax (IHT) on the value of assets inherited from the other, when the surviving member of a marriage or civil partnership would not suffer the same burden. The court held that the central question under the Convention was not whether different criteria could have been chosen for the grant of an IHT exemption, but whether the particular scheme chosen by the UK exceeded any acceptable margin of appreciation. The court found that the UK's scheme did not do so, even though it treated differently for tax purposes married couples and civil partners from other persons living together even in a long-term settled relationship. The difference of treatment was reasonably and objectively justified.

✔ Looking for extra marks?

In 'Coupledom' (2008) 158 *NLJ* 951, Augur Pearce considers the nature of civil partnerships and how civil partnerships differ from marriage or other contractual arrangements.

Do you think that civil partnerships are equivalent to marriage? Should marriage be available regardless of sexual orientation? You should consider the Government response to its consultation on equal marriage referred to earlier when answering this question.

Formalities

Whom can you marry?

You can marry:

- a person who was born of the opposite sex or who has a gender recognition certificate conferring the opposite sex on them; *and*
- who is aged 18 or more, or aged 16 or 17 with consent of those with parental responsibility (or with a court order of consent to marry); *and*
- who is not within the prohibited degrees of relationship; *and*
- who is not already married to, or in a civil partnership with, another.

Under **s 3(1) of the Civil Partnership Act** those wanting to enter into a civil partnership must satisfy the same criteria save that to enter into a civil partnership the parties must be of the same sex.

Prohibited degrees of relationship

A person can neither marry nor form a civil partnership with any person who is within the **prohibited degrees** of relationship. See Chapter 2, 'Prohibited degrees of relationship', p 21 for further details.

Formation of marriage or civil partnership

There are detailed provisions in the **Marriage Act 1949** relating to notices to be given, the premises on which marriages can take place, and the formalities attaching to the ceremony. The **Civil Partnership Act** sets out the provisions applying to civil partnerships.

When it was enacted, the **Civil Partnership Act 2004** provided that ceremonies could not take place on religious premises. The law has now changed so that civil partnerships can be conducted on religious premises where the religious organisation permits this and the premises have been approved for such ceremonies (**ss 6(1) and 6A Civil Partnership Act 2004**). However, religious organisations do not have to host civil partnership ceremonies.

Ending a marriage or civil partnership

For further information on the formalities involved in ending a marriage or civil partnership see Chapter 2, 'Introduction', p 18 and Chapter 3, 'Introduction', p 37.

Figure 1.1 Key differences between marriage and civil partnership

Marriage	Civil partnership
Between people of opposite sexes.	Between people of the same sex.
Can be a religious or civil ceremony.	Ceremony can take place on religious premises if those premises have been approved. However, religious organisations cannot be forced to perform ceremonies.
Formed by a declaration of words.	Formed by signing a civil partnership document.
A marriage can be annulled on the grounds of non-consummation.	A civil partnership cannot be annulled on the grounds of non-consummation.
Adultery is one of the facts that can be used to prove that a marriage has broken down irretrievably for the purposes of divorce.	Adultery cannot be used to prove irretrievable breakdown.

Common law marriage

A survey in 2004 for 'advicenow' (an internet-based advice organisation for cohabiting couples) found that 61% of 1,000 respondents thought that simply living together could give couples the same rights as marriage, and many refer to their relationship as a common law marriage.

However, even if there was ever such an institution (which is doubtful), the **Marriage Act 1753** (sometimes referred to as '**Lord Hardwicke's Act**') provided that no marriage was valid other than one performed by an ordained Anglican clergyman in the premises of the Church of England following the reading of banns or purchase of a licence. At the time, only Quaker and Jewish marriages were exempt. While other marriages, including those performed in Register Offices, and civil partnerships have since been recognised, nothing in law recognises cohabitation—however long—as establishing any sort of marriage-like status.

Cohabitation
What is cohabitation?

People do not naturally think of themselves as 'forming cohabitation'. Terms such as 'moving in together'; 'living together', or 'sharing a house' are more likely to be used. The difficulty with all of those phrases is that they are capable of covering relationships which have no family elements, such as students or others sharing a house or flat for convenience. The decision in *Langdon v Horton* (1951) drew this distinction:

Cohabitation

Langdon v Horton [1951] 1 KB 666

Two elderly ladies lived with their cousin, who was the tenant of a property, for about 30 years. The tenancy could pass under the **Rent Acts** to 'family members'. However, the court held that the two ladies had lived with their cousin for the sake of personal convenience and not because they were members of a family, and they were unable to inherit the tenancy.

In *Watson v Lucas* [1980] 1 WLR 1493, a woman lived with a man for some time, although he was still married to his wife. It was held that she was a member of his family for the purposes of the **Rent Acts**, so she could inherit his tenancy, because of the lasting relationship between them.

No formality is required to establish cohabitation. Indeed, it is not always easy to discern exactly when it commences, for example, a couple may regularly spend much of their time at each other's home and share living expenses, gradually sharing more and more aspects of their life, without any specific event to mark the transition to cohabitation.

Possible tests to establish whether cohabitees have acquired the status of a family are suggested in **Chios Property Investment Ltd v Lopez (1987)**—a 'sufficient state of permanence and stability' had been reached in the relationship to constitute a family.

Fitzpatrick v Sterling Housing Association Ltd [2000] 1 FCR 21

A gay couple, Mr Fitzpatrick and Mr Thompson, lived together for 18 years in a rented property, of which Mr Thompson was the tenant. The court held that Mr Fitzpatrick could inherit the tenancy as a 'family member' within the meaning of the **Rent Acts**. The test was to require 'a degree of mutual interdependence of the sharing of lives, of caring and loving, or commitment and support' and not 'a transient superficial relationship'. A majority of the court held that a sexual relationship was not a requirement.

Another way of inheriting a tenancy under the **Rent Act** was as the spouse of a tenant, which was extended in the Acts to include 'a person who was living with the original tenant as (their) wife or husband'. Mr Fitzpatrick failed on this ground, as the court held this could not include same-sex couples.

However, in *Mendoza v Ghaidan* (**2004**), the House of Lords held that the **Human Rights Act** had altered the position. **Article 8** (right to respect for private and family life) together with **Article 14** (prohibition of discrimination) required the court to read the **Rent Act** provision as if it said 'as if they were (their) wife or husband', which could extend to same-sex couples.

Ending cohabitation

No formality is required to bring cohabitation to an end. As with formation of the relationship, it is not always easy to discern when it ends.

An area in which the law is developing, and where there is some pressure for reform, is in relation to distribution of assets on the breakdown of a cohabiting couple. This is discussed further later. The basic position is that cohabitation establishes no property rights, and assets of a separating cohabiting couple would be split in accordance with common law rules covering disputes between any two individuals.

Key differences between married couples/ civil partners and cohabitants

For the sake of simplicity the following section only refers to married couples and not to civil partners. However, the same rules apply to civil partners as to married couples.

Rights to occupy the family home

Section 30 of the Family Law Act 1996 deals with a situation where one spouse (A) has a right to occupy the family home and the other (B) does not. In these circumstances, B has the rights set out in **s 30(2)**:

Section 30(2)

    (a) if in occupation, a right not to be evicted or excluded from the dwelling-house or any part of it by A except with the leave of the court given by an order under section 33;

    (b) if not in occupation, a right with the leave of the court so given to enter into and occupy the dwelling-house.

Cohabitants do not benefit from statutory rights to occupy the family home.

Domestic violence

Both spouses and cohabitants can apply for injunctions under the **Family Law Act 1996** (see Chapter 4, 'Civil law', p 56).

It is worth noting that a cohabitant applying for an occupation order, who does not have a right to occupy the property, is treated less favourably than a spouse in the same position.

Children

For a discussion of the current differences between the position of married and unmarried fathers, see Chapter 6, 'What is included in parental responsibility?' p 106.

Maintenance

Unlike the position for married couples or civil partners, a cohabitant cannot claim maintenance from their former partner after their relationship breaks down. This means that if someone has given up their career to raise a child, they have no claim to maintenance for themself. However, that person will have claims for the benefit of the child. For example, claims under **Schedule 1 of the Children Act 1989** and claims for child maintenance through the Child Support Agency (CSA).

✅ Looking for extra marks?

As you will see in Chapter 5 ('Introduction', p 78) the court has a wide discretion when making **financial orders** on divorce or dissolution of a civil partnership. Is it fair that cohabitants should not be entitled to maintenance, even where someone has sacrificed their career to raise a child? Should the length of cohabitation make a difference?

Dealing with property at the end of a relationship

A key issue on separation of a cohabiting couple is how to deal with the ownership of their former home. Unlike the position for married couples or those in civil partnerships, the courts do not have a statutory discretion to redistribute property when a relationship breaks down. This means that the law of trusts becomes very important.

Revision tip

You may remember from land law and trusts law that there are two aspects of property ownership: **legal ownership** and **beneficial ownership**.

In the case of registered land, the legal owner of property is the person in whose name it is registered. In the case of unregistered land the legal owner is the person to whom it is conveyed.

Beneficial ownership is the equitable ownership of the property and can be established in various ways, which are discussed later.

Where the parties hold legal ownership of a property jointly, the starting point is that they own the beneficial interest jointly. Following the case of *Stack v Dowden* **(2007)** (see 'Extent of the parties' shares', p 11), it is difficult to depart from this.

Where only one party has legal ownership the position is more complex. There are two key issues: did the parties *intend to share ownership* of the property? If they did intend to share ownership, *what share do they each have?*

Intention to share

A beneficial interest in a property can be established in the following ways:

1. **Express trust**: The most straightforward way to deal with the issue is to form an express agreement where the parties set out that they intend to share the property. Where there is

a declaration of trust this is conclusive unless it can be set aside or it is subsequently varied by agreement or affected by proprietary estoppel (***Pankhania v Chandegra* (2012)**)

2. **Resulting trust**: A party is presumed to have an interest under a resulting trust if s/he either contributes to the purchase price of a property which is put into another person's sole name or transfers a property to another person's name without receiving anything in return. It is possible to rebut this presumption. In ***Jones v Kernott* (2011)** the Supreme Court indicated that where you are looking at cohabiting couples you should generally look at constructive trusts, rather than resulting trusts, unless the couple are also business partners.

3. **Constructive trust**: To establish an interest under a constructive trust it is necessary to show:

   (a) a common intention that both parties should have a beneficial interest; *and*

   (b) the claimant has acted to his detriment on the basis of that common intention. Common intention can be established by evidence of an express agreement.

....

Eves v Eves [1975] 1 WLR 1338

Mr Eves told his cohabitant (who renamed herself Mrs Eves by deed poll) that, if she had been 21 years of age, he would have put the house into their joint names but that, as she was younger, it would have to be put into his name alone. In fact, he said this to avoid putting the property into joint names. She did a great deal of work to the house.

It was held that she had an interest in the property. The majority of the Court of Appeal inferred an agreement that Mrs Eves would contribute labour to a house in which she had a beneficial interest. Lord Denning based his judgment on what Mr Eves expressly stated rather than his unspoken intention.

....

The court may infer a common intention, though in ***Lloyds Bank PLC v Rosset* (1991)**, it was said that it was 'extremely doubtful' whether common intention could be found from anything less than a direct contribution to the purchase price.

However, ***Stack v Dowden* (2007)** suggests that carrying out improvements adding significantly to the value of the property should give rise to an interest in it.

4. **Proprietary estoppel**: To establish an interest by way of proprietary estoppel a claimant must show:

   (a) the defendant promised the claimant an interest in the property;

   (b) the claimant relied on that promise to his detriment; and

   (c) it would be unconscionable to deny the claimant relief.

Extent of the parties' shares

If the couple intended to share the property, the next question is the extent of their shares:

Key differences between married couples and cohabitants
✳✳✳✳✳✳✳✳✳✳✳

In relation to trusts, the onus is on the claimant to establish that they are entitled to a share or a greater share than the legal title provides.

....

Stack v Dowden [2007] UKHL 17

Stack v Dowden indicates that, although there is a presumption in resulting trusts that the parties hold the beneficial ownership in proportion to their financial contributions, this is not a rule of law. The court will ascertain the parties' shared intentions, actual, inferred, or imputed, with respect to the property in the light of their whole course of conduct in relation to it. All the facts of the case are relevant in determining the parties' intentions, but examples include the nature of the parties' relationship and whether they had children that they were both responsible for housing. On the facts of this case Ms Dowden was awarded 65% of the proceeds of sale. She had contributed significantly more to the purchase price and the parties had kept their finances completely separate throughout their relationship, despite the fact that they had four children together.

....

In proprietary estoppel cases, the courts will generally award the minimum share required to do justice between the parties—*Crabb v Arun District Council* (1976).

Changes over time

Where the parties make an express declaration of trust, they can later agree to vary their shares. The position is more complex where there is no express variation.

In *Stack v Dowden*, the court cited an example where an intention to vary shares might be inferred: if one party financed, or himself constructed, an extension or substantial improvement to the property, so that what they now have significantly differs from what they had when their shares were initially fixed.

....

Kernott v Jones [2011] UKSC 53

Mr Kernott and Ms Jones, who had two children, bought a property in joint names. Ms Jones paid the deposit and the rest of the purchase was funded by an interest-only mortgage. Mr Kernott paid most of the cost of an extension to the property. Household bills were split equally.

When they separated, Mr Kernott left the property and it was agreed that they owned it in equal shares. Subsequently, Ms Jones met all the bills for the house and the children. Mr Kernott cashed in a jointly-owned life insurance policy and used his share of it towards a new property for himself. Twelve years after the separation, the court had to decide whether it could infer a common intention to vary the parties' beneficial interests from their conduct since separation.

The Supreme Court held that the parties' shares had changed since separation and that Ms Jones now had a 90% share. The starting point where a family home is bought in joint names is that the parties' own the property as joint tenants in law and equity (the position is different where the house is owned in one party's sole name). It is possible to rebut this presumption with evidence of a different intention at the time the property was purchased or later on. If possible, the court will infer the parties' intention (ie work out what they actually intended) but if that is not possible then the court can impute an intention (ie attribute an intention to them) that each party is entitled to a fair share of the property. Each case will turn on its own facts but the judgments set out various matters the court might consider. You should note that whilst the judgments unanimously awarded Ms Jones 90%, Lady Hale and Lord Walker seemed to have done so on the basis of inferred intention whereas Lord Wilson and Lord Kerr seemed to feel imputing intention was necessary. Lord Collins felt that the difference between inference and imputation would hardly ever matter.

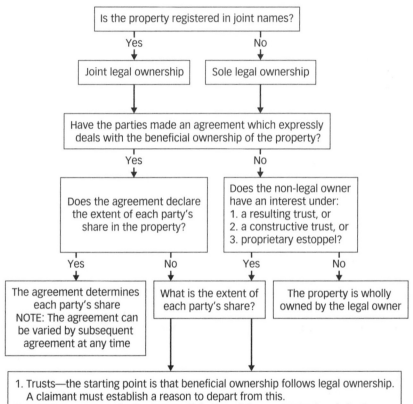

Figure 1.2 Determining interests in property

Inheritance

If a person dies leaving a will, their property will be divided in accordance with that will. However, if one spouse dies intestate (without leaving a will), the other has an automatic right to inherit their estate under the intestacy rules in **s 46 Administration of Estates Act 1925**. In contrast, a cohabitant has no automatic right to inherit.

A cohabitant, like a spouse, may be able to claim against their deceased partner's estate under the **Inheritance (Provision for Family and Dependants) Act 1975**. There are two possible grounds of claim open to cohabitants:

1. as a person maintained by the deceased under **s 1(1)(e)**; and

2. as a cohabitant of two years or more under **s 1(1)(ba)**.

In either case, while a cohabitant can only claim 'such financial provision as it would be reasonable in all the circumstances of the case for the applicant to receive for his maintenance', a spouse would be entitled to 'such financial provision as it would be reasonable in all the circumstances of the case…whether or not that provision is required for his or her maintenance'.

Is there a need for reform?

Reform of this area of law gives rise to considerable debate and exam questions often focus on whether the law should be reformed. It is important to consider carefully whether reform is needed and, if so, whether reform should be targeted—should all aspects of the law be reformed or should reform be confined to specific issues, for example property rights, or rights and responsibilities in relation to children?

Figure 1.3 Arguments for and against reform

Arguments for reform	Arguments against reform
Research shows that people do not base a decision to marry on legal considerations.	Giving rights to cohabitants would undermine marriage.
Many people believe in the common law marriage myth and act to their detriment, for example in giving up work to care for a child, without acquiring a right to maintenance for themselves if the parties separate.	All couples have the option to marry or enter into a civil partnership.
The law protects stronger parties who choose not to marry to avoid the financial implications. An opt-out scheme would offer the weaker party, who is unaware of the implications, the protection of a default regime. The onus would be on the stronger, and more informed party, to opt out.	One party may have deliberately chosen not to marry so as to avoid the financial implications of marriage. That person should not be subject to financial claims through another route.

Law Commission proposals

In July 2007, a Law Commission report on cohabitation made suggestions for a new regime for cohabitants who separate. A remedy would only be available where:

- the couple satisfied certain eligibility requirements;
- the couple had not agreed to disapply the scheme; and
- the applicant had made qualifying contributions to the relationship giving rise to certain enduring consequences at the point of separation.

✓ Looking for extra marks?

Consider whether you think the Government should accept the Law Commission proposals.

You may find it useful to read 'Back to the bad old days?' 158 *NLJ* 174 in which Sarah Greer considers the effect that the Law Commission proposals would have had on the outcome of the case of *James v Thomas* (2007) (the facts of which are set out in the article). You may also wish to consider Lady Hale's comments on the need for reform in the Scottish case of *Gow v Grant* [2012] UKSC 29.

✱ Key cases

Case	Facts	Principle
Kernott v Jones [2011] UKSC 53	Mr Kernott and Ms Jones bought a property in joint names. When the couple split Mr Kernott left the property and it was agreed that they owned it in equal shares. After their split Ms Jones met all the bills for the house and the children.	Ms Jones had a 90% interest in the property. The parties' intentions had changed since their separation.
Stack v Dowden [2007] UKHL 17	Ms Dowden had contributed significantly more to the purchase price and the parties had kept their finances completely separate throughout their relationship, despite the fact that they had four children together.	The starting point is that where legal ownership of a property is in joint names the beneficial interest was in joint names. Where legal ownership of a property was in sole names then the starting point is that the beneficial interest is solely owned. The claimant must justify departure from this. 'The search is to ascertain the parties' shared intentions, actual, inferred or imputed, with respect to the property in the light of their whole course of conduct in relation to it.' All the facts of the case are relevant in determining the parties' intentions.

Key debate

✱✱✱✱✱✱✱✱✱✱✱✱

Case	Facts	Principle
Wayling v Jones [1996] 2 FCR 41	Mr Wayling (W) and Mr Jones (J) cohabited for a number of years. J promised W that he would leave property to him in his will if he helped in running his business. W did assist and received very little money for doing so (described as 'pocket money' by the court). J did not leave W any property in his will. W claimed for proprietary estoppel.	It was held that W assisted in the business in reliance on J's promise. The court determined that the promise did not have to be the sole motivation for a person acting to their detriment. Once the link had been established it was for J's estate to prove that W had not relied on the promise, which it was unable to do.
Wilkinson and Kitzinger v Lord Chancellor [2006] EWHC 2022 (Fam)	A British lesbian couple lawfully married in Canada, then challenged the English court's failure to recognise their relationship as a marriage in this country, on the basis that it was discriminatory, because a heterosexual marriage abroad would have been recognised as such.	**Section 11(c) Matrimonial Causes Act 1973** together with public policy considerations and the terms of the **Civil Partnership Act 2004** itself meant that their action failed.

Key debate

Topic:	Should the law treat cohabitants in the same way as married couples?
Academics:	Anne Barlow and Grace James
Viewpoint:	The law should protect the function rather than the form of relationships.
Reading:	'Regulating Marriage and Cohabitation in 21st Century Britain' (2004) *MLR*, vol 67, pp 143–176.

? Exam questions

Problem Question

Jane and Robert have cohabited for 10 years and have an 11-year-old son called Ben. Robert paid solely for their house as Jane gave up her career as a doctor to care for Ben. However, Jane has bought many of the furnishings for the property. She has also been a full-time mother throughout Ben's life.

Robert and Jane's friends treat them as married, and some are not even aware that they are not as they refer to each other as 'husband' and 'wife'. Jane has felt for some time that the relationship is not working and wants some advice about how she goes about getting a 'divorce'.

Advise Jane about her position.

An outline answer is included at the end of the book.

Essay Question

Should cohabitees be entitled to the same property and inheritance rights as married couples and civil partners? If this were so, would there subsequently be any purpose to marriage and civil partnership?

 Scan here

Scan this QR code image with your mobile device to see an outline answer to this question or log onto www.oxfordtextbooks.co.uk/orc/concentrate

#2

Nullity

- Nullity is a way of ending marriages and civil partnerships.

- Once annulled, the marriage or civil partnership is treated as if it had not occurred.

- English law distinguishes between void marriages/civil partnerships and voidable ones.

- Void means the marriage/partnership was never a valid one. There is no need for a decree although the parties may apply for one if they wish to obtain a financial, pension, or property order.

- Voidable means that the marriage/partnership remains a valid one until the parties obtain a decree to annul it. It becomes void after the decree.

- The law of nullity in relation to marriages is set out in the **Matrimonial Causes Act 1973**.

- The law in relation to civil partnerships is set out in the **Civil Partnership Act 2004**.

Chapter overview

Comparison of grounds—void and voidable marriages

Void		Voidable	
Marriage Section 11 MCA 1973	**Civil Partnership Section 49 CPA 2004**	**Marriage Section 12 MCA 1973**	**Civil Partnership Section 50 CPA 2004**
Parties within prohibited degrees of relationship		Lack of consent due to duress, mistake, or otherwise	
Party under 16 years of age		Mental disorder	
Formalities not complied with		Respondent pregnant by another	
Party already married/in a civil partnership		Gender recognition certificate issued after marriage/civil partnership entered into	
Parties not of different sex	Parties not of the same sex	Acquired gender at time of marriage/civil partnership	
Polygamous marriage		Non-consummation (by reason of incapacity or wilful refusal)	
		Bars to pronouncing a marriage/civil partnership void	
		Section 13 MCA 1973	**Section 51 CPA 2004**
		• Conduct and unjust • Time limits • Knowledge of facts	

Introduction

Nullity is a way of ending a marriage or civil partnership. For marriages, the law is contained in the **Matrimonial Causes Act 1973** (MCA), which consolidated the **Nullity of Marriage Act 1971** and other Acts. **Section 11** contains the grounds on which the marriage will be void, **s 12** contains the grounds on which the marriage will be voidable, and **s 13** contains the bars (or defences) to a decree. The **MCA** applies to marriages which took place after 31 July 1971. It is very unlikely that you will be asked about marriages which took place before that date.

The law of nullity in relation to civil partnerships is contained in the **Civil Partnership Act 2004** (CPA). **Section 49** contains the grounds on which the civil partnership will be void, **s 50** contains the grounds on which it will be voidable, and **s 51** contains the bars to a decree.

The bars to the grant of a decree of nullity only apply to **voidable marriages** or civil partnerships. This is because void marriages or civil partnerships were never valid ones so there can be no bar or defence to a petition of nullity.

One explanation for the difference between void and voidable marriages may be the state interest in the institution of marriage. Void marriages may be seen to be so defective that public policy demands they are not viewed as a marriage. In contrast the defects in voidable marriages are less severe from a public policy perspective but impact on the parties. Public policy reasons do not demand that the marriage should never have existed but fairness to the parties demands that they should be able to bring it to an end.

The difference between nullity and divorce/ dissolution of civil partnership

A marriage or civil partnership which is **annulled** is not a valid one. Divorce or dissolution is necessary if the marriage or civil partnership is a valid one but has irretrievably broken down.

Unlike divorce, you do not have to be married for a year before you can petition for a decree of nullity.

The difference between a void marriage and a non-marriage

A **void marriage** will appear to be a valid marriage but a **non-marriage** will not resemble a marriage and will have no legal consequences whatsoever. Thus the court has no power to award any financial order to either party, as it does when the marriage is void.

In the case of *Hudson v Leigh* (2009), Bodey J held that in deciding what constituted a non-marriage the following factors should be taken into consideration. He stressed that these were non-exhaustive:

1. whether the ceremony or event set out or purported to be a lawful marriage;

2. whether it bore all or enough of the hallmarks of marriage;

3. whether the three key participants (most especially the officiating official) believed, intended, and understood the ceremony as giving rise to the status of lawful marriage; and

4. the reasonable perceptions, understandings, and beliefs of those in attendance.

Figure 2.1 Main differences between void and voidable marriages/civil partnerships

Void	Voidable
There is no need for a decree. Either party can remarry or enter a new civil partnership without a decree.	A decree is necessary to end the relationship.
A decree is possible after the death of either or both parties.	A decree is only possible during the lifetime of the parties.
A third party can take nullity proceedings (eg a trustee of a marriage settlement).	Only the couple themselves can take proceedings.

Sham marriages

This is when a couple marry, and intend their marriage to be valid, but do not intend to live together as husband and wife. The marriage could be for the purpose of allowing one party to gain residence in a country, to gain a work permit, or to claim benefits. **Sham marriages** are neither voidable nor void.

In *Vervaeke v Smith* (1983), the purpose of the marriage was for the wife to avoid being deported. The couple did not intend to live together. It was held that such marriages will be valid.

 Looking for extra marks?

Do you think sham marriages should be upheld as valid marriages? What are your reasons for this? If you think that sham marriages should not be upheld would they be better viewed as void or voidable marriages?

Grounds on which a marriage may be void—s 11 MCA

Although a decree is not strictly necessary to end a void marriage, the parties may apply for one if they wish to obtain a financial, pension, or property order.

Section 11 MCA

(a) It is not a valid marriage under the provisions of the Marriage Acts 1949 to 1986 because:

    (i) the parties are within the *prohibited degrees of relationship*; or

    (ii) either party is *under the age of sixteen*; or

    (iii) the parties have intermarried in disregard of certain *requirements as to the formation of marriage*;

Grounds on which a marriage may be void—s 11 MCA

✳✳✳✳✳✳✳✳✳✳

(b) at the time of the marriage either party was *already lawfully married*;

(c) the parties are not respectively *male and female*;

(d) in the case of a *polygamous marriage* entered into outside England and Wales, either party was at the time of the marriage domiciled in England and Wales.

Note: Being **domiciled** in England means a person normally lives there and intends to remain there.

Prohibited degrees of relationship—s 11(a)(i)

The law forbids certain relatives from marrying each other. These may be blood relatives (consanguinity) or non-blood relatives (affinity).

Note: Unlike many other countries it is possible to marry your cousin under English law.

The rules relating to affinity were relaxed by the **Marriage (Prohibited Degrees of Relationship) Act 1986** to allow marriage between a step-parent and step-child if both are over 21 at the date of marriage and there has never been a parent/child relationship between them.

The former prohibition on marriages between a former parent-in-law and their son- or daughter-in-law was lifted by the **Marriage Act 1949 (Remedial) Order 2007** (SI No 438) following the ruling in the case of ***B and L v UK* (2006)**. In this case the European Human Rights Court ruled that preventing a man from marrying his former daughter-in-law interfered with his right to marry and found a family under **Article 12 of the European Convention on Human Rights**.

Figure 2.2 Prohibited degrees of relationship

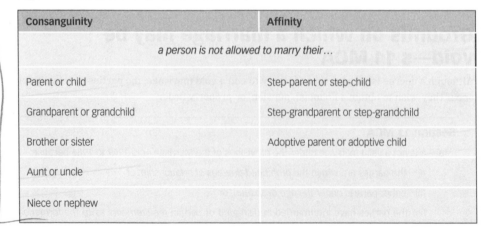

Consanguinity	Affinity
a person is not allowed to marry their…	
Parent or child	Step-parent or step-child
Grandparent or grandchild	Step-grandparent or step-grandchild
Brother or sister	Adoptive parent or adoptive child
Aunt or uncle	
Niece or nephew	

✓ Looking for extra marks?

Now that former parents and children in law are allowed to marry, is it justifiable to retain the remaining prohibited degrees of consanguinity and affinity? Lawrence Schäfer argues that retaining the prohibited degrees of consanguinity is justifiable to prevent genetic defects in any offspring but retaining the prohibited degrees of affinity may be in breach of **Article 12**. ('Marrying an in-law? The future of prohibited degrees of affinity and consanguinity in English law' [2008] *Child and Family Law Quarterly* 219).

Either party is under 16—s 11(a)(ii)

A person cannot marry if they are less than 16 years old. Those who are between the ages of 16 and 18 require the consent of a parent or guardian to their marriage. If they are subject to a care order, consent from the local authority is also required. Under some circumstances a court may give consent.

Revision tip

If the parties are aged 16 or 17 and they do not obtain the appropriate consent, the marriage will still be a valid one. Remember this if you answer a question on nullity in your examination. However you could point out that they would have made a false statement to the registrar and they could be prosecuted for doing so.

The parties have married in disregard of certain requirements as to the formation of the marriage—s 11(a)(iii)

This would include, for example, that there is no valid marriage, certificate, or licence, the appropriate notice had not been given, or the building in which the ceremony took place was not an approved one.

For the marriage to be void the couple must have 'knowingly and willingly' disregarded the requirements—*Gereis v Yagoub* (1997). In this case the couple knew that their marriage had been conducted without the required notice, by an unauthorised person and in an unauthorised building. The marriage was void.

In view of the decision in *Hudson v Leigh* (2009) it is possible that the court would consider the marriage in *Gereis v Yagoub* (1997) to be a non-marriage rather than a void marriage if the case was decided today.

✓ Looking for extra marks?

Under the **Equality Act 2010**, civil partners will be permitted to form their civil partnership on religious premises. However, there is no obligation on religious organisations to host such ceremonies.

bigamy
✓

Either party was already lawfully married or in a civil partnership—s 11(b)

A person must have legally ended their present marriage or civil partnership before they can enter into another one. Failure to do so will mean that they are committing bigamy, an offence under **s 57 Offences Against the Person Act 1861**.

A problem may arise if a person wishes to remarry and they do not know the whereabouts of their current spouse. One solution may be for them to apply under **s 19 MCA** for a decree of presumption of death and dissolution of the marriage. The petitioner has to show that their spouse has been missing for seven years or more and they have reasonable grounds to believe their spouse is dead.

The parties are not a male and a female—s 11(c)

Although two people of the same sex may enter into a civil partnership, they may not marry. However, a transsexual who has had their new gender legally recognised may marry a person of the opposite sex to their acquired gender. This has not always been the case in English law.

....

Corbett v Corbett [1971] P83, 105–6

The case concerned whether a marriage between a male, and a male to female transsexual was a valid one. The marriage was held void under **s 11(c)** on the grounds that a person's sex is determined at birth and cannot be altered by medical or surgical means.

....

The law changed following the cases of *Goodwin v UK* **(2002)** and *Bellinger v Bellinger* **(2003)** and the subsequent passing of the **Gender Recognition Act 2004** (see Chapter 1, 'One man and one woman', p 3).

Polygamous marriages—s 11(d)

Polygamous marriages are not permitted under the law of England and Wales. Therefore, if either party entered into a polygamous marriage abroad and were domiciled in England and Wales at the time, the marriage will be void.

Grounds on which a civil partnership may be void—s 49 CPA

The grounds for a civil partnership being void are similar to those for a void marriage but are contained within **s 49 Civil Partnership Act 2004**.

Section 49 CPA

(a) The parties are not of the same sex.

(b) Either is already married or in a civil partnership.

(c) Either is under 16.

(d) They are in the prohibited degrees of relationship.

(e) The necessary formalities have not been complied with.

The parties must be of the same sex and there is no provision in relation to polygamous civil partnerships.

Grounds on which a marriage may be voidable—s 12 MCA

A decree is necessary to end a voidable marriage and the marriage will continue until a decree is obtained.

Section 12 MCA

(a) The marriage has not been consummated owing to the *incapacity* of either party to consummate it;

(b) The marriage has not been consummated owing to the *wilful refusal* of the respondent to consummate it;

(c) Either party to the marriage did not validly *consent* to it, whether in consequence of duress, mistake, unsoundness of mind or otherwise;

(d) At the time of the marriage either party, though capable of giving valid consent, was *suffering* (whether continuously or intermittently) from *mental disorder* within the meaning of the Mental Health Act 1983, of such a kind or to such an extent as to be unfitted for marriage;

(e) At the time of the marriage the respondent was suffering from *venereal disease* in a communicable form;

(f) At the time of the marriage the respondent was *pregnant* by some person other than the petitioner;

(g) An *interim Gender Recognition Certificate* under the Gender Recognition Act 2004 has, after the time of the marriage, been issued to either party to the marriage;

(h) The respondent is a person whose gender at the time of the marriage has become *the acquired gender* under the Gender Recognition Act 2004.

****

Grounds (a) to (f) derive from the **Nullity of Marriage Act 1971**, while grounds (g) and (h) were added by the **Gender Recognition Act 2004**.

Consummation

The first two grounds relate to **consummation** of the marriage. Consummation is an act of sexual intercourse between a male and a female.

....

D v A [1845] 1 Rob Ecl 279

The wife's vagina was deformed and the husband was unable to fully penetrate her. The marriage was annulled. Dr Lushington held that intercourse must be 'ordinary and complete' intercourse and not 'partial and imperfect'.

....

The use of contraceptives does not prevent the marriage from being consummated:

....

Baxter v Baxter [1948] AC 274

The wife, fearing pregnancy, refused to have intercourse with her husband without the use of a condom. The court held that the marriage had been consummated.

....

If the couple have intercourse before they marry but not afterwards, this does not consummate the marriage:

....

Ford v Ford (1987) 17 Fam Law 232

A couple married while the husband was in prison. They had previously had a sexual relationship. When the husband was released he refused to have intercourse with his wife and said he did not wish to live with her. The wife was granted a decree of nullity on the grounds of his wilful refusal.

....

Revision tip

Either party can petition on their own incapacity. However it is not possible for a person to petition on their own wilful refusal. Remember this if you are asked in your examination to advise one of the parties on what grounds they may petition for a decree.

Incapacity—s 12(a)

The incapacity must be incurable and permanent. It will be considered incurable if medical treatment would be dangerous or if the respondent refuses to undergo treatment to cure it—*S v S* **(1955)**.

It may be that the incapacity is only in relation to the spouse. So for example a man may be impotent with his wife but capable of having intercourse with another. However, there must be more than a lack of attraction or a mere dislike of the other spouse—*Singh v Singh* (**1971**). There must be 'invincible repugnance'—*G v G* (**1924**).

Wilful refusal—s 12(b)

This was defined in ***Horton v Horton*** (**1947**) as 'a settled and definite decision come to without just excuse'. In this case the wife was reluctant to have intercourse but took advice from her parents and her priest in an attempt to overcome the problem. The husband's petition was dismissed.

Settled and definite decision

In considering whether the respondent has made *a settled and definite decision* not to consummate the marriage, the court will look at all the whole history of the marriage.

....

Potter v Potter (1975) 5 Fam Law 161

In this case, the wife underwent surgery to cure a physical defect which had prevented her having intercourse with her husband. The husband subsequently made a further attempt at intercourse which failed because of the wife's emotional state. He refused to try again and the wife petitioned on the grounds of his wilful refusal. Her petition failed on the grounds that his failure to consummate was not a deliberate decision but a loss of ardour.

....

Without just excuse

A petition will not be granted if the respondent can show that there was a *just excuse* for not consummating the marriage. For example, in ***Kaur v Singh*** (**1972**), even though the couple had been through a civil ceremony, the husband's failure to organise a religious ceremony which was necessary for the marriage to be recognised within the couple's religion, amounted to wilful refusal.

Revision tip

Note that incapacity concerns a physical or psychological inability to consummate the marriage. Wilful refusal occurs if either party, although capable of having intercourse, decides that that they do not wish to do so.

Consent—s 12(c)

Lack of consent may be due to *duress, mistake, unsoundness of mind*, or *otherwise*.

Duress

A marriage which is entered into because of fear or some sort of threat may be voidable.

Grounds on which a marriage may be voidable—s 12 MCA

✳✳✳✳✳✳✳✳✳✳✳✳

Szechter v Szechter [1971] 2 WLR 170

In this case it was held that the test for duress was whether there was a 'threat of immediate danger to life limb or liberty'. In this case the man married the woman so that she could escape a prison sentence in Poland which due to her ill health could have been a threat to her life. The petition was granted.

This objective test set a high hurdle to cross. A person may be coerced into a marriage against their wishes but in most cases there will not have been a threat to life, limb, or liberty, even less an immediate threat. Thus it would be difficult to show duress in the case of most forced marriages.

Hirani v Hirani (1983) 4 FLR 232

In this case, a woman was told that unless she went through an arranged marriage she would be ostracised by her community. This was enough to amount to duress. The court held that it was not necessary to apply the test in **Szechter** in order to show duress. The test should be *whether the threat or pressure is such as to overbear the will of the individual petitioner so as to destroy the reality of consent*, a subjective test.

For an example of a case in which family obligations did not amount to duress see *Singh v Singh* (1971) in the 'Key Cases', p 33.

Revision tip

Note the difference between an arranged marriage and a forced marriage which was discussed in Chapter 1, 'Voluntary', p 2.

Mistake

This must be either mistake as to the *nature of the ceremony* or mistake as to the *identity of the other person*. No other type of mistake will count.

Mehta v Mehta [1945] 2 All ER 690

In this case the wife believed that the ceremony was one of conversion to Hinduism whereas it was actually a ceremony of conversion and marriage. A decree based on mistake as to the nature of the ceremony was granted.

The mistake must relate to the person's identity and not to the person's attributes.

C v C [1942] NZLR 356

A woman met and married a man who claimed to be Michael Miller, a famous Australian boxer. She subsequently discovered that he was not Miller and applied to have the marriage annulled. This was refused because the mistake related to his attributes and not to his identity. She had married the man she intended to marry so the marriage was valid.

Unsoundness of mind

A petition will only be granted under this ground if the unsoundness of mind exists at the time of the marriage. There must be a failure to understand the nature of the marriage contract and the duties and responsibilities involved.

In the Estate of Park (deceased) [1953] 2 All ER 1411

The relatives of an elderly widower who had remarried argued that the marriage was void because he had lacked the necessary mental capacity. The court held that the test should be whether the person is 'capable of understanding the nature of the contract into which he is entering'. Although he was forgetful, he had been determined to marry his second wife. The marriage was held to be a valid one.

Or otherwise

This allows for mistake through factors other than those already mentioned. It could include, for example, where one of the parties was so drunk that they could not validly consent to the marriage. See, for example, *Sullivan v Sullivan* (1812) 2 Hag Con 238 at 246.

Mental disorder—s 12(d)

This would cover any mental illness as defined in the **Mental Health Act 1983**. The illness must be of an extent that makes it impossible for the couple to have a normal married life. The petition must be brought within three years of the date of the marriage. If the illness arises after the marriage has taken place then a petition of nullity would not be possible and the remedy would be divorce.

Revision tip

This ground differs from mistake due to unsoundness of mind in that it covers those who understand the nature of marriage, but owing to their illness they cannot perform the necessary duties. Those who are of unsound of mind may not understand that they are getting married nor the duties attached to it. It is much easier to show mental disorder than unsoundness of mind.

✔️ *Looking for extra marks?*

If your exam question concerns the reform of the law of nullity, you should consider whether it should still be possible to annul a marriage on the grounds of mental illness. Society's attitudes towards this sort of illness have changed since the Act came into force.

Grounds on which a marriage may be voidable—s 12 MCA

✳✳✳✳✳✳✳✳✳✳

Venereal disease—s 12(e)

The respondent must have been suffering from a communicable venereal disease (a sexually transmitted disease) at the time of the marriage and the petitioner must have been unaware of it. The petition must be brought within three years of the date of the marriage.

✅ *Looking for extra marks?*

Should this sort of illness still be a ground to annul a marriage? These days sexually transmitted diseases can in most cases be treated by drugs. Is it justifiable for this ground to exist in relation to marriages but not in relation to civil partnerships?

Pregnancy by another—s 12(f)

This is sometimes referred to as *pregnancy per alium*. The woman must be pregnant at the time of the marriage by someone other than her husband. He must be unaware of this. The petition must be brought within three years.

✅ *Looking for extra marks?*

Note the gender discrimination here. There is no corresponding ground for a woman to petition if another woman is pregnant by the husband at the time of the marriage. It may be possible for her to use the 'or otherwise' option under mistake.

The next two subsections were added by the **Gender Recognition Act 2004**.

An interim gender recognition certificate has been issued to either party—s 12(g)

The marriage can be annulled if one of the parties has obtained an interim gender recognition certificate after the marriage has taken place. The application to annul the marriage must be made with six months of the certificate being granted.

The respondent has an acquired gender—s 12(h)

If one of the parties has acquired a gender recognition certificate before the marriage and the other party is unaware of it then the marriage may be annulled.

✅ *Looking for extra marks?*

You could question whether either of these grounds should be available to annul a marriage. Should it be possible to annul a long marriage, where the parties may have had a family because one of them obtains an interim gender recognition certificate? It was a valid marriage while it lasted. Does it go against the spirit of the **Gender Recognition Act** to allow a marriage to be annulled where a person has not declared that they are in possession of a gender recognition certificate? Would divorce be a more appropriate solution under these circumstances? ⌐

Grounds for a civil partnership being voidable—s 50 CPA

The grounds for a *civil partnership being voidable* are similar to those for a voidable marriage but are contained within **s 50 Civil Partnership Act 2004.** However, it is not possible to annul a civil partnership on the grounds of non-consummation or venereal disease.

Section 50 CPA

(a) either of them did not validly *consent* (due to duress, mistake, unsoundness of mind or otherwise);

(b) either of them, though capable of giving a valid consent, was *suffering from mental disorder* of such a kind or to such an extent as to be unfitted for civil partnership;

(c) the respondent was *pregnant by some person* other than the applicant;

(d) an *interim gender recognition certificate* has, after the time of its formation, been issued to either civil partner;

(e) the respondent is a person whose gender at the time of its formation had become the *acquired gender* under the 2004 Act.

Voidable marriages—bar to nullity

If one of the bars contained within **s 13 MCA** can be established then the decree may not be granted.

Section 13(1)

(a) That the petitioner, with knowledge that it was open to him to have the marriage avoided, so conducted himself in relation to the respondent as to *lead the respondent to believe that he would not seek to do so* and

(b) that it would be *unjust* to the respondent to grant the decree.

Both (a) and (b) must be satisfied.

··

D v D (Nullity) [1979] Fam 70

The wife refused to consummate the marriage. The husband petitioned on the grounds of her wilful refusal. However, he had agreed to adopt children during the marriage, indicating that he wished the marriage to continue. However, as the wife agreed to the petition it was not unjust to grant it.

··

Section 13(2)

This refers to *time limits*. The court will not grant a decree under:

- **s 12(c)**—consent
- **s 12(d)**—mental disorder
- **s 12(e)**—venereal disease
- **s 12(f)**—pregnant by another
- **s 12(h)**—acquired gender,

unless the proceedings were started within three years of the date of the marriage.

The period may be extended by the court if the petitioner had been suffering from some type of mental disorder during the three-year period.

In relation to **s 12(g)** (gender recognition certificate), the court will not grant a decree unless proceedings were started within six months of the interim gender certificate being issued.

Section 13(3)

This refers to *knowledge of the facts*. The court will not grant a decree under **s 12(e), (f), or (g)**, if the petitioner was aware of the facts at the time of the marriage.

The bars in relation to civil partnerships are the same as for marriages but are to be found in **s 51 CPA**.

The future of nullity

There are far fewer nullity petitions than divorce petitions. For example, in 2008 135,994 divorces were granted against 200 decrees for nullity. A popular exam topic is whether the law should be reformed or retained. In 1970 the Law Commission Report considered whether the concept of voidable marriages should be abolished, and those seeking to end their marriage on voidable grounds should divorce instead. It decided against this option because it considered that for many people divorce has a stigma attached to it and because certain religious groups see a distinction between annulment and divorce. It saw no advantage to abolishing voidable marriages. Do these arguments still apply today? See *Report on Nullity of Marriage*, Law Com No 33 (1970).

✳ Key cases

Case	Facts	Principle
Bellinger v Bellinger [2003] UKHL 21	Mrs Bellinger was a male to female transsexual whose husband was aware of her background and supported her application. She applied for a declaration that her marriage was valid on the grounds that she was a female on the date that she married. Her appeal to the House of Lords was dismissed.	Recognising her as a female would mean giving a new meaning to the words male and female. It was not for the court to do this. It was up to Parliament to legislate on whether post-operative transsexuals could marry in their acquired gender. NOTE that following **Goodwin** and **Bellinger**, Parliament passed the **Gender Recognition Act 2004**.
Goodwin v UK [2002] 2 FLR 487	A male to female transsexual complained to the ECHR that she was still legally recognised as a man in relation to employment, pensions, social security, and who she could marry. It was held that her **Article 8** (respect for private and family life) and **Article 12** (right to marry and found a family) rights had been breached.	A test which relied on biological factors (as in **Corbett**) should no longer be used to deny transsexuals the right to legal recognition of their new gender.
Hirani v Hirani [1983] 4 FLR 232	In order to terminate their 19-year-old daughter's relationship with a Muslim man, her parents who were Hindus, arranged for her to marry a Hindu man whom their daughter had never met. She lived with her parents and was financially dependent upon them. They told her that unless she married him they would no longer support her. The marriage was never consummated and the wife applied for a decree of nullity based on duress. At first instance, the judge, using the test from **Szechter**, held that there was no threat to 'life, limb or liberty' and so no duress. On appeal this was overturned and her petition was granted. The threats and pressure by her parents clearly amounted to duress.	The test for duress is not whether there is a threat to life, limb, or liberty, but whether the threats or pressure overbear the will of the individual and destroy the reality of consent.
Kaur v Singh [1972] 1 All ER 292	A Sikh couple went through a civil marriage ceremony. In accordance with their religion they would not live together until a religious ceremony had taken place. It was the husband's duty to do this. He refused to make the arrangements. The wife was awarded a decree based on her husband's wilful refusal.	Failure to organise a religious ceremony, which was essential to ensure recognition of that marriage within that couple's religion, amounted to wilful refusal.

Key debate

✶✶✶✶✶✶✶✶✶✶✶

Case	Facts	Principle
Singh v Singh [1971] 2 WLR 963	The parents of a 17-year-old girl arranged her marriage to a man she had never met. She reluctantly went through with the ceremony but said that she only did so out of respect for her parents and in accordance with her religion. However, she refused to have intercourse with him. She petitioned for a decree of nullity based on the grounds of duress or alternatively on her own incapacity to consummate due to 'invincible repugnance'. The decree was refused.	Going through with a marriage out of respect to her parents and her religion did not amount to duress. It must be shown that her will had been overborne or her consent had been obtained by fear. In relation to incapacity there must be more than a lack of attraction or mere dislike of the other person. Not wishing to be married to someone is not enough to amount to 'invincible repugnance'.

(**”**) Key debate

Topic:	As consummation is not a ground for annulling a civil partnership, should it be abolished as a ground for annulling a marriage?
Academic:	Rebecca Probert
Viewpoint:	Abolition would prevent transsexual marriages being vulnerable and lengthy legal debates on the meaning of consummation would cease.
Reading:	'How would *Corbett v Corbett* be decided today?' (2005) *Fam Law*, vol 35, 382–385

(**?**) Exam questions

Problem Question

Guy, who wants to become a Member of Parliament, believed that he would not be considered as a candidate unless he was married. So he persuaded Sarah, a party worker, to marry him. He told her that unless she married him, she would lose her job if he was elected. Sarah who is financially supporting her elderly parents, reluctantly agreed. The marriage took place 10 months ago. Guy has declined to consummate the marriage. This is because he is in love with Harold with whom he has been having a secret relationship for the past two years.

One month after the marriage, Sarah discovered that she was pregnant with Bill's child. The child was conceived prior to her marriage to Guy. In an attempt to make Guy believe he was the father of the child she drugged his evening meal and pretended the next day that intercourse had taken place, although in reality it had not. When the child was born it had brown eyes, whereas Guy and Sarah both have blue eyes. Guy suspects that the child is not his and as he has failed to be selected as a parliamentary candidate, has decided to be open about his relationship with Harold. Sarah wants to resume her relationship with Bill.

Advise whether, and on what grounds Sarah or Guy could petition for a decree of nullity.

An outline answer is included at the end of the book.

Essay Question

'It is sometimes suggested that there would be much to be said for abolishing the concept of the voidable marriage (with the attendant full hearings and sometimes unpleasant medical examination) and allowing the parties to seek a divorce based on the breakdown of their marriage...' (Cretney, *Principles of Family Law*, p 84).

In light of this comment, do you think the law of nullity should be reformed?

 Scan here

Scan this QR code image with your mobile device to see an outline answer to this question or log onto www.oxfordtextbooks.co.uk/orc/concentrate

#3

Divorce, dissolution, and judicial separation

Key Facts

- Divorce is the legal end of a marriage. A civil partnership is ended by dissolution.

- The only ground for a divorce or dissolution is irretrievable breakdown.

- Five facts can be used to prove a marriage has irretrievably broken down: adultery, behaviour, desertion, two years' separation with consent, and five years' separation.

- You cannot use adultery to prove that a civil partnership has irretrievably broken down, but the other four facts can be used.

- Behaviour, adultery, and desertion are fault-based: one party is blamed for the breakdown of the marriage. The two types of separation do not involve blaming one party.

- Under the current law, behaviour and adultery allow for the quickest divorces. This means that divorce based on fault is quicker than no-fault divorce. This has led to a number of calls for reform.

- The **Family Law Act 1996** aimed to introduce a system of no-fault divorce. The divorce provisions did not come into force. The domestic violence provisions contained within the same Act did come into force.

- Judicial separation can be used as an alternative to divorce. It grants the court power to make orders relating to finances and to children but it does not bring the marriage to an end.

Chapter overview

The ground and facts for divorce/dissolution

Divorce Matrimonial Causes Act 1973	Dissolution of civil partnership Civil Partnership Act 2004
Ground on which a decree can be granted	
Irretrievable breakdown—**s 1(1)**	Irretrievable breakdown—**s 44(1)**
Facts on which the ground must be based	
Adultery and intolerability—**s 1(2)(a)**	
Behaviour—**s 1(2)(b)**	Behaviour—**s 44(5)(a)**
Desertion—**s 1(2)(c)**	Desertion—**s 44(5)(d)**
Two years' separation with consent—**s 1(2)(d)**	Two years' separation with consent—**s 44(5)(b)**
Five years' separation—**s 1(2)(e)**	Five years' separation—**s 44(5)(c)**

Introduction

Divorce is the legal end of a marriage. The law is set out in the **Matrimonial Causes Act 1973** (MCA). Divorce is brought to an end by a decree absolute.

A civil partnership is brought to an end by a dissolution order under the **Civil Partnership Act 2004** (CPA). This has the same effect on a civil partnership as a decree absolute has on a marriage. The procedures for obtaining the decrees are the same in divorce and **dissolution**. The key differences between divorce and dissolution are highlighted later in the chapter.

Revision tip

Note that a **decree nisi** is granted before the decree absolute is granted. A decree nisi is a provisional decree showing the parties are entitled to a divorce. It does not free either party from the marriage: for that they must apply to make it absolute.

For civil partnerships the two stages are a **conditional dissolution order** and a final dissolution order.

✱✱✱✱✱✱✱✱✱✱

A person who applies for a divorce is called the petitioner and the other party to the marriage is called the respondent. A person applying for dissolution of a civil partnership is called the applicant and the other party is called the respondent.

Marriages and civil partnerships can also be brought to an end by a decree of nullity (see further Chapter 2, 'Introduction', p 18). Alternatively the parties can seek judicial separation. This does not bring the marriage to an end but many of its other effects are similar to divorce or dissolution.

Very few divorces are contested. If both parties agree to divorce, then the procedure is straightforward. The divorce petition is filled in, the respondent files an acknowledgement of service and then the petitioner signs a statement confirming the contents of the petition. There is usually no need for the parties to go to court. If everything is in order, the judge will allow the decree to go ahead.

Bar on petitions within one year of marriage

A petitioner cannot present a petition within one year of marriage. However, the petitioner can rely on matters that occurred during the first year of marriage in the petition (**s 3 MCA**).

✔ *Looking for extra marks?*

Consider how long you think it should take for a couple to be able to divorce. At present the one-year bar is in place and the separation facts impose further waiting periods. Should there be a minimum period the parties must stay married before they divorce? Should divorce take the same amount of time regardless of which fact is used? Baroness Deech considers that where adultery and behaviour are used there should be a delay before the parties can remarry ('Divorce—A Disaster?' [2009] *Fam Law* 1048).

The ground for divorce or dissolution

The only ground for divorce is that the marriage has broken down irretrievably. This is set out in **s 1(1) MCA**. The ground for dissolution of a civil partnership is the same (**s 44(1) CPA**).

Irretrievable breakdown must be proved by one of five facts in the case of divorce or four facts in the case of a civil partnership. However, one of the facts alone is not enough. One of the facts must exist and there must be irretrievable breakdown (*Buffery v Buffery* (1988)).

The five facts

These are set out in **s 1(2) MCA**:

Section 1(2) MCA

(a) that the respondent has committed adultery and the petitioner finds it intolerable to live with the respondent;

(b) that the respondent has behaved in such a way that the petitioner cannot reasonably be expected to live with the respondent;

(c) that the respondent has deserted the petitioner for a continuous period of at least two years immediately before the petition is presented;

(d) that the parties to the marriage have lived apart for a continuous period of at least two years immediately before the petition is presented and the respondent consents to a decree being granted;

(e) that the parties to the marriage have lived apart for a continuous period of at least five years immediately before the petition is presented.

Adultery and intolerability—s 1(2)(a)

Adultery is 'a voluntary act of sexual intercourse between the husband or wife and a third party of the opposite sex' (*Dennis v Dennis* **(1995)**). Intercourse must be between a man and a woman. So homosexual intercourse and non-penetrative sex would not count. A petitioner cannot rely on his or her own adultery.

Revision tip

The **Civil Partnership Act** does not provide for adultery to evidence irretrievable breakdown of a civil partnership, even if one of the partners has sexual intercourse with a person of the opposite sex. The petitioner would need to rely on the behaviour fact.

Intercourse must be voluntary, so a person who is raped would not be committing adultery, although they would need to show it was involuntary (*Redpath v Redpath* **(1950)**).

If the respondent denies that adultery has taken place, then it would be up to the petitioner to prove that it has. Circumstantial evidence may be enough, for example that the parties had spent the night together, although such evidence is rebuttable.

The requirements of adultery and intolerability are separate and do not have to be linked— *Cleary v Cleary* **(1974)**.

Intolerability is subjective: the issue is whether this particular petitioner finds it intolerable to live with this particular respondent—*Goodrich v Goodrich* **(1971)**

Effects of continued cohabitation

• If the parties cohabit for less than six months after the petitioner finds out about the final act of adultery this is ignored when deciding if the petitioner finds it intolerable to live with the respondent (**s 2(2) MCA**);

• If the parties cohabit for six months or more after the petitioner finds out about the final act of adultery then the petitioner cannot rely on the adultery (**s 2(1) MCA**).

Behaviour—s 1(2)(b)

This fact is not 'unreasonable behaviour' as it is often abbreviated. It is whether the petitioner can reasonably be expected to live with the respondent following their behaviour.

The test has objective and subjective elements. In *Livingstone-Stallard v Livingstone-Stallard* (1974), Dunn J explained that the question was 'would any right-thinking person come to the conclusion that this husband has behaved in such a way that this wife cannot reasonably be expected to live with him, taking into account the whole of the circumstances and personalities of the parties'.

'Behaviour' includes a wide range of conduct. For example:

- physical violence (*Bergin v Bergin* (1983));
- criticism, disapproval, and boorish behaviour (*Livingstone-Stallard v Livingstone-Stallard*);
- a collection of trivial acts (*O'Neill v O'Neill* (1975))
- an association falling short of adultery. In *Wachtel v Wachtel (No 1)* (1973) the judge was not convinced the wife had committed adultery but allowed the husband to amend his petition so as to rely on behaviour;
- negative behaviour such as prolonged silences and periods of inactivity (*Thurlow v Thurlow* (1975)).

Behaviour does not always suggest the respondent is blameworthy. For example, the petitioner can still establish behaviour where the respondent's behaviour is caused by illness. In these cases the court will consider 'all the obligations of the married state' including the duty to accept and share burdens on the family resulting from the illness. However, the court will also consider the impact on the petitioner and make a judgment about whether the behaviour is enough to allow the petition (*Thurlow v Thurlow*).

It has been suggested that a petitioner cannot rely on the respondent's behaviour where his or her own has been the same. For example, a violent petitioner could reasonably be expected to live with a violent respondent (*Ash v Ash* (1972)).

Not all behaviour is enough. In *Pheasant v Pheasant* (1972) the court refused to accept that the wife's failure to give the husband spontaneous, demonstrative affection fulfilled the test.

Effects of continued cohabitation

- If the parties have lived together for a period or periods totalling less than six months after the final incident of behaviour, that is ignored in deciding whether the petitioner can reasonably be expected to live with the respondent (**s 2(3) MCA**).

- If the parties have lived together for a period or periods totalling six months or more the court will consider whether the petitioner has proven that that it is not reasonable to expect her to live with the respondent (***Bradley v Bradley* (1973)**). Note that in that case the wife had nowhere else to go).

Desertion—s 1(2)(c)

The petitioner must show the following:

The parties have not lived in the same household for a period of two years.

Le Brocq v Le Brocq [1964] 1 WLR 1085

The wife stopped sharing a bedroom with the husband and put a bolt on her bedroom door. She continued to prepare the husband's evening meal but there was no other communication between them. The court held there was no desertion as there was no separation of households. The meals were all cooked in one kitchen and the wife bought the food, which the husband paid for.

There is no good reason for them living apart.

Glenister v Glenister [1945] 1 All ER 513

In this case it was found that the wife had not committed adultery. However, the court found that her conduct gave the husband reasonable cause to believe she had. He had returned home one night to find three men in the house, and one of them in the wife's bedroom. The husband's reasonable belief that the wife had committed adultery gave him reasonable cause to leave which meant that he had not deserted her.

See also ***G v G* (1964)**. The husband was mentally ill and his behaviour scared the children. This was held to be good reason for the separation and so the wife's refusal to live with the husband was not desertion.

The respondent intends to stay permanently separated.

Perry v Perry [1963] 3 All ER 766

The wife suffered delusions that the husband was trying to kill her and she left the matrimonial home. It was held that she did not have the mental capacity to form an intention to desert. However, note **s 2(4) MCA**, which deals with the situation where a deserting party does not have the capacity to *continue* the intention to desert. The court can treat the intention as continuing if it is satisfied that, had the person not been incapable, it would have inferred the intention on the evidence presented.

The parties do not consent to the separation.

....

Joseph v Joseph [1953] 2 ALL ER 710

In this case the husband deserted the wife. She was granted a Get (a Jewish divorce which has no effect under English law). She later petitioned for divorce on the basis of the husband's desertion. The court held that in applying for a Get she had consented to the husband's separation. Her consent to the separation brought the desertion to an end.

....

Effects of continued cohabitation

If the parties resume living together for a period or periods totalling less than six months this will not prevent the petitioner from relying on desertion. However, periods when the parties lived together will not be counted towards the two-year period (**s 2(5) MCA**).

Two years' separation and consent—s 1(2)(d)

If the parties agree that they want to divorce and are not going to rely on fault of either party then this fact can be used.

You should note that the date on which the parties separate does not count for the purposes of the two-year period. The petition can be filed on the day after the second anniversary of the date the parties separated.

What is 'separation'?

Separation has a mental element as well as a physical element.

The mental element

In *Santos v Santos* (1972) the court held that the parties could not be regarded as 'living apart' where they both recognised the marriage as continuing. The court must consider the parties' attitudes towards the marriage to see whether, at some stage, the petitioner ceased to recognise the marriage as continuing, regarding it a mere shell, and had no intention of returning to the respondent.

The physical element

Many couples cannot afford to run two households. This means that when they separate it is not possible for one of them to move out into rented accommodation or to buy a new house. Where the couple is still living together it can be more difficult to prove they have separated. The key is for the parties to prove that they are not living with each other in the same household (**s 2(6) MCA**).

In *Fuller (Otherwise Penfold) v Fuller* (1973) the court found that the husband and wife were living apart, when he shared a home with his wife and her new partner as their lodger.

In *Mouncer v Mouncer* (1972) the parties did not sleep together, but ate together and shared the cleaning. They were not living apart.

In contrast, in *Hollens v Hollens* (1971) the parties continued to live together but did not talk and they did not eat together. They were found to be living apart.

Consent

The respondent must consent to the divorce. Consent must be freely given and it can be withdrawn at any time. The petitioner must give the respondent enough information for the respondent to understand the consequences of consenting to the divorce. The parties must also have the capacity to consent (*Mason v Mason* (1972)).

The respondent must be given enough information to understand the steps he must take to consent to the divorce (**s 2(7) MCA**). The fact of consent is usually proved by the respondent signing an acknowledgement of service. This is a document in which the respondent acknowledges he has received the petition and he answers various questions about it. Consent will not be inferred.

Effects of continued cohabitation

- If the parties resume living together for a period or periods totalling less than six months this will not prevent the petitioner from relying on separation. However, periods when the parties lived together will not be counted towards the two-year period (**s 2 (5) MCA**).

Five years' separation—s 1(2)(e)

This allows the petitioner to divorce his or her spouse without their consent. However, there are defences to a divorce under this fact.

Separation has the same elements when this fact is relied upon as when there is consent.

Effects of continued cohabitation

- If the parties resume living together for a period or periods totalling less than six months this will not prevent the petitioner from relying on separation. However, periods when the parties lived together will not be counted towards the five-year period (**s 2(5) MCA**).

Defence—s 5 (see s 47 CPA)

Under **s 5 MCA**, a court can refuse to grant a divorce if the grant would:

> **Section 5 MCA**
>
> (1)   cause the respondent grave financial or other hardship; and
>
> (2)   be wrong in all the circumstances.

Other bars to divorce

Financial arrangements (this only applies to two and five years' separation)

Under **s 10(2) MCA** the respondent can apply to the court for consideration of his financial position after divorce. Following this assessment, **s 10(3)** states that the court cannot make a decree absolute unless it is satisfied that:

> **Section 10(3) MCA**
>
> (a)   the petitioner should not be required to make any financial provision for the respondent; or
>
> (b)   the financial provision made by the petitioner for the respondent is reasonable and fair or the best that can be made in the circumstances.

Religious marriage

If the marriage is a religious marriage the parties may have to cooperate to take the steps needed to end their marriage under religious law. If one party refuses to cooperate **s 10A MCA** allows the court to order that decree *nisi* will not be made absolute until both parties make a declaration to the court that the steps have been taken. It must be reasonable and just in all the circumstances for the court to make this order (**s 10A(3)(a)**).

Orders relating to children

Section 41 MCA allows the court to refuse to make a decree absolute (or grant a judicial separation) in cases where there are children if the court feels:

> **Section 41 MCA**
>
> (1)   the court is likely to be required to exercise powers under **the Children Act 1989**;
>
> (2)   the court is not able to exercise those powers without considering the case further; and
>
> (3)   there are exceptional circumstances making it desirable in the interests of the child that the court should give a direction under **s 41**.

Divorce reform: problems with the current law

It is confusing and unjust

The idea of proving the ground of 'irretrievable breakdown' on the basis of one of the facts is not an obvious one and may confuse. Parties may have a marriage that has broken down irretrievably but be unable to prove this on the basis of adultery or behaviour. If so, the parties are forced to rely on the separation grounds and so must have lived apart for at least two years. This means that fault-based divorce is faster, which may be seen as unjust. Additionally, it may encourage the parties to petition on a fault-based ground when they might not otherwise have done so.

It does not promote ongoing relationships

Most divorce petitions are based on behaviour. Blaming one party for the breakdown of the marriage does not encourage the parties to move forward and continue any kind of relationship. Particularly where children are involved, it is important that the parties can be civil and can communicate going forward. Additionally, blaming one parent for the breakdown of a marriage may create problems for the relationship between that parent and their child. Even when there are no children involved it is likely that the parties will have mutual friends and their lives will be relatively intertwined. It is equally unhelpful in these situations for the parties to have no ongoing relationship.

The problem is also seen where separation is the fact used. Many couples cannot afford to maintain two homes so they may have to continue to live together. Where this happens the parties must demonstrate that they are living apart. As can be seen from the case law outlined earlier, the law encourages parties to avoid any kind of ongoing relationship.

Conflict of fact and reality

The focus on proving facts can distort a situation. Both parties may have behaved very badly but the behaviour of the person who petitions is not taken into account. It is possible for parties to cross-petition, which means that both petition for divorce, but this is rare in practice and increases legal costs.

Distorted bargaining positions

If there is insufficient evidence to petition on the basis of adultery or behaviour and one party refuses to consent then the other party must petition on the basis of five years' separation. If one party is keen to divorce quickly then the other could use the threat of a drawn-out divorce as a negotiating tool in discussions about financial settlement or children.

Is no-fault divorce a better solution?

Different time periods reflect the different reasons for a divorce

Fault-based divorce should be faster because the fault involved proves that the marriage is truly at an end. Where a divorce is based on consent there should be a longer period to give the parties time to reflect on their decision. Whilst adultery and behaviour are facts that prove the end of a marriage unquestionably, in other circumstances there might be the possibility of saving the relationship.

One counter to this argument is that there may be many other, equally important, reasons why marriages fail. Ultimately a marriage is brought to an end because it has broken down irretrievably. To say that some ways of proving this are more convincing than others is very simplistic. It also undermines the ability of the parties to consent to the end of their marriage.

Failure to reflect the views of the parties

A petitioner who cites adultery or behaviour may view the respondent as to blame for the divorce. No-fault divorce means that both parties are seen as equally responsible for the breakdown of the marriage. The petitioner may feel this is unfair and unjust and may want friends and family to know 'the truth'.

Message to society

If one party has behaved particularly badly, for example if there has been domestic violence, there may be good reason to highlight this as blameworthy behaviour to send a message to society. No-fault divorce means this is not possible.

Undermining marriage

If a marriage can be ended for any reason then it undermines the idea of a commitment for life. The parties could divorce on a whim and do not have the same incentive to try and make the marriage work.

Family Law Act 1996

This Act introduced a no-fault system of divorce. However, the Act was never brought into force and the Government has indicated its intention to repeal the Act (see the 2013 Children and Families Bill). The 1996 Act is notable as a failed attempt to introduce no-fault divorce and it is important to take account of this failure of reform in any consideration of how the law should be reformed (if it should be reformed at all).

General principles

Section 1 outlined the aims of the Act:

Section 1

(a) to support the institution of marriage;

(b) to encourage the parties to take all practicable steps to save a marriage which has broken down;

(c) where a marriage has broken down irretrievably, to end the marriage with minimal distress to any children, with any questions dealt with in a way likely to promote a good continuing relationship between the parties and any children, and without unnecessary costs; and

(d) to remove or diminish the risk of violence to the parties and any children in so far as reasonably practicable.

The procedure under the 1996 Act

Note that this is a simplified version of the procedure which assumes that there are no complications along the way.

Reasons for failure of the Act

The Government carried out a pilot study to see how well the information meetings would function. The findings of the study were that the procedure under the **1996 Act** did not help to fulfil the aims of the Act, in particular the aim to save marriages:

- the results showed that those who were uncertain when they went to an information meeting left the meeting being more inclined to divorce;

- generally only the petitioner attended the meetings. Marriage counselling and **mediation** need the involvement of both spouses; and

- the procedures in the Act were seen to be complex and it was felt they would cause delays and uncertainty.

Mediation

✳✳✳✳✳✳✳✳✳✳

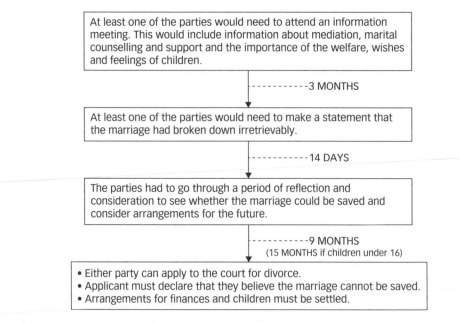

At least one of the parties would need to attend an information meeting. This would include information about mediation, marital counselling and support and the importance of the welfare, wishes and feelings of children.

----------3 MONTHS

At least one of the parties would need to make a statement that the marriage had broken down irretrievably.

----------14 DAYS

The parties had to go through a period of reflection and consideration to see whether the marriage could be saved and consider arrangements for the future.

----------9 MONTHS
(15 MONTHS if children under 16)

- Either party can apply to the court for divorce.
- Applicant must declare that they believe the marriage cannot be saved.
- Arrangements for finances and children must be settled.

Figure 3.1 Timescales under Family Law Act 1996

✔ Looking for extra marks?

Consider what the aims of divorce law should be. In particular, consider whether it is appropriate for the law of divorce to try and save marriages or improve the quality of the relationship between the parties, particularly where there are dependent children. You may find it useful to refer to Chapter 17 of the Final Evaluation Report on the Research by Newcastle University into the **Family Law Act 1996** provisions on information meetings. You can find the Report at webarchive.nationalarchives.gov.uk/+/http://www.dca.gov.uk/family/fla/fullrep.pdf.

Mediation

What is mediation?

Mediation is an alternative to the court process. The parties try to reach an agreement between themselves and an independent third party, the mediator, helps them to do this. The parties may still be represented by lawyers but the aim of the process is to avoid going to court. Equally the parties may choose not to have lawyers and may go through the process themselves.

The key use for mediation in divorce is in agreeing the terms of the financial settlement (see further Chapter 5, 'Financial provision on divorce or dissolution', p 77 on this topic). Governments are often very keen to promote mediation as a way to reduce court costs. An emphasis on mediation can be seen in the **1996 Act** and the 2013 Children and Families Bill provides that anyone who wants to make certain family law applications must attend a mediation information and assessment meeting (MIAM) first (unless certain exceptions apply). The aim of an MIAM is to give people information about alternatives to the court process and give them the chance to consider using those alternatives.

Revision tip

You should note that mediation is not linked to reconciliation. The mediation process aims to achieve an agreement so the parties can move forward. It is not concerned with getting the parties back together.

The advantages

- It promotes cooperation between the parties. The court process can be far more adversarial.

- The process is more flexible than the court process so the parties can focus on the particular issues that are important to them rather than those a court feels are important.

- Family law is a particularly private area of law and it may be more appropriate to settle matters privately than in a court where this is possible.

- It may reduce legal costs, particularly if the parties do not have lawyers. Court time is very expensive as the parties may have to pay for both a barrister and a solicitor to attend.

- If the parties are not faced with the pressure and stress of a court environment they may be more likely to reach an agreement suitable to both of them. The pressure of court is more likely to lead to snap decisions and if the parties cannot agree a judge will impose a decision on them.

The problems

- Where the parties have unequal bargaining power mediation may lead to an unfair result. Domestic violence is a key example of this but there may be inequality in a far wider range of situations. For example, where one party has always managed the finances the other may be used to deferring to them in financial decisions and may feel intimidated to challenge them.

- Mediation can take as long as a court hearing so if the parties do have solicitors the costs can be as high. If mediation fails there may need to be a court hearing as well so the costs could be greater.

cial separation

✳✳✳✳✳✳✳✳

Mediation may not give enough consideration to children's needs and wishes. Courts must consider what is best for children. Mediation is not as structured and there is no obligation to consider children.

- Judges have at least some prescribed qualifications whereas mediators can be from a range of backgrounds. Not all mediators will be suitable for all divorces. For example, where there are lots of complex financial assets involved a mediator may not have the experience to understand these properly.

✅ *Looking for extra marks?*

Mediation is not the only alternative to the court process. Other options are collaborative law and family law arbitration. 'The Evolving Role of the Family Lawyer: The Impact of Collaborative Law on Family Law Practice' [2011] *CFLQ* 370–392 gives an overview of the features of collaborative law and considers the impact it might have on family law in some detail. 'Arbitration in Family Financial Proceedings: The IFLA Scheme Part 1' [2012] *Fam Law* 1353–1360 provides more information about family law arbitration.

Judicial separation

Some couples may seek a **judicial separation** rather than a divorce, although the number is very few in reality. This does not bring the marriage to an end. For this reason you do not need to prove that the marriage has broken down irretrievably. You do, however, need to establish one of the five facts (**s 17 MCA**).

Civil partners can obtain a separation order which is equivalent to judicial separation. To obtain this you need to prove one of the four facts.

The main effects of judicial separation are:

- the parties no longer have to live together;
- the courts can make orders relating to the parties' finances and any children; and
- if one of the parties dies without making a will the other will not be entitled to inherit.

Unlike divorce, judicial separation does not remove any benefits that the parties may have under the pension scheme of the other spouse.

Why seek judicial separation?

- The parties may have moral or religious objections to divorce.
- The parties may not have been married for a year.
- One of the other bars to divorce might apply.
- The parties may not be able to prove that the marriage has broken down irretrievably.

Judicial separation does not prevent the parties from obtaining a divorce later. If the parties want to be married again they can request that the courts rescind their judicial separation.

Revision tip

Note that, because judicial separation does not bring the marriage to an end, neither party is free to remarry. This could be a particular problem where the reason for the judicial separation is that one of the parties has a religious or moral objection to divorce. If the other has no such objection then he or she will be unable to remarry if they obtain a judicial separation rather than a divorce.

(✱) *Key cases*

Case	Facts	Principle
Cleary v Cleary [1974] 1 All ER 498	The husband and wife reconciled for five–six weeks after the wife's adultery. She stayed in contact with the other man during that period. The husband petitioned for divorce and said he could no longer live with the wife because there was no future in the marriage. Lord Denning held that adultery and intolerability were two separate limbs. Although the husband forgave the adultery he found it intolerable to live with the wife because of her behaviour after the adultery. Therefore both limbs of the test were established.	Adultery and intolerability do not have to be linked.
Fuller v Fuller [1973] 2 All ER 650	The wife had left the husband and moved in with Mr Penfold. She called herself Mrs Penfold and they lived together as if they were married, although she remained married to the husband. When the husband became unwell he moved in with the wife and Mr Penfold as their lodger, paying them for his bedroom. He ate some meals with the family and the wife did all the washing. The court considered they were living apart. The wife lived with Mr Penfold as his wife. The husband was a lodger in the house.	Living together means living together as husband and wife.
Hollens v Hollens (1971) 115 SJ 237	The husband and wife had a violent argument. Although they continued to live together they did not speak or eat together again. Divorce granted.	A couple may live in the same premises as long as all common life has ceased.

Key debate

✳✳✳✳✳✳✳✳✳✳✳

Case	Facts	Principle
Livingstone-Stallard v Livingstone-Stallard [1974] 2 All ER 766	The couple married when he was 56 and she was 24. The husband patronised the wife and continually criticised her. He became very angry after she gave sherry to a photographer who visited the house when he was not present. She left him after a violent argument and was successful in her petition for divorce under **s 1(2)(b)**.	The test for behaviour is 'would any right thinking person come to the conclusion that this husband has behaved in such a way that this wife cannot reasonably be expected to live with him, taking into account the whole of the circumstances and the character and personalities'.
Mouncer v Mouncer [1972] 1 WLR 321	In this case the wife left the shared bedroom to share with their daughter and the husband shared with their son. The parties ate together, not always in the company of the children, and the wife cooked the meals. The parties shared the cleaning and cleaned the entire house. The wife did not do the husband's washing and he only remained at the matrimonial home to live with and help look after the children. They were regarded as living together in the same household.	All common life between a couple must cease before they can be said to be living apart.
Santos v Santos [1972] Fam 247	The husband lived in Spain and the wife in England. The wife had visited the husband for short periods and shared a bed. Petition for divorce under **s 1(2)(d)** dismissed.	Living apart involves a mental element as well as a physical element.

⑩ Key debate

Topic:	Should everyone resolve their finances on divorce outside the court process?
Academic:	Robert Dingwall
Viewpoint:	Government calls to promote mediation in divorce ignore lack of evidence that mediation is effective or that lawyers promote conflict in divorcing couples.
Reading:	'Divorce mediation: should we change our mind?' (2010) *Journal of Social Welfare and Family Law* 32: 2, 107–117

Academic:	Lord Wilson of Culworth
Viewpoint:	There are good reasons why some cases need to be determined by the court. However, alternative methods of resolving disputes should be supported
Reading:	'Family Dispute Resolution' [2012] *Fam Law* 289–293

Topic:	**Should the civil partnerships and marriages be regulated by one Act?**
Academics:	Sarah Beresford and Caroline Faulks
Viewpoint:	This article argues that the **MCA 1973** should be repealed and all such relationships should be regulated by the **CPA 2004**.
Reading:	(2009) *Liverpool Law Review* 30:1–12

② Exam questions

Problem question

Tom and Fred have been in a civil partnership for 11 months. Tom recently became very suspicious of Fred's behaviour and went through the text messages in his phone. This led him to believe that Fred was having an affair. When Tom confronted Fred about this Fred confessed that he had been having a relationship with Elizabeth, a colleague from work. Fred swore this had been a stupid mistake and that his relationship with Elizabeth was over. Tom was devastated and confided in Matt, the couple's next door neighbour. Tom and Matt became very close and Tom has recently told Fred that he and Matt want to enter into a civil partnership. Fred does not think that his relationship with Tom is over and wants them to reconcile.

Advise Tom about how he could bring his civil partnership to an end.

An outline answer is included at the end of the book.

Essay question

'The present divorce law (**Matrimonial Causes Act 1973**) is unsatisfactory. Although it appears to retain some fault grounds, it is in reality 'no fault' divorce; but also with much bitterness involved. It is quick and impersonal, and gives insufficient attention to the children.' (www.famyouth.org.uk/bulletin.php?number=103

Is this a fair reflection of the current law? Should the law of divorce be reformed?

 Scan here

Scan this QR code image with your mobile device to see an outline answer to this question or log onto www.oxfordtextbooks.co.uk/orc/concentrate

#4

Domestic violence

Key Facts

- **Domestic violence** is not limited to physical abuse.

- **Non-molestation orders** under the **Family Law Act 1996** (FLA) prohibit a person from molesting a person they are associated with, or a relevant child. Breach of an order is a criminal offence but, if criminal proceedings are not taken, breach can be dealt with in the civil courts as a contempt of court.

- **Occupation orders** regulate the occupation of property. Various categories of applicant can seek occupation orders. The orders they can obtain depend on whether they are married, whether they have an interest in the property, and other factors. Breach of an order is dealt with as a contempt of court.

- Non-molestation orders and occupation orders can be applied for on an *ex parte* basis (without notice to the respondent).

- In some circumstances it may be possible to accept an undertaking (a formal promise to the court) instead of making an order.

- If the parties are not associated persons protection may be available under the **Protection from Harassment Act 1997**.

Chapter overview

Non-molestation orders

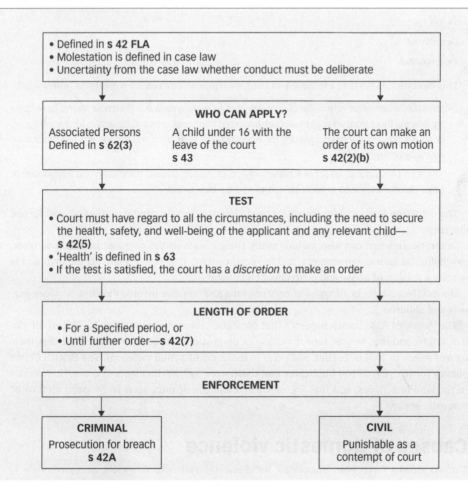

- Defined in **s 42 FLA**
- Molestation is defined in case law
- Uncertainty from the case law whether conduct must be deliberate

WHO CAN APPLY?

| Associated Persons Defined in **s 62(3)** | A child under 16 with the leave of the court **s 43** | The court can make an order of its own motion **s 42(2)(b)** |

TEST

- Court must have regard to all the circumstances, including the need to secure the health, safety, and well-being of the applicant and any relevant child— **s 42(5)**
- 'Health' is defined in **s 63**
- If the test is satisfied, the court has a *discretion* to make an order

LENGTH OF ORDER

- For a Specified period, or
- Until further order—**s 42(7)**

ENFORCEMENT

| **CRIMINAL** Prosecution for breach **s 42A** | **CIVIL** Punishable as a contempt of court |

Introduction

As from March 2013 the Government's definition of domestic violence and abuse is extended to include people aged 16 and 17. The definition is:

> Any incident or pattern of incidents of controlling, coercive or threatening behaviour, violence or abuse between those aged 16 or over who are or have been intimate partners or family members

regardless of gender or sexuality. This can encompass, but is not limited to, the following types of abuse:

- psychological
- physical
- sexual
- financial
- emotional

This definition is further explained on the Government's *directgov* website as follows:

- 'Controlling behaviour is: a range of acts designed to make a person subordinate and/or dependent by isolating them from sources of support, exploiting their resources and capacities for personal gain, depriving them of the means needed for independence, resistance and escape and regulating their everyday behaviour.'
- 'Coercive behaviour is: an act or a pattern of acts of assault, threats, humiliation and intimidation or other abuse that is used to harm, punish, or frighten their victim.'

The definition also includes 'honour'-based violence, female genital mutilation, and forced marriage.

Domestic violence can also include many things, such as the constant breaking of trust, psychological games, harassment, and financial control. It is rarely a one-off incident and is usually a pattern of abuse and controlling behaviour.

It can affect adults in all types of relationships and can also involve violence between parents and children.

The Women's Aid charity suggests that domestic violence accounts for 16–25% of all violent crime, and that 89% of repeat victims of domestic violence are women (note that their figures relate to 2004 or earlier, and refer to incidents of actual violence). The British Crime Survey for the year 2010/11 indicates that there were 392,000 incidents of domestic violence in England and Wales, and that 7% of women and 5% of men aged 16–59 were victims of domestic abuse.

Causes of domestic violence

Various causes have been suggested for domestic violence. A widely accepted view is summed up by the National Center for Victims of Crime (USA):

Domestic violence is about power and control. The abuser wants to dominate in order to establish and maintain authority and power. Perpetrators of domestic violence are usually not sick or deranged, but have learned abusive, manipulative techniques and behaviors that allow them to dominate and control others and obtain the responses they desire.

Other causes which have been suggested may be separate causes, or may be interwoven with aspects of power and control—alcohol abuse; other drug abuse; personality issues leading to excessive reactions to conflict, mental illness, frustration, or stress because of poverty or unemployment.

Dealing with domestic violence

It is clear that domestic violence is a significant issue. A number of civil and criminal law remedies are relevant to deal with domestic violence:

Civil law

- Non-molestation and occupation orders under the **Family Law Act 1996**.
- Injunctions under the **Protection from Harassment Act 1997**.
- Domestic violence protection notices and orders under ss 24–33 of the **Police & Security Act 2010** (being piloted in three police areas).
- Orders under the **Forced Marriages (Civil Protection) Act 2007**.

Criminal law

- Offences of violence under the **Offences Against the Person Act 1861**.
- Public order offences under the **Public Order Act 1986**.
- Offences of harassment under the 1997 Act (which also provides for restraining orders to be made).

Revision tip

If you have an essay question in your exam you could be asked whether the law is adequate to cope with the problem of domestic violence. It is useful to have an overview of the causes of domestic violence, the remedies available, and any other initiatives that are being undertaken. It is important that you are familiar with the civil remedies contained within the **Family Law Act** and the **Protection from Harassment Act** if you are going to answer a problem question.

Other steps

Steps which have been taken to try to ensure that domestic violence is dealt with more effectively include:

- establishing over 120 Specialist Domestic Violence Courts, which deal only with cases of domestic violence, with specially trained magistrates and court officers;
- appointment of nearly 1,000 Independent Domestic Violence Advocates (IDVAs) who work with victims to assess risk, discuss the range of suitable options, and develop coordinated safety plans;

- specially tailored programmes, such as the Integrated Domestic Abuse Programme (IDAP), have been developed by the National Offender Management Service (NOMS) as community order requirements for those convicted of domestic abuse offences;

- about 250 Multi-Agency Risk Assessment Conferences (MARACs) have been established in England and Wales to coordinate responses of police, social services, health, probation, and education services to domestic abuse;

- various public bodies have published their policies on dealing with domestic violence, such as:

  - ACPO's Guidance (originally issued in 2004) was updated in 2008 and reissued by the National Policing Improvement Agency under the slightly different title 'Guidance on Investigating Domestic Abuse'.

  - The Crown Prosecution Service published a 'Policy for Prosecuting Cases of Domestic Violence' in March 2009. Annex A of this Policy contains a very full list of offences relevant to dealing with domestic violence.

  - The President of the Family Division issued the *Practice Direction: Residence and Contact Orders: Domestic Violence and Harm* (2009).

✅ Looking for extra marks?

In March 2011 the Government launched 'Call to end violence against women and girls: Action Plan'. This set out a number of actions the Government will take to tackle violence against women and girls. Note that the violence being considered in this document is not just domestic violence.

Civil law remedies

The main remedies in relation to domestic violence are contained within **Part IV of the Family Law Act 1996**. Non-molestation orders are intended to prohibit molestation and occupation orders regulate the occupation of the family home. The Law Commission had proposed the Act on the basis that 'the sooner the range, scope and effect of (existing) powers are rationalised into a coherent and comprehensive body of statute law the better'. However, media opposition while the Bill was in Parliament (notably from the *Daily Mail*) led to amendments which have made the provisions highly technical and complex, particularly in relation to occupation orders.

Non-molestation orders

These orders are in the nature of injunctions, forbidding a domestic violence perpetrator from repeating certain behaviour.

Under **s 42 FLA** the respondent is prohibited from:

- molesting an associated person; and
- molesting a relevant child.

Molestation

This is not defined in the **FLA**, but has been defined in case law.

See *Vaughan v Vaughan* **(1973)**, *Horner v Horner* **(1982)**, *C v C* **(1998)** in 'Key Cases', p 73 for some examples of conduct indicating the courts' interpretation of what might or might not constitute **molestation**.

There is some uncertainty in the case law about whether conduct must be deliberate.

....

Banks v Banks [1999] 1 FLR 726

The wife suffered from manic depression and dementia. She was verbally and physically aggressive but this was not something she could control, so that a non-molestation order would serve no practical purpose, even if the wife could understand the order.

....

In contrast, in *G v G (Occupation Order: Conduct)* **(2000)** the Court of Appeal considered this issue in the context of an occupation order and it was held that:

Plainly, the court's concentration must be upon the effect of conduct rather than on the intention of the doer. Whether misconduct is intentional or unintentional is not the question…The effect is what the judge must assess. Tiny wounds may be inflicted with great malice: great blows may be struck unintentionally.

✅ *Looking for extra marks?*

Consider whether you think non-molestation orders should be granted in cases where the conduct in question is not deliberate.

Do you think there is a difference between cases where the perpetrator does not intend their actions and those in which the perpetrator cannot control their actions?

Who can apply for a non-molestation order?

1. Associated persons—**s 42(2)(a) FLA**.
2. A child under the age of 16 with leave of the court—**s 43 FLA**.
3. The court can make a non-molestation order even though no application has been made—**s 42(2)(b)**.

Associated persons

This is defined in **s 62(3) FLA**. The following 10 headings indicate those who are included in the term associated persons.

1. They are or have been married to each other

2. They are or have been civil partners of each other

Who can apply for a non-molestation order?

✶✶✶✶✶✶✶✶✶✶✶

3. They are cohabitants or former cohabitants

Cohabitant is defined in **s 62(1) FLA** as two people who are not married or in a civil partnership but who are living together as husband and wife or as if they were civil partners.

....

G v G [2000] 2 FLR 533

A man and woman lived separately but spent several nights a week together and talked of marrying. When the man sold his house the money was put into a joint account, most of which was spent on the woman's home. The man eventually moved in. It was held that the parties were former cohabitants, as three of the 'signposts' set out in the earlier case of **Crake v Supplementary Benefits Commission** (1982) were present:

1. the parties had a sexual relationship;

2. there was evidence that the parties lived in the same household; and

3. there was substantial evidence that the parties operated a joint account; into which the man's proceeds of sale had been paid and which was spent on the woman's property.

....

4. They live or have lived in the same household

Note that they must have not lived in the same household merely because one of them is the other's employee, tenant, lodger, or boarder.

5. They are relatives

A list of relatives is set out in **s 63(1)**. It includes a wide variety of relatives, extending as far as first cousins.

6. They have agreed to marry (it does not matter if the agreement has been terminated)

Section 44 FLA sets out the evidence a court will accept of an agreement to marry:

- evidence in writing—the agreement to marry does not need to be in writing, but there does need to be some written evidence, for example a wedding invitation;
- the gift of an engagement ring; or
- a ceremony in the presence of one or more people who are there to witness the ceremony—commentators generally consider that an engagement party would not be enough.

7. They have entered into a civil partnership agreement (it does not matter if that agreement has been terminated)

The agreement must be evidenced in the same way as an agreement to marry, with the exception that the gift from one party to another does not have to be an engagement ring.

8. They have or have had an intimate personal relationship with each other which is or was of significant duration

The court will decide whether the relationship meets these criteria. This covers a long-standing relationship which may, or may not, be a sexual relationship, but which is an intimate and personal one. It does not include long-term platonic friends or 'one-night stands'.

See Paragraph 24, Section 4 of the explanatory notes to the **Domestic Violence, Crime and Victims Act 2004** (an Act which amended the **FLA**).

9. They are both parents of a child or they both have or have had parental responsibility for a child

10. They are parties to the same family proceedings, other than proceedings under Part IV FLA

✅ *Looking for extra marks?*

In 'The End of Domestic Violence' (2006) 99(5) *MLR* 770, Helen Reece considers the definition of associated persons and considers that the extended definition does not aim protection at the right people.

Relevant child

This is defined in **s 62(2) FLA** and includes any child:

- who lives with, or may reasonably be expected to live with, a party to the proceedings;
- who is subject to an adoption or Children Act order;
- whose interests the court considers relevant.

Child applicants

Under **s 43(2)** the court will grant leave for the child to apply for an order if it is satisfied that the child has sufficient understanding to make the application.

When will an order be made?

The test for a non-molestation order is set out in **s 42(5) FLA**. The court will have regard to all circumstances including the need to secure the health and well-being of the applicant and any relevant child. Even if the test is satisfied the court is not obliged to make an order.

Length of the order

A non-molestation order may be made for a specified period or until a further order is made—**s 42(7) FLA**.

Enforcement of orders and the effect of breach

Under **s 42A FLA** it is an offence to breach the terms of a non-molestation order without reasonable excuse. The Crown Prosecution Service will decide whether to prosecute.

The police have the general powers to arrest for an offence, under the **Police and Criminal Evidence Act 1984**, and a power of arrest cannot be attached to the order itself.

Previously, the victim had to decide whether to bring proceedings for contempt of court. Now, if (and only if) there are no criminal proceedings, the applicant *may* enforce the order as a contempt of court, and apply to the court for a warrant of arrest—**s 47(8) FLA**.

✅ Looking for extra marks?

Do you think decisions in the area of domestic violence should be made by the victim?

In deciding whether to prosecute, the Crown Prosecution Service must apply their 'reasonable prospect of conviction' and 'public interest' tests. Might this process reduce the focus on the effect of the conduct on the victim?

You made find it helpful to read Jonathan Herring's consideration of this issue in *Family Law* (5th edn) at p 317.

Occupation orders

Applications for occupation orders can be made under **ss 33, 35, 36, 37, or 38 of the FLA**. Applications under **s 33** can only be made by a person entitled to occupy the property—an *entitled* applicant. This may be because of a beneficial estate or interest or contract or matrimonial home rights.

Applications under the other sections can be made by those who are not entitled to occupy the property—non-entitled applicants.

You should note that occupation orders have the potential to remove somebody from their home. This may be a significant infringement of their property rights. There are two forms of order:

- Declaratory orders—The court may declare that the person is entitled to occupy the property because of a beneficial estate, interest or contract, or matrimonial home rights. Applications can only be made by an entitled applicant.

- Regulatory orders—Available to all applicants. These regulate the occupation of the family home, possibly by ousting one person and allowing another to go into occupation.

✅ Looking for extra marks?

Consider the consequences of non-molestation orders and occupation orders for the respondent. Which do you think are more serious and why? Do the tests for occupation and non-molestation orders reflect this?

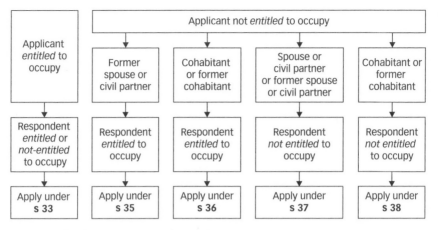

Figure 4.1 Parties to occupation order applications

Who can apply for an occupation order?

Figure 4.1 indicates which section of the **FLA** applies, depending on the status of the applicant and the respondent. The parties must be associated but the range of associated persons is much narrower than those who can apply for a non-molestation order, ie they must be entitled or non-entitled applicants.

The significant harm test

The significant harm test is found in **s 33(7) FLA**, and applies to applications for occupation orders.

This balances the harm that the applicant or relevant child is likely to suffer, because of the respondent's conduct, if an order is not made, with the harm likely to be suffered by the respondent or relevant child if the order is made.

There are two stages for the court to consider:

- Will the applicant (and any relevant child) suffer 'significant harm' without an order?
- If making an order will cause significant harm to the respondent (and any relevant child), where does the 'balance of harm' lie?

Harm, in relation to an adult, means 'ill-treatment or the impairment of (physical or mental) health'. In relation to a child the meaning is extended to include the impairment of development—**s 63(1) FLA**.

Ill-treatment is not limited to physical ill-treatment and includes sexual abuse of a child.

Significant in relation to an adult means 'considerable, noteworthy or important'—Booth LJ, in ***Humberside County Council v B* (1993)**. This is a **Children Act 1989** case. Significant

The significant harm test

✱✱✱✱✱✱✱✱✱✱

harm is not defined in the **FLA** but, as it is a term taken from the **1989 Act**, case law under that Act can be used to glean its meaning.

Two cases suggest that the balancing exercise required by the test may make the courts reluctant to make an order.

B v B [1999] 2 FCR 251

A married couple lived with their young daughter and the husband's son from a previous relationship. Because of the husband's violence the wife left with the daughter, and they were placed in temporary council accommodation, The woman sought an occupation order in respect of the home where the husband was living with his son. Her application failed because the son would suffer greater harm than the wife and daughter.

Chalmers v Johns [1999] 2 FCR 110

The parties cohabited for 25 years and had an adult son and a seven-year-old daughter. The parties had a tempestuous relationship and the woman and daughter eventually left after various minor incidents of violence. They were placed in temporary council accommodation. The woman applied for an occupation order. She failed to establish significant harm, so the matter was decided on the exercise of discretion. An occupation order was refused, on the basis that these were draconian orders overriding property rights and should be restricted to exceptional cases.

Applying for an occupation order

The property which is the subject of the application must be a dwelling house *and* must be, or have been, the actual home of the parties, or their intended home. Obligations can be imposed in respect of the home, for example to repair and maintain or pay rent—**s 40**.

The court must take various factors into account in deciding whether or not to make an order. There are common factors, and some which relate only to specific sections:

Figure 4.2 Factors to be considered in occupation order applications

s 33, s 37, s 38 applications—s 33(6), s 37(4), s 38(4)	s 35 applications—s 35(6)	s 36 applications—s 36(6)
(a) the housing needs and housing resources of each of the parties and of any relevant child		
(b) the financial resources of each of the parties		
(c) the likely effect of any order, or of any decision by the court not to exercise its powers…on the health, safety or well-being of the parties and any relevant child		
(d) the conduct of the parties in relation to each other and otherwise		

(e)	the length of time that has elapsed since the parties ceased to live together	the nature of the parties' relationship and in particular the level of commitment involved in it
(f)	the length of time that has elapsed since the marriage or civil partnership was dissolved or annulled	the length of time during which they have cohabited
(g)	the existence of any pending proceedings for property adjustment orders, financial relief, or relating to ownership of the home	whether there are or have been any children who are children of both parties or for whom both parties have or have had parental responsibility
(h)		the length of time which has elapsed since the parties ceased to live together
(i)		the existence of any pending proceedings for financial relief or relating to ownership of the home

Section 33 applications—entitled applicants

Only entitled applicants can apply under **s 33**. Current spouses and civil partners always have (at least) home rights, and so are always entitled.

- if the significant harm test in **s 33(7)** is made out in favour of the applicant, the court *must* grant an occupation order;

- if the significant harm test is *not* made out in favour of the applicant, the court has a *discretion* to grant an order, and must then consider the factors in **s 33(6)** (see 'Applying for an occupation order', Figure 4.2, p 64);

- an order can be declaratory (confirming the applicant has a right to occupy) or regulatory (defining the extent to which the applicant can actually occupy and/or exclude the respondent);

- a regulatory order may:
    - require the respondent to permit the applicant to enter and remain in the property or part of it;
    - regulate occupation by either or both parties;
    - prohibit, suspend, or restrict the respondent in exercising any right to occupy;
    - restrict or end any home rights of the respondent;
    - require the respondent to leave the property or part of it; or

- exclude the respondent from a defined area around the property;
- orders can be made for a specified period *or* until a specified future event *or* until further order—**s 33(10)**.

Section 35 applications—former spouses/civil partners no rights to occupy, but respondent does

A non-entitled former spouse or former civil partner can apply for an order against a respondent who is entitled to occupy.

- in deciding whether to make any order, the court must consider the factors in s 35(6)—(see 'Applying for an occupation order', Figure 4.2, p 64)
- if an order is made, certain provisions are *mandatory*:

Figure 4.3 Mandatory provisions in s 35 orders

If applicant is in occupation	If applicant is not in occupation
giving the applicant the right not to be evicted or excluded from the home or any part of it by the respondent	giving the applicant the right to enter into and occupy the home
prohibiting the respondent from evicting or excluding the applicant	requiring the respondent to permit the exercise of that right

- in deciding whether or not to include discretionary provisions in an order, the court must consider the significant harm test together with five other factors—the 'usual' four which apply to every section, as well as the time that has elapsed since the parties lived together;
- discretionary provisions may be included in an order to:
    - regulate occupation of the home by either of the parties;
    - prohibit, suspend, or restrict the respondent's right to occupy;
    - require the respondent to leave the home or part of it;
    - exclude the respondent from defined area around the home;
- orders can last up to six months. Extensions each of up to six months can be granted.

Section 36 applications—cohabitant/former cohabitant not entitled to occupy, but respondent is

A non-entitled cohabitant or former cohabitant can apply for an order against a respondent who is entitled to occupy.

- In deciding whether to make an order, the court must consider the factors in s 36(6) (see 'Applying for an occupation order', Figure 4.2, p 64).
- If an order is made, the same provisions as for **s 35** are mandatory and discretionary.
- In deciding whether to include discretionary provisions, the court must consider the significant harm test together with the four factors which apply to every section.
- Orders can last up to six months, and can be extended once for up to six months.

Revision tip

Note that to add discretionary provisions to an order under **s 36**, the court must consider just the 'usual' four factors; under **s 35**, it must also consider 'the time elapsed since the parties lived together'.

Section 37 applications—neither spouse/civil partner is entitled

A non-entitled current/former spouse or civil partner can apply for an order against a respondent who is not entitled to occupy, that is, neither party has a right to occupy (for example, where they may be squatters).

- In deciding whether to make an order, the court must consider the 'usual' four factors, together with the significant harm test.
- If an order is made, there are no mandatory provisions. The order may:
  - regulate the occupation of the home by the parties;
  - prohibit, suspend, or restrict the respondent's right to occupy;
  - require the respondent to leave the home or part of it;
  - exclude the respondent from a defined area around the home.
- Orders can last up to six months, and may be extended on one or more occasions for up to six months.

Section 38 applications—neither cohabitant entitled

A non-entitled cohabitant or former cohabitant can apply for an order against a respondent who is not entitled to occupy, that is, neither party has a right to occupy (for example, they may be squatters).

- In deciding whether to make an order, the court must consider the 'usual' four factors, together with the significant harm test.

Section 38 applications—neither cohabitant entitled

****

- If an order is made, there are no mandatory provisions. The order may:
  - require the respondent to permit the applicant to enter and remain in the home or part of it;
  - regulate the occupation of the home by the parties;
  - require the respondent to leave the home or part of it;
  - exclude the respondent from a defined area around the home.
- Orders can last up to six months, and can be extended once for up to six months.

Figure 4.4 Summary of occupation order applications

Section	33	35	36	37	38
Applicant	Entitled	Non-entitled			
		Former spouse/ civil partner	Cohabitant/ former cohabitant	Spouse/ civil partner or former spouse/civil partner	Cohabitant/ former cohabitant
Respondent	Entitled or non-entitled	Entitled		Non-entitled	
Process	Court considers the *'usual' four factors* in **s 33(6)** Court then considers the *significant harm* test before deciding whether to make an order	Court considers the *seven factors* in **s 35(6)** (first four are the 'usual' ones). If an order is then made, it must include mandatory provisions. Court then considers the *first five* of those factors *and* the *significant harm test* to decide whether to include discretionary provisions	Court considers the *nine factors* in **s 36(6)** (first four are the 'usual' ones). If an order is then made, it must include mandatory provisions. Court then considers the *'usual' four factors and* the *significant harm test* to decide whether to include discretionary provisions	Court considers the *'usual' four factors* (**ss 37(4)** and **38(4)** respectively) *and* the *significant harm test* to decide whether to make an order	

Provisions in order	Orders *may* declare applicant's rights under **s 33(4)** Orders *may* include any of the regulatory provisions in **s 33(3)**	Any order *must* include mandatory provisions in **s 35(3) or (4) or 36(3) or (4)** respectively An order *may* also include discretionary provisions in **s 35(5) or 36(5)**		An order *may* include discretionary provisions in **s 37(3) and 38(3)** respectively (which are in similar terms)	
Duration of order	A specified period; until a specified event; or until further order	Up to 6 months; extensions of up to 6 months each are possible	Up to 6 months; single extension of up to 6 months possible	Up to 6 months; extensions of up to 6 months each are possible	Up to 6 months; single extension of up to 6 months possible

Enforcement of orders and the effect of breach

The court must attach a power of arrest to an occupation order if it appears that the 'respondent has used or threatened violence against the applicant or any relevant child' unless they will be adequately protected without a power of arrest—**s 47(2)(b)**.

Breach of an occupation order is punishable as a contempt of court.

✅ *Looking for extra marks?*

Where the applicant has an interest in the property then cohabitants are treated in the same way as spouses or civil partners. However, where the applicant is a cohabitant who does not have an interest in the property then spouses and civil partners are treated differently. For example, where cohabitants are concerned, the court is not under a duty to make an order if the significant harm test is satisfied, the court must consider the nature of their relationship and the maximum duration of orders is shorter.

Consider whether you think these differences can be justified.

Ex parte orders

A court may grant a non-molestation or occupation orders where the respondent has not been given notice of the hearing—**s 45 FLA 1996**.

The court must consider the following factors in deciding whether to make an order:

- any risk of significant harm to the applicant or a relevant child, because of the respondent's behaviour if the order is not made immediately;

- whether the applicant will be deterred or prevented from pursuing the application if an order is not made immediately; and

- whether there is reason to believe that the respondent is aware of the proceedings but is deliberately evading service and that the applicant or a relevant child will be seriously prejudiced by the delay involved.

Undertakings

An **undertaking** is a formal promise to the court which can be enforced—**s 46(4) FLA**. Breach of an undertaking may be a contempt of court.

The court can accept an undertaking in any case instead of an occupation order or a non-molestation order—**s 46(1) FLA**. However, there are two limitations on accepting undertakings:

- an undertaking cannot be accepted instead of making a non-molestation order if the respondent has used or threatened violence against the applicant or a relevant child and an order is needed to protect them by making any breach punishable as an offence under **s 42A—s 46(3A) FLA**; and

- an undertaking cannot be accepted instead of making an occupation order where a power of arrest would be attached to the order (**s 46(3)**).

There are advantages and disadvantages to undertakings:

Figure 4.5 Advantages and disadvantages of undertakings

Advantages	Disadvantages
Undertakings avoid the time, expense, and stress of court proceedings for both the applicant and the respondent	Undertakings cannot have a power of arrest attached—**s 46(2) FLA**
The applicant gets the protection of a promise that is enforceable as a court order	Breach of an undertaking cannot be prosecuted as a criminal offence under **s 42A FLA**, as that section makes no reference to undertakings
The respondent does not have a court order against him or her	

Protection from Harassment Act 1997

This Act was designed to deal with 'stalkers', but it has often been used in relation to incidents between parties who are not associated persons. Amendments made to the 1997 Act by the **Protections of Freedom Act 2012** create offences which are more specifically designed to cover 'stalking'.

Offence under s 2

Section 2 creates an offence if a person pursues a course of conduct which amounts to harassment of another and which he knows or ought to know amounts to harassment.

Section 7(2) provides that harassment *includes* alarming a person or causing them distress, but this is not an exhaustive definition.

A course of conduct must consist of at least two incidents—**s 7(3)(a)**.

....

Lau v DPP [2000] All ER (D) 244

In November, a former boyfriend slapped his former girlfriend across the face, and in the following March he threatened her new boyfriend. The court held this was not a course of conduct amounting to harassment. The fewer the occasions and the wider apart they were, the less likely they were to constitute harassment.

....

Offences under s 4

Section 4 makes it an offence for a person to pursue a course of conduct which causes another to fear violence, if he knows or ought to know the conduct will cause the other person to fear violence.

Offences under s 2A and s 4A

Section 111 and **s 112 of the Protection of Freedoms Act 2012** inserted **s 2A** and **s 4A** into the **1997 Act**. The offences created require proof of the same elements as the existing **s 2** and **s 4** offences, but with the additional requirement that the acts or omissions in the course of conduct are 'ones associated with stalking'. **Section 2A(3)** provides a number of examples of acts or omissions which are 'associated with stalking', while emphasising that those are merely examples, and that other acts or omissions may constitute stalking.

✅ *Looking for extra marks?*

Consider when and why the Crown Prosecution Service might charge a **s 2A** (or **s 4A**) offence rather than a **s 2** (or **s 4**) offence, when evidence to support the additional 'stalking' element will be needed, but the maximum penalty remains the same.

Restraining orders

These may be imposed on a person who has been convicted of an offence under **s 2** or **s 4**. If necessary to protect a person from harassment they can be imposed on a person who has been convicted or acquitted of any offence—**s 12 Domestic Violence Crime & Victims Act 2004**.

Civil proceedings under the Protection from Harassment Act 1997

A civil claim can be brought against anyone who pursues a course of conduct against the claimant which amounts to harassment and which the perpetrator knows or ought to know amounts to harassment. Damages may be awarded for any anxiety caused by the harassment and any financial loss resulting from it—**s 3**.

Other offences

Domestic abuse which involves actual violence may constitute an offence, ranging from murder or manslaughter to common assault. In addition, threats of violence may amount to an offence under the **Public Order Act 1986**.

Revision tip

Annex A to the CPS 'Policy for Prosecuting Cases of Domestic Violence' (March 2009) contains a very full list of offences relevant to dealing with domestic violence.

Problem questions are unlikely to expect detailed consideration of these aspects of the criminal law but it is worth being aware of their existence.

Domestic Violence Protection Notices and Orders (DVPNs)

Sections 24–33 of the Crime and Security Act 2010 provide for the police to issue DVPNs, and to apply to a court for a Domestic Violence Protection Order (DVPO).

A DVPN can operate as an immediate non-molestation and occupation order, breach of which is an offence.

If the police obtain a DVPO, this can contain similar provisions and last for between 14 and 28 days, which is intended to be sufficient time for the victim to make their own applications for non-molestation and occupation orders.

Forced Marriage (Civil Protection) Act 2007

This Act added **s 63A** to the **Family Law Act 1996,** to give family courts power to make Forced Marriage Protection Orders (injunctions) to protect a person from being forced into a marriage or to protect them if they have *been* forced into a marriage.

An order can forbid families from:

- taking a person abroad for marriage;
- taking their passport away;
- intimidating someone into agreeing to marry.

It can also require family members to reveal the whereabouts of a person who is being forced into marriage. The police can apply for a Forced Marriage Protection Order, a breach of which can be punished by two years' imprisonment.

✅ Looking for extra marks?

'Something needs to change, and it is people's attitudes. Perpetrators believe they have the right to treat their partners in such a way. Invariably they believe their partners are lesser citizens.' (said by a worker at Women's Aid, Cardiff)

Consider whether there are further legislative and policy changes which could be effective in preventing and/or dealing with incidents of domestic violence. Can such changes alter such attitudes?

With an ageing population, might the incidence of domestic violence towards the elderly become more of an issue? Are other legislative and policy changes needed to tackle that abuse?

✱ Key cases

Case	Facts	Principle
B v B [1999] 2 FCR 251	The parties were married with a young daughter. The husband had a son from a previous relationship. The husband's violence caused the wife to leave with the daughter and they were both rehoused in temporary council accommodation.	There should be no occupation order as it would result in greater harm to the son than the wife and daughter. The husband would be considered intentionally homeless so the council would not accommodate him long-term and the son's education would suffer. The case was unusual on the facts.
C v C (Non-molestation Order: Jurisdiction) [1998] Fam 70	There was no direct correspondence between the husband and the wife, but the wife had communicated with journalists and unflattering stories were published about the husband.	The behaviour did *not* amount to molestation. It was significant that s 42 dealt with domestic violence. Here the parties were divorced and the husband was essentially seeking a gagging order.
Chalmers v Johns [1999] 2 FCR 110	The parties cohabited for 25 years and had an adult son and a seven-year-old daughter. The parties had a tempestuous relationship and the woman and daughter eventually left the jointly owned home after various minor incidents of violence. They were rehoused in temporary local authority accommodation. The woman applied for an occupation order under s 33 as an entitled person.	Applying the two-part significant harm test—was the applicant or a relevant child likely to suffer significant harm attributable to the respondent's conduct if no order were made? If 'yes', an order must be made, unless the harm to the respondent or the child is likely to be as great (balance of harm).

Key cases

✳✳✳✳✳✳✳✳✳✳✳✳✳

Case	Facts	Principle
		If not, the court had a broad discretion, based on all the circumstances of the case, including the s 33(6) items. Significant harm was *not* established; a discretionary order was refused. These were draconian orders overriding property rights and should be restricted to exceptional cases.
Chechi v Bashier [1992] 2 FLR 489	There was a dispute between two brothers and their families, who did not live together.	This fell within Part IV FLA: the family relationship overlay and magnified the dispute. A non-molestation order was refused on the facts.
G v G [2000] 2 FLR 533	The parties had their own homes but spent a number of nights a week together and talked of getting married. The man sold his house and put the money into a joint account. Most of the money was spent on the woman's house (which would have become the matrimonial home). After a period of renting the man moved in with the woman.	The parties had a sexual relationship; there was evidence they lived in the same household; there was substantial evidence of a joint account, and the sale proceeds of the man's house were paid into it and spent on the woman's property. Statutes should be given a purposive construction where domestic violence is concerned. The parties were held to be cohabitants, so that they were associated persons
Horner v Horner [1982] 2 All ER 495	The husband had previously been violent to the wife and after they separated he harassed her in various ways, for example, by handing her threatening letters and intercepting her on her way to the station.	This was molestation, which did not necessarily imply violence or threats of violence. It applies to any conduct which can properly be regarded as such a degree of harassment as to call for the intervention of the court.
Re J (Abduction: Wrongful Removal) [2000] 1 FLR 78	Although not a domestic violence case, the principle is relevant to all *ex parte* hearings	An *ex parte* order did not deprive the respondent of the right to a fair trial. She could apply to the court to have the order set aside. In addition, the *ex parte* application had been followed by a full hearing with both parties present.

Case	Facts	Principle
Vaughan v Vaughan [1973] 3 All ER 449	The wife had petitioned for divorce. While the parties were together, the husband had been violent and had 'pestered' her. However, the application for a non-molestation order was based on early morning and late night calls to the wife's house and calling at her workplace. The husband admitted that he knew the wife was frightened of him and that being pestered in these circumstances must have had an impact on her health.	This behaviour did amount to molestation

⑨ Key debate

Topic:	How should the law deal with domestic violence?
Academic:	Byron James
Viewpoint:	Criminal law is not the appropriate way to deal with domestic violence.
Reading:	'In Practice: Prosecuting Domestic Violence' [2008] *Fam Law* 456

Topic:	How should the law deal with domestic violence?
Academics:	Shazia Choudry and Jonathan Herring
Viewpoint:	Human rights can be used to justify the state taking an interventionist approach to domestic violence.
Reading:	'Righting Domestic Violence' (2006) *Int J Law Policy Family 20(1)*, 95

② Exam questions

Problem question

Adam and Susan have been in a relationship for five years. They live together with their two-year-old daughter, Amy, in a small flat which is in Adam's name. He paid the initial deposit and continues to pay the mortgage. Before Amy was born, Susan paid all the couple's other outgoings which amounted to more than the mortgage payments. However, Susan has not worked since Amy was born and Adam pays for everything.

Exam questions

✻✻✻✻✻✻✻✻✻✻

Recently Susan was admitted to hospital after burning herself on an iron. Susan explained that this was an accident which happened during a particularly heated row. Adam has never been violent to Susan but, since Amy was born, Adam has been highly critical of everything that Susan does. He does not like her leaving the flat without him and he sometimes locks her in, suggesting that she would go off with other men if he didn't. Susan wants to leave Adam but is scared of what he might do. She fears that she might have to leave Amy with Adam if she did escape, because Susan has nowhere to live if she does leave.

Advise Susan about the options open to her.

An outline answer is included at the end of the book.

Essay question

Is the range of possible legal responses to domestic violence sufficient to protect victims?

 Scan here

Scan this QR code image with your mobile device to see an outline answer to this question or log onto www.oxfordtextbooks.co.uk/orc/concentrate

#5

Financial provision on divorce or dissolution

Key facts

- On divorce, nullity, judicial separation, or dissolution of a civil partnership the court has wide statutory powers to redistribute property. This is different from the situation where a cohabiting couple split up (see Chapter 1, 'Ending cohabitation', p 8).

- Civil partners are treated in the same way as married couples but the law is governed by the **Civil Partnership Act 2004** (CPA) rather than the **Matrimonial Causes Act 1973** (MCA).

- The court has a wide discretion in reaching a decision.

- The court will consider all the circumstances of the case, and in particular the factors in **s 25 MCA**, before deciding what combination of orders to make.

- Case law in this area often focuses on 'big money' cases, where the courts have outlined some general principles that should be applied where resources exceed needs. These principles are likely to have little relevance in most cases.

- Any award must be fair. In deciding this, the court should consider the three principles of financial needs, compensation, and sharing.

- Nuptial agreements (agreements between the parties which include 'pre nups') are one of the circumstances of the case. The courts are now likely to give effect to these agreements if the parties entered into them freely and understood the effects, unless it would be unfair in the circumstances to hold the parties to the agreement.

- Parents are obliged to support their children financially. The **Child Support Act 1991**, the **Children Act 1989**, the **MCA**, and the **CPA** all provide regimes for child support.

Chapter overview

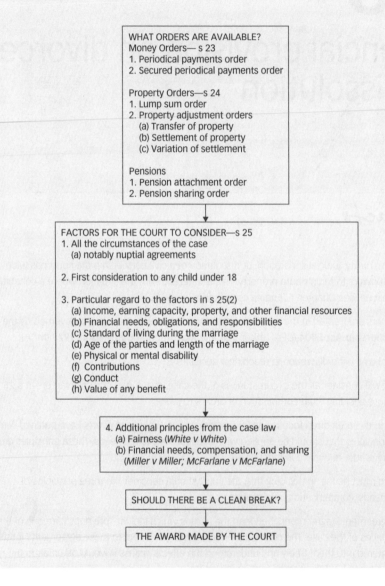

WHAT ORDERS ARE AVAILABLE?
Money Orders— s 23
1. Periodical payments order
2. Secured periodical payments order

Property Orders—s 24
1. Lump sum order
2. Property adjustment orders
   (a) Transfer of property
   (b) Settlement of property
   (c) Variation of settlement

Pensions
1. Pension attachment order
2. Pension sharing order

FACTORS FOR THE COURT TO CONSIDER—s 25
1. All the circumstances of the case
   (a) notably nuptial agreements

2. First consideration to any child under 18

3. Particular regard to the factors in s 25(2)
   (a) Income, earning capacity, property, and other financial resources
   (b) Financial needs, obligations, and responsibilities
   (c) Standard of living during the marriage
   (d) Age of the parties and length of the marriage
   (e) Physical or mental disability
   (f) Contributions
   (g) Conduct
   (h) Value of any benefit

---

4. Additional principles from the case law
   (a) Fairness (*White v White*)
   (b) Financial needs, compensation, and sharing
     (*Miller v Miller; McFarlane v McFarlane*)

SHOULD THERE BE A CLEAN BREAK?

THE AWARD MADE BY THE COURT

Introduction

In most cases of divorce or dissolution a couple will have limited financial resources. When these are divided there will not be enough money for the couple to maintain their previous lifestyle. In these cases the court's concern is to provide for housing and everyday expenses of the parties and any children involved.

There is a great deal of case law in this area about the principles that should guide the court's discretion. These have little relevance to the majority of cases where the court is concerned with meeting everyday needs. The case law has more relevance to so-called big money cases.

A court can make various orders and will decide what combination of orders to make by reviewing the facts of the case and considering the factors in **s 25 MCA** (or **Schedule 5, Part 5 CPA**) and the relevant case law.

Note that this area of law is no longer referred to as ancillary relief. From 6 April 2011 the **Family Procedure Rules 2010** (FPR 2010) apply. They detail the procedures to be followed in family cases (replacing the **Family Proceedings Rules 1991**), and now refer to applicants seeking a **financial order** (**rule 2.3 FPR 2010**).

Interim financial relief—s 22 MCA

Often the parties will have different financial resources. For example, where a husband has been the sole earner and the wife has stayed at home to raise their children, she may not have any income when the parties separate. She will not be able to afford to wait until the couple's financial arrangements are finalised, and could apply for maintenance pending suit under **s 22 MCA** (for civil partnerships the provision is **Schedule 5, Part 8 CPA**).

Either party can apply for maintenance pending suit. An order can be made at any time after the petition has been filed and before a final order has been granted. These are usually granted for the purpose of maintenance, but can be for other things, such as legal fees—*A v A (Maintenance Pending Suit: Provision for Legal Fees)* **(2001)**. You should be aware that when **s 49 of the Legal Aid Sentencing and Punishment of Offenders Act 2012** is brought into force, it will insert a new section into the **MCA** dealing with the payment of legal fees.

Money orders—s 23

In all cases except judicial separation these orders do not take effect until the final decree has been granted. This means that if one of the parties dies after an order is made but before the grant of a decree absolute, his or her estate will not benefit from the order.

For the sake of simplicity, only references to the **MCA** are included in the following discussion. The equivalent provisions in the **CPA** are in **Schedule 5**.

Periodical payments order—s 23(1)(a)

The court can order payments of a specified amount for a specified time. They may be long term or for a specified period of time to allow the recipient to become self-sufficient. For example, in *Parlour v Parlour* (2004), the wife was awarded high **periodic payments** for a relatively short period so she could save for her future. Her husband, a footballer, had high earnings at the time of the divorce, but these would decline relatively soon.

Secured periodical payments order—s 23(1)(b)

A court can order **secured periodical payments** which means that the payments are tied to certain property, for example the matrimonial home or a share portfolio. This security can be used in two ways:

1. The property can generate money to make the payments. An example would be a share portfolio where the shares pay dividends.

2. If the payer fails to meet the payments then the property can be sold so that payment can be made.

These orders are rarely made. If there is property that can be used as security it is often considered better to use that property to make a lump sum payment.

Who can benefit from these orders?

A court can make these orders in favour of either party to the marriage.

It is possible to order periodical payments in favour of a child of the family unless payments are being made under the **Child Support Act**.

Periodical payments can be varied up or down. Either party can apply to the court for a variation. For example, if the paying party gets a pay rise, the receiving party may apply to court for increased payments.

They end on remarriage and may be reduced in the event of cohabitation depending on the finances of the parties at that time—*K v K (Periodical Payment: Cohabitation)* (2006).

Lump sums—s 23(1)(c)

The court can order that one party pays a specified sum of money to the other. Although the court can only make one order for a lump sum, **s 23(3)(c)** **MCA** allows this lump sum to be paid by instalments if there is insufficient money to pay it in one lump. It is also possible to draft an order providing for a series of lump sums (whilst these are separate lump sums, there is still only one court order). Unlike periodical payments, lump sum payments by instalments will survive remarriage.

Property orders—s 24

Transfer of property—s 24(1)(a)

The court can order that one party transfers particular property to the other. For example, the court could order the wife to transfer her share in the matrimonial home to the husband or it could order one civil partner to transfer his car to the other.

Settlement of property—s 24(1)(b)

The court can order one party to the marriage to settle a particular item of property for the benefit of the other or for their children. Examples of this power being used in practice are **Mesher orders** (named after the case of **Mesher v Mesher (1980)** and **Martin orders** (from **Martin v Martin (1978)**).

A **Mesher order** is an order that the parties hold the property as tenants in common in equity. The property is not sold until a particular event occurs. This event might be:

- the children reach the age of 17;
- the children complete their full-time education;
- the wife dies or remarries; or
- the court makes a further order.

Until one of these events occurs the resident parent (the parent who lives with the children) and the children can live in the property. When the event happens the property is sold and the sale proceeds are divided between the parties.

Disadvantages of a *Mesher* order

1. The non-resident parent cannot use the house and does not get the benefit of the sale proceeds until one of the events occurs;
2. the fact that the parties own property together means there is a tie between them;
3. by the time the property is sold the resident parent is likely to be middle-aged and may not be in a good position to buy a new property. For example, it may be difficult to get a mortgage where you do not have many years of your working life left; and
4. children are often still dependent on their parents after the age of 17 or completing full-time education and may still need a home.

A *Martin* order is a variation on a *Mesher* order.

....

Martin v Martin [1978] Fam 12

The court accepted that the husband and wife had equal shares in the equity of the property (although it did not specify whether they were joint tenants or tenants in common). The resident parent was allowed to stay in the house for the rest of her life, until she remarried, or until she voluntarily decided to move out.

....

✱✱✱✱✱✱✱✱✱✱✱

Variation of settlement—s 24(1)(c)

A court can vary a settlement which was made on the parties to a marriage whether it was made before or after the marriage took place.

Who can benefit from these orders?

A court can make these orders in favour of either party to the marriage, or in favour of a child of the family.

Sale of property—s 24A

Where the court makes one of the orders under **s 23 or s 24 MCA** the court can make a further order for the sale of particular property in which either or both of the parties would have an entitlement to the proceeds of sale.

Pensions

The court can make two different types of order relating to pensions: a pension attachment order or a pension sharing order.

Pension attachment order—s 25B(4)

This is an order that, once the pension has become payable, part of that pension will be paid to the other partner.

Disadvantages of pension attachment orders

1. The parties remain tied together until, and beyond, the point of retirement;
2. depending on the age of the parties, the order may take effect in the distant future. This means there is no certainty about the value of the pension or what the parties' financial positions will be by then;
3. the payments depend on what the payer puts into the pension fund and will not be made until the payer decides to retire.

Pension sharing order—s 21A(1)

This order avoids some of the problems of pension attachment orders. Essentially it allows one party's pension to be shared with the other party. This means that the person who has the benefit of the order gets a percentage of the pension as their own.

Revision tip

It is not possible to have a pension sharing order if a pension attachment order has already been made.

Figure 5.1 Summary of financial orders on divorce, nullity, dissolution

Section nos refer to MCA 1973	MONEY ORDERS				PROPERTY ORDERS		PENSION ORDERS	
	Periodical payments s 23(1)(a)	**Secured periodical payments s 23(1)(b)**	**Lump sum s 23(1)(c)**	**Transfer of property s 24(1)(a)**	**Settlement of property s 24(1)(b)**	**Pension attachment** *(or 'earmarking'* s 25B(4)	**Pension sharing s 21A(1)**
Brief description	Payments of a specified amount for a specified time	Payments of a specified amount for a specified time tied to property	Payment of a specified sum of money. **s 23(3)(c)** *allows payment to be by instalments*	Transfer of specified property	Direction to settle property in favour of another person	Once a pension is payable, a percentage of it is to be diverted to the other party	A percentage of one party's pension is transferred to the other
Who can benefit?	Child of the family if CSA inapplicable	Child of the family if CSA inapplicable	Either party	Either party	Either party	Either party	Either party
	Either party	Either party	Any child of the family	Any child of the family	Any child of the family	Parties only	Parties only

Pensions

****

Variation possible?	YES s 31(2)(b)	YES s 31(2)(c)	NO but instalments can be varied: s 31(2)(d)	NO	YES s 31(2)(e) + Any settlement on the parties (pre- or post-nuptial) can be varied under s 24(1)(c)	YES provided the order was made before decree absolute: s 31(2)(dd)	NO
		YES s 31(2)(c)	NO but instalments can be varied: s 31(2)(d)	NO	YES s 31(2)(e) + Any settlement on the parties (pre- or post-nuptial) can be varied under s 24(1)(c)	YES provided the order was made before decree absolute: s 31(2)(dd)	NO
Effect of payer's death	Payments cease: s 28(1)(a)	Payments do not necessarily cease: s 28(1)(b)	Any unpaid sum is a debt from payer's estate to payee	Payee can require payer's estate to effect the transfer	Payee can require payer's estate to effect the settlement	Pension payments are likely to cease at death	Payments do not cease, subject to the pension's rules

NOTE: Orders take effect at decree absolute. If the payee dies *before* then, their estate will not benefit from the order. The effects above occur if the payer dies *after* decree absolute.

Factors the court will take into account in making an award

The court will decide what combination of orders to make on divorce or dissolution by considering the following:

1. the statutory factors in **s 25 MCA** (or **Schedule 5, Part 5 CPA**);

2. relevant case law; and

3. whether there should be a clean break between the parties.

The statutory factors in outline

Section 25(1) states that when the court decides whether to and how to exercise its powers to make a financial award it must consider all the circumstances of the case.

The first consideration is the welfare of any child who is under the age of 18—**s 25(1)**.

Section 25(2) then sets out eight further factors that the court must have regard to:

Section 25(2)

(a) The income, earning capacity, property and other financial resources which each of the parties to the marriage has or is likely to have in the foreseeable future. This includes any increase in earning capacity which, in the court's opinion, it would be reasonable for one of the parties to take steps to achieve.

(b) The financial needs, obligations and responsibilities of the parties. This includes their current position and their likely position in the foreseeable future.

(c) The family's standard of living before the marriage broke down.

(d) The age of the parties and the length of their marriage.

(e) Any physical or mental disability of either party.

(f) Contributions made to the welfare of the family, including domestic contributions. These contributions can be those already made or contributions which the parties are likely to make in the foreseeable future.

(g) Any conduct of the parties, during the marriage or after separation, which the court thinks it would be inequitable to ignore.

(h) The value of any benefit, for example a pension, that either of the parties will lose the chance of acquiring because of the divorce.

Principles from the case law

It is helpful to consider the principles from the case law first as these will guide the court when it considers how to apply the statutory factors to the facts of a case. In most cases the court's primary concern is the needs of the parties and it will not need to look beyond these. However, exam questions often ask about big money cases so it is useful to consider the case law alongside the statutory factors.

Fairness

White v White [2001] 1 All ER 1

A wealthy married couple had two farms. One was bought in joint names with the help of money from Mr White's father; the second was inherited by Mr White and was not in joint names. The wife had been the primary carer of the children.

- Fairness meant looking at all circumstances of the case.
- There should be no discrimination between the money-earner and the home-maker who had looked after children.
- Generally, the court should only depart from equality with good reason (not a presumption, but a cross-check to ensure division is fair).

Mrs White was awarded around two-fifths of the value of the assets. The contribution from Mr White's father to the first farm had been important initially, but did not carry much weight 33 years later. However, the contribution in relation to the second farm was significant.

Financial needs, compensation, and sharing

Miller v Miller; McFarlane v McFarlane [2006] 3 All ER 1, HL (two joined appeals)

The Millers were married for just under three years and had no children. The court awarded Mrs Miller £5m, including the matrimonial home. This was less than one-third of the value of the shares in a company the husband had set up during the marriage and one-sixth of the husband's total worth. The award reflected the work the husband had put in to his business before the marriage.

The McFarlanes were married for 16 years. The wife had given up a successful career to look after the children. In doing so she would be economically disadvantaged and would be supporting the husband, at least indirectly. The court awarded Mrs McFarlane periodical payments of £250,000 a year, well in excess of her needs, to reflect an element of compensation.

The principles

Several elements of fairness were identified:

- *Financial needs* created by the marriage. The one who takes on the domestic role may be less able to support themselves financially when the marriage ends.

- *Compensation*: for example to compensate the wife who has had time out of the workforce supporting her family, and whose future employment prospects may suffer as a result.

- *Sharing*: marriage is a partnership of equals so the 'yardstick of equality' will be applied (as an aid, not a rule) regardless of the length of the marriage.

✅ Looking for extra marks?

The Law Commission is currently reviewing the law in this area. It is considering:

1. What is meant by 'needs' and how far one party should be required to meet the financial needs of the other on dissolution or divorce; and

2. Whether the law should treat property inherited by one party/owned by one party before the relationship differently from other property.

At present, there are no proposals for reform but you can find the consultation paper, with summaries at http://lawcommission.justice.gov.uk/consultations/matrimonial_property.htm

You should be aware that this consultation follows on from a 2011 Law Commission consultation on matrimonial property agreements, which is discussed further later in the chapter.

Section 25 factors in detail

These are explained in detail in the following paragraphs.

All the circumstances of the case—s 25(1)

Nuptial agreements

In the leading case of **Radmacher (formerly Granatino) v Granatino (2010)** the Supreme Court examined **'nuptial agreements'**, which includes any agreement between the parties about their finances before or during marriage. A wealthy German woman married a French banker who later gave his career up to return to university. Their ante-nuptial agreement was in German. He signed it without waiting for a translation and took no independent legal advice. The person who drew up the agreement explained the key provisions to the husband before he signed it.

The court held that the husband had understood the effect of the agreement. He chose not to take independent legal advice, so he could not rely on its absence. He knew the wife had substantial wealth but showed no interest in the extent of it, and would have signed the agreement anyway. He had no needs that made it unfair to hold him to the agreement. There was no element of compensation as he gave up work for his own benefit, not because of his family. He had agreed not to share in the wife's family money and it was fair to hold him to that.

✅ Looking for extra marks?

There have been a number of cases since **Radmacher** in which the courts have considered what weight to give to pre-nuptial agreements. For a summary see Heenan 'Pre-nuptial agreements: where are we now?' (2012) 162 *NLJ* 796–797 (7518).

Arguments for and against giving effect to nuptial agreements

Figure 5.2 Arguments for and against giving effect to nuptial agreements

For	Against
• it allows a party to protect property they have inherited;	• it could lead to one party suffering financial hardship on divorce;
• it could help prevent 'gold diggers' profiting;	• the parties are unlikely to have thought of everything that might happen in the future. Agreements that don't take account of changes in circumstance are unfair; and
• it may offer some comfort to wealthy people who want to be sure their partners are not marrying them for their money; and	• it undermines the idea of marriage as being for life.
• it allows the parties to settle their affairs at a time when they have a good relationship and their decisions are not informed by bitterness.	

Radmacher emphasised that the courts may, but do not have to, give effect to nuptial agreements and parties cannot agree to oust the court's jurisdiction—*Hyman v Hyman* (1929).

Revision tip

Some of the issues surrounding **pre-nuptial agreements** are discussed by George, Harris and Herring in 'Pre-Nuptial Agreements: For Better or for Worse?' [2009] *Fam Law* 934. The article was published before the Supreme Court judgment in *Radmacher* but it is still a useful discussion of some of the key issues.

At the moment *Radmacher* represents the law in this area. Lady Hale's dissenting judgment is worth reading because of her considerable experience in family law cases. She disagreed with the majority and suggested that reform should be left to Parliament.

✔️ *Looking for extra marks?*

In 2011, the Law Commission launched a consultation on reform of the law relating to matrimonial property agreements. You can find the consultation paper, with a summary and a press release at www. lawcom.gov.uk/marital_property.htm. At present, there are no proposals for reform.

The welfare of any child under 18

The welfare of any child under 18 is the 'first' consideration. This is not the same as the 'paramount' consideration—the term used in the **Children Act 1989** which means that it is the overriding consideration, but it is the most important consideration—*Suter v Suter and Jones* (1987).

In *B v B (Financial Provision: Welfare of Child and Conduct)* (2002), the sale proceeds of the matrimonial home were awarded to the wife, as she was caring for the child.

Income, earning capacity, property, and other financial resources—s 25(2)(a)

This includes the parties' current resources as well as those they are likely to have in the foreseeable future. A court could consider the steps the parties should reasonably take to increase their earning capacity.

A key issue is: what property should be taken into account? If one party inherits a large sum of money or some property, or earned a great deal of money before the marriage, there may be arguments about whether the other should share in it. Some of the key areas of debate are set out in the following paragraphs.

Inherited property

In *White v White* (2001), where the parties' needs could not be met without using inherited property or other pre-marriage assets, the fact that those assets were pre-marriage property would have little weight.

In *K v L* (2010), before the marriage, the wife inherited shares in a company and these provided the sole income for the couple and their three children. The husband was awarded £5m of the total assets of £57m, which generously met his reasonable requirements and more. It was relevant that the inherited shares had been kept separate from their other income.

Family or marital property

In *Miller v Miller; McFarlane v McFarlane* (2006), the judges took two different approaches to pre-marriage and marriage assets:

- *Marital property* is 'the financial product of the parties' common endeavour', so it would exclude property inherited or received as a gift by one of the parties. However, there is no precise boundary between marital property and other types of property and the matrimonial home would normally be marital property, even if one party brought it to the marriage. No matter how long the marriage, each party should be entitled to share in marital property. However, in a short marriage, fairness might require that one party should not share in the other's non-marital property. With a longer marriage the weight given to the contribution of non-marital property may be reduced.

- *Family assets* is a narrower concept and: 'refers to those things which are acquired by one or other or both parties, with the intention that there should be continuing provision for them and their children during their joint lives, and used for the benefit of the family as a whole.'

- It would include the family home and contents, the parties' earning capacities, assets obviously acquired for the benefit of the whole family (such as holiday homes, insurance policies, and family savings) and a business or joint venture in which they both work. However, business or investment assets generated solely or mainly by one party's efforts are more difficult to classify. A lot of money may be made in a very short time in business (as Mr Miller had done), but domestic contributions take longer to develop into contributions to the welfare of the family. Where assets were not family assets or had not been generated by the parties together, the length of the marriage might offer good reason to depart from equality.

Resources of a third party

The court will not take the resources of a third party into account directly. This means that if one of the parties has a new partner, the court cannot take that partner's income into account. However, the court might take the view that the partner's contribution to household expenses would reduce the needs of the spouse or civil partner.

Financial needs, obligations, and responsibilities—s 25(2)(b)

Needs vary depending on the parties and the nature of their lives together. The needs of a wealthy couple are likely to be interpreted far more generously than those of a couple who have very little.

It is important that both parties are rehoused, particularly where one of them is looking after a child. The court will look at the parties' outgoings and consider whether these are reasonable. For example, if the parties have very little money between them, it is likely to be unreasonable for one of them to pay out large amounts of money for an expensive car.

Standard of living before the marriage broke down—s 25(2)(c)

In most cases the parties' standard of living will fall, as the costs of running two households will be greater than the costs of running a single household jointly. However, in big money cases this factor will be relevant as the basic needs of the parties will be met.

The age of the parties and the length of their marriage—s 25(2)(d)

The court is more likely to order a clean break where the couple are young, childless, and have been married for a short period of time, as it will be much easier for them to get on with their lives than it would if the marriage was a long one and there were children. However, the time that they actually lived together during the marriage will be relevant.

In *Krystman v Krystman* (1973), the parties had been married for 26 years, but only cohabited for two weeks after marriage and neither had made any real effort to contact the other since. They married because the wife was pregnant, but she lost the baby. The wife was held not to be entitled to any financial provision when they eventually divorced.

Pre-marital cohabitation

The court will take a period of pre-marital cohabitation into account in deciding on the length of the marriage.

In *CO v CO* (2004), the parties cohabited for eight years prior to their four-year marriage and both their children had been born during the period of cohabitation. The court gave full weight to the fact that the period of cohabitation had moved seamlessly into marriage. To ignore cohabitation of this type would lead to unfairness.

In *McCartney v Mills McCartney* (2008), the parties kept their finances separate before marriage. The court accepted that, prior to marriage, the parties had spent 'many, many nights together', had taken holidays together, and had a very close relationship but 'that does not…in this case, equate with a settled, committed relationship moving seamlessly into marriage'.

Physical or mental disabilities—s 25(2)(e)

This is closely connected to the needs of the parties. If one of them has a disability it is likely that their financial needs will be greater.

Contributions—s 25(2)(f)

Both financial and non-financial contributions will be considered. *White v White* **(2001)** stressed that there should be no bias in favour of the money-earner as against a home-maker. Some later cases justified departing from the yardstick of equality on the basis of an outstanding financial contribution by one of the parties.

Conduct—s 25(2)(g)

Conduct must be very serious for it to be taken into account. It must be 'obvious and gross'— *Wachtel v Wachtel (No 1)* **(1973).**

In *Miller v Miller; McFarlane v McFarlane* **(2006)**, Mr Miller's affair with a younger woman was not conduct that should be taken into account.

In *H v H (Financial Relief: Attempted Murder as Conduct)* **(2006)**, the husband attempted to murder the wife in front of their children and was sentenced to 12 years' imprisonment. This was taken into account.

✅ *Looking for extra marks?*

In 'Ancillary Relief and Sexual (Mis)Conduct: Negating Need: *K v L*' [2010] *Fam Law* 642, Andrew Commins considers how conduct was treated by the courts in *K v L* **(2010)**. In particular, he considers that in that case conduct overrode the other statutory factors in **s 25 MCA**.

How do you think the courts should treat conduct?

Consider the arguments for and against no-fault divorce in Chapter 3, 'Is no-fault divorce a better solution?', p 44. Would a system of no-fault divorce be compatible with taking conduct into account under **s 25**?

The value of any benefit which the parties will lose the chance of acquiring—s 25(2)(h)

The most important benefit is likely to be a pension. If one party has a significant pension and the other has very little or no pension (for example, because that person has raised their children), then there could be a significant imbalance. The powers the court has to deal with pensions were outlined earlier.

Clean break

A **clean break** is a once-and-for-all order that ends financial ties between the parties. It is not possible to have a clean break in relation to obligations to maintain children.

A clean break would mean that if one of the parties won the lottery a week after the order was made there would be no possibility for the other to claim a share.

The court must consider whether to make a clean break order in every case— **s 25A(1)**.

Advantages and disadvantages of a clean break

Figure 5.3 Advantages and disadvantages of a clean break

Advantages of a clean break	Disadvantage of a clean break
The parties can move on with their lives.	
The parties can pursue careers without fear of later claims on their increased income.	Order cannot be adjusted if circumstances change, for instance, if one party loses their job.
Avoids difficulties associated with periodical payments, such as failure to pay; payments ending on death or remarriage.	

Even where there are advantages to the particular couple in ordering a clean break, there may be factors which make it inappropriate:

Factors which may make a clean break appropriate or inappropriate

Figure 5.4 Factors which may make a clean break appropriate or inappropriate

Clean break may be appropriate	Clean break may be inappropriate
Short, childless marriage	Insufficient assets or assets are tied up
Both parties have established careers	Where there is a young family
Big money cases	Financial imbalance between the parties
Relationship has totally broken down	Uncertainty over payee's financial future

Variation of orders and appeals

Variation

Section 31 MCA allows the court to vary or discharge the financial orders outlined in **s 31(2)**. **Lump sum orders** and property adjustment orders cannot be varied, although a lump sum by instalments can be varied. Orders are sometimes drafted as a series of lump sums, rather than a lump sum by instalments, to try and avoid them being varied (a single lump sum can't be varied whereas a lump sum by instalments can be). However, case law suggests that a series of lump sums might not protect against variation.

Variation of orders is usually sought where there has been a change in the financial circumstances of one of the parties. Under **s 31(7)** the court must consider all the circumstances of the case and first consideration is given to the welfare of a child of the family who is under 18 as well as other matters listed in that section.

Appeal

An alternative method of challenging an order is by appeal. Very strict time limits apply.

The leading case on this is *Barder v Barder (Calouri Intervening)* **(1988)**. See 'Key Cases', p 98.

Orders in favour of children

These are explained in detail in the following paragraphs.

The Child Support Act 1991

The current system of child support, as outlined here, has applied since March 2003.

What is child maintenance?

The Child Support Agency (CSA) describes child maintenance as: 'Regular, reliable financial support that helps towards the child's everyday living costs'. The parent who does not have main day-to-day care of the child (the non-resident parent) pays child maintenance to the parent who does have main day-to-day care (the parent with care).

The parties can arrange child maintenance:

1. through the CSA;

2. by private agreement between the parties; or

3. under a court order.

If the parties have a court order governing child support arrangements, the CSA cannot arrange child support during the 12 months after the date of the order.

Who does it apply to?

1. Payments are made in respect of a 'qualifying child'

   - one or both of the child's parents must be non-resident—**s 3(1) Child Support Act 1991**

- the child must be under 16, or under 19 and receiving full-time, non-advanced education.

2. Payments are made by the 'non-resident parent'
   - does not live in the same household as the child; and
   - the child lives with a person with care—**s 3(2) 1991 Act**.

Parents of a qualifying child are responsible for his or her maintenance—**s 1(1), 1991 Act**. **Section 1(3)** imposes a duty on a non-resident parent to make any payments due under the Act.

Revision tip

Only natural parents are required to pay child maintenance (**s 54** defines parent as the mother or father of the child in law). Step-parents do not have to pay child maintenance under these provisions. Married and unmarried natural parents who are non-resident must pay child support.

3. Payments are made to the person with care
   - the person the child lives with;
   - who usually provides day-to-day care (alone or jointly); and
   - who is not within a prescribed category—**s 3(3) and (4) 1991 Act**.

Shared care

If a qualifying child stays with a non-resident parent, the child maintenance paid by the non-resident parent may be reduced—**Schedule 1 paragraph 7 1991 Act**.

Reform

Changes to the way in which child maintenance is calculated started to take effect in December 2012. The changes are being rolled out gradually and only initially affected families in which there are four or more children. The changes are outlined in **Schedule 4 of the Child Maintenance and Other Payments Act 2008**.

✅ Looking for extra marks?

The **Child Support Act** uses a very rigid formula to work out the amount payable by a non-resident parent. This is very different to the situation when the courts make a financial award in favour of the parties following divorce or dissolution. Do you think certainty or discretion is the better approach? Is there a good reason for different approaches in these different types of cases? It is worth bearing in mind that the Law Commission consultation on 'Matrimonial Property, Needs and Agreements' raises the possibility of a formula for financial awards on divorce.

The Children Act 1989

Under the **Children Act 1989** the court has power to make various orders.

The following orders can be made under **Schedule 1, paragraph 2**:

1. periodical payments order;
2. secured periodical payments order;
3. lump sum order;
4. settlement of property order; or
5. an order to transfer property.

These can be made whether the parents are married or unmarried. The child must be a child of the family. This means payers are not limited to legal parents, and a step-parent could be ordered to make payments in favour of a step-child.

Relationship with child support

Where a non-resident parent is paying child support they cannot also be ordered to make periodical payments under the **Children Act** unless their net weekly income exceeds the upper limit (**s 8 Child Support Act 1991**).

The Matrimonial Causes Act and Civil Partnership Act

These Acts also allow a court to make various orders in favour of a child of the family.

Where a court is making an order in favour of a child of the family rather than in favour of one of the parties, then the court must consider the factors in **s 25(3) and (4) MCA**, rather than those in **s 25(2)**.

Relationship with child support

Where a non-resident parent is paying child support they cannot also be ordered to make periodical payments unless their net weekly income exceeds the upper limit (**s 8 Child Support Act 1991**).

✅ Looking for extra marks?

The Child Support Act only applied to legal parents. It does not cover step-parents. **The Children Act**, the **Matrimonial Causes Act**, and the **Civil Partnership Act** all allow orders to be made against step-parents. Which parent do you think should have the obligation to maintain their children? Should natural parents have to pay regardless, even if they have no relationship with their child and that child has been raised by a resident parent and a step-parent?

（✱) **Key cases**

Case	Facts	Principle
Barder v Barder (Calouri Intervening) [1988] AC 20	The wife killed herself and the couple's two children shortly after a final order was made. The husband applied for leave to appeal out of time.	The House of Lords held that leave to appeal out of time would only be granted if: 1. new events since the order have invalidated the basis of the order or fundamental assumptions underlying it to the extent that, if leave was given, the appeal would be certain or very likely to succeed; 2. the new events occurred very shortly after the order was made. It was suggested this would be no more than a few months; 3. the application for leave to appeal out of time was made reasonably promptly; and 4. the grant of leave to appeal out of time should not prejudice third parties who acquired relevant property in good faith and for paying full value.
Imerman v Tchenguiz [2010] EWCA Civ 908	In financial remedy proceedings the parties have a duty to disclose their assets. In this case, the wife's brothers downloaded huge numbers of documents belonging to the husband as they feared the husband would not be truthful in his disclosure.	The Court of Appeal held that these documents could not be used by the wife as to allow her to do so would breach the husband's right of confidentiality.
Miller v Miller; McFarlane v McFarlane [2006] 3 All ER 1	The Millers were married for just under three years and had no children. The husband ran a very profitable company and was estimated to be worth £32m, of which £15m consisted of shares in his company. The wife received one-sixth of the assets which reflected the effort the husband had put into the business before the marriage. The McFarlanes were married for 16 years. At marriage, both were professionals earning similar amounts. After their second child was born the wife gave up work to look after the children. There was insufficient capital to achieve a clean break but the husband had substantial income.	There are three elements to fairness: needs, compensation, and sharing.

Key debates

✱✱✱✱✱✱✱✱✱✱✱✱

Case	Facts	Principle
	The court noted that the husband's earnings after marriage resulted from the parties' earlier joint efforts. The wife had given up a successful career. In looking after the children she would be economically disadvantaged and would be supporting the husband, at least indirectly. The court awarded her periodical payments of £250,000 a year, well in excess of her needs, to reflect an element of compensation.	
Radmacher (formerly Granatino) v Granatino [2010] UKSC 42	A wealthy German woman married a French banker who later gave up work to return to university. Their ante-nuptial agreement was drawn up in German. The husband signed it without allowing time for it to be translated, and without having independent legal advice. The key provisions were explained to the husband before he signed it.	An agreement between the parties was one factor in the process of quantifying a claim 'and, perhaps, in the right case…the most compelling factor'.
White v White [2001] 1 All ER 1	A farming couple were married for 33 years. They contributed similar amounts to purchase their first farm and took out a mortgage and received a loan which later became a gift, from Mr White's father. Mr White inherited the second farm which was not put into joint names nor treated as part of the partnership, though they farmed it as part of their business. Both were involved in the business, but Mrs White was the children's primary carer when they were young.	Fairness is the guiding principle. There should be no bias in favour of the money-earner as against a home-maker. The judge should check the award against 'the yardstick of equal division'. There should only be a departure from equality where there are good reasons to do so.

⑨⑨ Key debates

Topic:	Marriage as a contract
Academic:	Jonathan Herring
Viewpoint:	The case of *Radmacher* signals a shift from marriage as a status towards marriage as a contract
Reading:	(2010) 'The death knell of marriage' *New Law Journal*, vol 160, 1551

Topic:	Should the courts divide assets at the end of a marriage according to what is fair?
Academic:	Jonathan Herring
Viewpoint:	The wider interests of society may be more important than achieving fairness between the parties.
Reading:	'Why Financial Orders on Divorce Should Be Unfair' (2005) *Int J Law Policy Family* 19 (2): 218
Academic:	Ruth Deech
Viewpoint:	Underlying the law on maintenance payments is the idea that women are dependent on men. Her view is that women have the choice whether to give up work to care for children
	The wider interests of society may be more important than achieving fairness between the parties.
Reading:	'What's a Woman Worth?' [2009] *Fam Law* 1140

⑦ Exam questions

Problem Question

Geraldine and Rufus are aged 45 and married 15 years ago. Geraldine comes from a very wealthy family and inherited a manor house when she was 18. She has lived there ever since and Rufus moved in 20 years ago. The manor house is worth around £15 million. Rufus also owns a flat in Kensington worth around £1 million.

Rufus started divorce proceedings after discovering Geraldine's affair with Max, a 25-year-old client of her firm. Geraldine is still seeing Max but has no plans to cohabit with him as their relationship is not very serious. However, she fears that she might be pregnant. Max is worth around £500 million and earns in excess of £25 million a year.

Geraldine earns around £200,000 as a partner in a law firm. Rufus is a well-established and highly successful actor and earns around £520,000 a year net through film and voice-over work. They have two children, Sebastian, aged 16, and Henry, aged 18, who live with Geraldine and stay with Rufus one night per week.

About six months ago Rufus was contacted by his first girlfriend, Emmeline, on Facebook. Since leaving Geraldine he has been in regular contact with Emmeline and he proposed to her on Twitter last Friday. Emmeline has accepted and Rufus is keen to marry her as soon as possible. He wants to resolve financial issues between him and Geraldine and wants a clean break so that he can start a new life with Emmeline.

Advise Rufus about the possible terms of a financial settlement.

An outline answer is included at the end of the book.

Exam questions

✱✱✱✱✱✱✱✱✱✱

Essay Question

'Marriage still counts for something in the law of this country and long may it continue to do so.'

Consider this comment by Baroness Hale in the **Radmacher** case. Should pre-nuptial agreements be taken into account in divorce cases?

 Scan here

Scan this QR code image with your mobile device to see an outline answer to this question or log onto www.oxfordtextbooks.co.uk/orc/concentrate

#6
The Children Act— the private law

Key Facts

- Private law matters concerning children (that is, disputes between individuals, not involving public bodies) are covered by the **Children Act 1989**, particularly **s 1** and **s 8**.

- Parental responsibility means all the rights, duties, powers, responsibilities, and authority which by law a parent of a child has in relation to that child and his property.

- Married parents and unmarried mothers have parental responsibility in respect of their children. Generally, unmarried fathers do not—but this can be acquired in several ways.

- **Section 8 of the 1989 Act** provides for courts to make residence, contact, specific issue, and prohibited steps orders to resolve disputes over aspects of parental responsibility.

- When dealing with any matter relating to a child's upbringing, the child's welfare must be a court's paramount consideration. The court must have regard to a welfare checklist, the 'delay' principle and the 'no order' principle in making its decisions.

- A child's views can be considered and they can bring proceedings themselves (with the leave of the court) if they are of sufficient age and understanding to do so.

- Children Act orders generally last until a child is 16 years old, but residence orders have effect until they are 18.

Note: section numbers in this chapter refer to sections of the 1989 Act, unless it is made clear that another Act is being referred to.

Chapter overview

Children Act 1989—private law

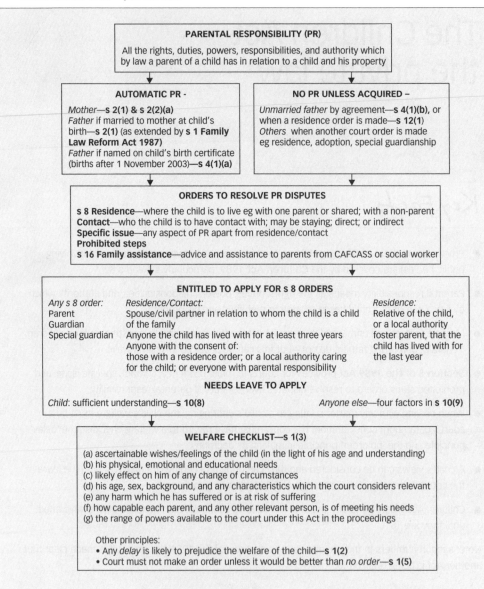

PARENTAL RESPONSIBILITY (PR)

All the rights, duties, powers, responsibilities, and authority which by law a parent of a child has in relation to a child and his property

---

AUTOMATIC PR -

Mother—**s 2(1) & s 2(2)(a)**
Father if married to mother at child's birth—**s 2(1)** (as extended by **s 1 Family Law Reform Act 1987**)
Father if named on child's birth certificate (births after 1 November 2003)—**s 4(1)(a)**

NO PR UNLESS ACQUIRED –

Unmarried father by agreement—**s 4(1)(b)**, or when a residence order is made—**s 12(1)**
Others when another court order is made eg residence, adoption, special guardianship

---

ORDERS TO RESOLVE PR DISPUTES

s 8 Residence—where the child is to live eg with one parent or shared; with a non-parent
Contact—who the child is to have contact with; may be staying; direct; or indirect
Specific issue—any aspect of PR apart from residence/contact
Prohibited steps
s 16 Family assistance—advice and assistance to parents from CAFCASS or social worker

---

ENTITLED TO APPLY FOR s 8 ORDERS

Any s 8 order:
Parent
Guardian
Special guardian

Residence/Contact:
Spouse/civil partner in relation to whom the child is a child of the family
Anyone the child has lived with for at least three years
Anyone with the consent of:
those with a residence order; or a local authority caring for the child; or everyone with parental responsibility

Residence:
Relative of the child, or a local authority foster parent, that the child has lived with for the last year

NEEDS LEAVE TO APPLY

Child: sufficient understanding—**s 10(8)**   *Anyone else*—four factors in **s 10(9)**

WELFARE CHECKLIST—s 1(3)

(a) ascertainable wishes/feelings of the child (in the light of his age and understanding)
(b) his physical, emotional and educational needs
(c) likely effect on him of any change of circumstances
(d) his age, sex, background, and any characteristics which the court considers relevant
(e) any harm which he has suffered or is at risk of suffering
(f) how capable each parent, and any other relevant person, is of meeting his needs
(g) the range of powers available to the court under this Act in the proceedings

Other principles:
• Any *delay* is likely to prejudice the welfare of the child—**s 1(2)**
• Court must not make an order unless it would be better than *no order*—**s 1(5)**

Introduction

The **Children Act 1989** introduced the concept of parental responsibility (PR), which balances duties and responsibilities against rights, powers, and authority.

For example, a parent has a duty to ensure that their child is properly educated, while they have the power to decide whether that education is to be provided by a public or private sector school or home education; they have a responsibility to provide a home, but have the right to decide where that home is to be.

The **Children Act** marked a change in the emphasis of the law. It moved from the idea that children were their parents' possessions and towards the idea that children had rights of their own. This is discussed further later in the chapter.

The Act designates who automatically has PR and how others may acquire it. It provides that PR may be shared between a number of people as well as shared with a local authority. When relationships break down it is inevitable that disputes will arise over the exercise of aspects of PR, and **s 8** provides a range of orders to resolve those disputes.

A 'child' is defined (except for certain maintenance purposes) in **s 105** as a person under 18 years of age.

Section 91 states that **s 8** orders (apart from residence orders which last until the age of 18) last only until a child is 16, though **s 9(6)** allows a court to make orders for older children in exceptional circumstances.

The rights of the child

In the past children were believed to be incapable of having rights and their parents, in particular their father, would have had complete control to make decisions about them and to administer corporal punishment. The idea of children's rights emerged in the middle of the nineteenth century.

The **Children Act** is an example of the change in attitude. When the Bill was being considered in Parliament, Lord Mackay said:

> Your Lordships will have noted a change of terminology…[t]he fundamental concept in this area of law is no longer to be expressed variously in terms of rights, duties, authority or even powers of parents, but simply as 'parental responsibility'. The phrase…emphasises that the days when a child should be regarded as a possession of his parent—indeed when in the past they had a right to his services and to sue on their loss—are now buried forever. The overwhelming purpose of parenthood is the responsibility for caring for and raising the child to be a properly developed adult both physically and morally.

In addition to the **Children Act** there have been a number of other key developments in the area of children's rights. For example:

Who is the legal parent of the child?

****

Figure 6.1 Key developments in children's rights

Gillick v West Norfolk & Wisbech Area Health Authority (1986)	Children under 16, of sufficient age and understanding, 'Gillick competent', could be prescribed contraceptive advice and treatment without knowledge or permission of their parents.
UN Convention on the Rights of the Child—Article 12	The views of the child should be taken into account in any decision made by adults which affects them. The weight given to those views will depend upon the age and maturity of the child.
The Children Act 1989	Under **s 1(3)(a)** the court must take into account the 'ascertainable wishes and feelings of the child in light of his age and understanding' when considering an order under **s 8**.
The European Convention on Human Rights	Children have rights as well as adults.
Mabon v Mabon and Others (2005)	Children have a right to separate legal representation in family law disputes.

You should note that although, following ***Gillick***, mature children have the right to consent to medical treatment, they may not have the right to refuse it if the court considers it is not in their best interests to do so.

You may find it useful to read the cases of ***Re L*** (1998) and *(Axon) v Secretary of State for Health* (2006). A summary of these cases can be found in the 'Key Cases', p 119 at the end of the chapter.

Who is the legal parent of the child?

The mother

The woman who gives birth to the child will be the legal mother, even if she is acting as a surrogate and the embryo was created using the egg of another woman (**s 33 Human Fertilisation and Embryology Act 2008** (HFEA 2008)).

You should note that surrogacy arrangements are not legally enforceable, regardless of who provides the egg or sperm and the birth mother may change her mind and decide to keep the baby.

If the birth mother wishes to go through with the surrogacy arrangement, her parental rights will be transferred to the commissioning couple by means of a parental order (**s 54 HFEA 2008**).

Parental orders may be made in favour of a married couple, civil partners, or those living together in an enduring family relationship provided they are not within the prohibited degrees of relationship. Single people may not have a parental order made in their favour.

A woman may also become the legal mother of a child that she adopts.

The father

The position in relation to a child's father is more complex:

Figure 6.2 Who is legally a father?

Type of father	Legal father?
Genetic father	Generally speaking, the genetic father is the legal father.
	The position is more complex where a man has donated sperm to a licensed clinic. In these circumstances a man is not the legal father of the child if the sperm is used in accordance with his consent **(s 41(1) HFEA 2008)**.
Presumptions of paternity	There is a rebuttable presumption that a man is a child's father in the following circumstances:
	1. Where the man is married to the woman who gives birth to the child it is presumed that he is the father.
	2. If a man is named as a child's father on the birth certificate it is presumed that he is the child's father **(*Brierley v Brierley* (1918))**.
IVF treatment	1. Where a man is married to a woman who undergoes IVF treatment but he does not provide the sperm he will be the father unless he did not consent to the treatment **(s 35 HFEA 2008)**.
	2. Where a man is not married to a woman undergoing IVF treatment he may also be treated as the father if both parties consent to the man being treated as the father of the child **(s 36 and s 37 HFEA 2008)**.
Parental orders	A man may become the legal father of a child if there is a parental order in his favour.
Adoptive father	A man may become the legal father of a child that he adopts.

The other parent

Unlike the **Human Fertilisation and Embryology Act 1990**, the **2008 Act** gives legal recognition to lesbian parents. In the following situations no man will be treated as the father of the child:

1. If the woman undergoing treatment is in a civil partnership, then her partner will be treated as a parent of the child unless she does not consent to the treatment (**s 42 HFEA 2008**).

2. Where the woman undergoing IVF treatment is not married to that other she may also be treated as a parent if both parties consent to her being treated as the parent of the child (**s 43 and s 44 HFEA 2008**).

✅ *Looking for extra marks?*

The main legislation in relation to assisted reproduction is the **Human Fertilisation and Embryology Act 2008** which amends the 1990 Act of the same name. For a fuller discussion of the provisions of the 2008 Act, see Rachel Fenton, Susan Heenan, and Jane Rees, 'Finally fit for Purpose? The Human Fertilisation and Embryology Act 2008' (2010) *Journal of Social Welfare and Family Law*, Vol 32(3), 275–286.

Keep in mind that PR and being a parent are separate concepts. Someone can be a parent, but not have PR, and a person may acquire PR without being a parent.

Parental responsibility

Parental responsibility (PR) is defined in **s 3** as:

> all the rights, duties, powers, responsibilities and authority which by law a parent of a child has in relation to a child and his property.

✅ *Looking for extra marks?*

In the **Children (Scotland) Act 1995**, parental responsibility is defined in terms of:

- responsibility for the child's health, development, and welfare;
- responsibility to provide the child with direction and guidance suitable to their stage of development, and the right to control, direct, or guide the child's upbringing;
- the right to have the child living with him or otherwise to regulate the child's residence;
- the right and responsibility, if the child is not living with the parent, to maintain personal relations and direct contact with the child on a regular basis; and
- the right and responsibility to act as the child's legal representative.

Is this much fuller definition any clearer and/or more useful or (because it still does not spell out *all* aspects of PR) merely longer?

What is included in parental responsibility?

Figure 6.3 lists just some examples of the elements which make up PR and indicates which court order will deal with any dispute relating to it.

Figure 6.3 How elements of parental responsibility may be regulated

Element	May be regulated by:
Providing a home for the child	Residence order
Deciding where the child's home is to be	Residence order
Keeping in contact with the child	Contact order
Consenting or refusing to consent to medical treatment	Residence order
Changing the name of the child (most usually the surname)	Residence or prohibited steps order
Which school a child attends, whether public sector or private, or home education	Residence or prohibited steps order
Taking the child abroad	Residence or prohibited steps order
Acting as the child's legal representative	A grant of leave to the child to bring proceedings himself if he is of sufficient age and understanding to do so

You should remember that any aspect of the upbringing of a child will involve an exercise of PR. In respect of each aspect, there will be powers or rights balanced by duties and responsibilities. It is useful to consider the balancing element when any aspect of PR is being discussed.

✅ Looking for extra marks?

Whether or not a person has PR does not affect any obligation which is otherwise imposed on them in relation to the child, for example, to maintain the child—**s 3(4)**. This means that an unmarried father who is the biological parent of a child must pay child maintenance regardless of whether he has PR.

John Eekelaar comments on this point and other areas where the exercise of rights and responsibilities is not dependent on PR in 'Rethinking parental responsibility' [2001] *Fam Law* 426.

Who has parental responsibility?

- The mother of a child, whether or not she is married to the child's father, automatically has PR—**ss 2(1) and 2(2)(a)**.
- The father of a child who is married to the child's mother automatically has PR—**s 2(1)**.
- The father of a child who is not married to the child's mother will automatically have PR if he is entered on the child's birth certificate as the child's father (in relation to births registered after November 2003).

✔ *Looking for extra marks?*

In November 2009, the **Registration of Births (Parents Not Married and Not Acting Together) Regulations** were published in draft for consultation, with a view to taking effect in January 2011 but, by March 2012, implementation was still 'under consideration'. As drafted, the Regulations would generally make it compulsory for the father, whether the parents are married or not, to be registered on the child's birth certificate, unless it would be impossible, impracticable, or unreasonable to do so. This would automatically bestow PR on most unmarried fathers.

- Any other father of a child who does not marry the mother does not have PR, unless he acquires it by a parental responsibility agreement or a court order. If a father is granted a residence order in respect of a child, the court is required to give parental responsibility for that child to the father—**s 4**.
- A court order must also be made where a lesbian couple undertake IVF together and there is no-one who fulfils the legal definition of a father—**s 4ZA**.
- Other individuals can acquire PR by a court order, for example, on the making of a residence order in their favour—**s 12(2)**.
- A local authority acquires PR in respect of a child when a care order is made—**s 33(3)(a)**.

Acquiring parental responsibility

Parental responsibility agreement

By **s 4(1)(b)**, a father will acquire PR for his child if he and the mother enter into a parental responsibility agreement. To be effective, this must be in a prescribed form, signed, witnessed, and recorded at the Principal Registry of the High Court.

Section 4A makes a similar provision in relation to step-parents.

Court order

The father can apply to the court for a PR order—**s 4(1)(c)**.

An order must be made in favour of a father if he is granted a residence order in respect of a child. Even if the father does not specifically apply for PR when he applies for residence the court must grant PR—**s 12(1)**.

Similar provisions apply to a second female parent where a child is born following IVF treatment—**s 4ZA; s 12(1A)**.

In deciding whether to order PR under **s 4(1)(c)** to a father, the court will take into account:

- the degree of commitment shown towards the child;
- the degree of attachment between the child and the father; and
- the father's reasons for applying.

See *Re H (Minors) (Parental Responsibility) (No 3)* (1991).

The views of the child will be taken into account if they are of sufficient age and understanding, and also if it is clearly distressing to the child. In *Re G (A Child) (Domestic Violence: Direct Contact)* (2001), a four-year-old became very upset at any mention of the father. PR was not granted.

Special guardians and *adoptive parents* acquire PR when the special guardianship or adoption order is made; a *guardian* appointed by the court, by the mother, or by another guardian acquires PR when they are appointed.

Sharing parental responsibility

More than one person can have PR in respect of a child at any one time; for example, separated married parents each retain PR for their child. They can agree how PR is to be exercised. If they cannot agree on this, either can apply to the court for a **s 8** order to decide the issue.

Even if a person has PR for the child, they cannot act in a way which would be incompatible with any order made under the **1989 Act** in respect of the child—**s 2(8)**.

While a care order is in force, a local authority controls the extent to which parents and others can exercise their PR. However, the local authority's PR is itself limited. For example, it cannot change the child's religion, nor consent to adoption—**s 33**. (This is covered more fully in Chapter 7, 'Care order or supervision order?', p 133.)

Delegated parental responsibility

A person who does not have PR, but has care of the child, may do what is reasonable in the circumstances to safeguard and promote the child's welfare—**s 3(5)**.

This would include school teachers, foster parents, a babysitter, and a parent hosting a party for a number of their own child's friends. For example, if a child was injured while in the care of such a person, that person would have the right (and responsibility) to act as a parent in seeking medical assistance, administering first aid, consoling the child, and so on.

Revision tip
The common law right of parents to physically punish their children (ie reasonable chastisement) has been effectively limited by **s 58 Children Act 2004**. CPS guidelines state that there should be no more than 'a reddening of the skin'. However, the power of teachers to administer corporal punishment has been removed altogether by **s 548 Education Act 1996** (as substituted by **s 131 School Standards and Framework Act 1998**).

Losing parental responsibility

Revocation of PR

It is fairly unusual for the courts to revoke parental responsibility. *Re P* **(1995)** and *CW v SG* **(2013)** are the only two reported cases where this has happened; as you can see, the facts are fairly extreme.

Re P (Terminating Parental Responsibility) [1995] 1 FLR 1048

The father had seriously injured the child, with long-term effects on the child's physical and mental health. The court approached the case by examining whether it would grant PR if the father were now seeking it. It concluded that the father would not exercise any aspect of PR in a way which would promote the welfare of the child, so it was appropriate to bring his PR (which had been acquired by agreement) to an end.

CW v SG [2013] EWCA 854 (Fam)

The father was sentenced to four years' imprisonment for sexual offences against two of the child's half-sisters. PR was terminated because the child's emotional security would be imperilled if the father had further involvement in his life.

Revocation of residence order

If a residence order in favour of a non-parent is revoked, their parental responsibility comes to an end. **Section 12(2)** makes their PR incidental to the residence order, and does not bestow a separate status.

Adoption

An adoption order extinguishes the PR of everyone who held it before the order, and vests PR in the adoptive parents (see Chapter 8, 'Adoption orders', p 151).

Special guardianship

A **special guardianship order** does not extinguish existing PR, but puts it into abeyance for as long as the special guardianship order continues, so that the special guardian can exercise

PR to the exclusion of others. (Special guardianship is dealt with in Chapter 8 on Adoption ('Special guardianship order—s 14A of the Children Act 1989', p 152.)

Section 8 orders

While orders are mainly available to resolve disputes between parents about their children, s 8 orders can be made in favour of other people, such as grandparents, relatives, foster parents, or the child himself if they are of sufficient age and understanding.

In any divorce, dissolution, judicial separation, or nullity proceedings, the court must examine the arrangements proposed for any children of the family and consider whether it should exercise any of its powers to make orders under the 1989 Act for the children—**s 41 Matrimonial Causes Act 1973**. Note that this provision will be repealed under the Children and Families Bill. Arrangements for children will no longer be scrutinised as part of the divorce process, but may be dealt with in separate proceedings at any time.

Section 11(7) allows a court to attach conditions to any **s 8** order.

Under the Children and Families Bill residence and contact orders under **s 8** will be replaced with 'child arrangements orders'. These will regulate 'arrangements relating to (a) with whom the child is to live, spend time, or otherwise have contact with, and (b) when a child is to live, spend time or otherwise have contact with any person'.

Residence order

This is an order setting the arrangements as to the person with whom the child is to live— **s 8(1)**.

Revision tip

As mentioned earlier, under **s 12(1) and (2)**, if a court makes a residence order in favour of a father who does not already have PR, it must make a separate PR order in his favour.

If anyone who is not a parent has a residence order in their favour, the residence order itself confers PR. The difference is to ensure that PR for a non-parent ends if residence ends, whereas a father retains it unless it is specifically revoked by a court.

In *In the Matter of G (A Child)* **(2008)**, Ward LJ underlined the changed approach brought about by the **Children Act**: 'The whole purpose of the Act is getting rid of the concept of custody and access...all of that should have been swept away, so that you have an order which conveys no right but simply regulates a factual state of affairs.'

Shared residence

A residence order may be made in favour of more than one person and the 'order may specify the periods during which the child is to live in the different households concerned'—**s 11(4)**.

Losing parental responsibility
★★★★★★★★★★

Despite the wording of this provision, which clearly points to the possibility of the child's residence being shared between the parties, for many years the courts seemed to be firmly against the idea of shared residence orders.

In *A v A (Minors) (Shared Residence Order)* **(1994)** it was held that a shared order should only be made if there was something unusual about the case. A residence order to one parent with generous contact with the other was to be preferred.

The approach of the courts has changed considerably:

....

Re AR (Relocation) [2010] EWHC 1346 (Fam), [2010] 2 FLR 1577

Mostin J held that, 'A shared residence order is nowadays the rule rather than the exception, even where the quantum of care undertaken by each parent is decidedly unequal...' Also, 'If one were to draw up a hierarchy of human rights protected by the ECHR, near the top would be the right of a child, while he or she is growing up, to have a meaningful participation by both of his parents in his upbringing.'

....

....

T v T [2010] EWCA Civ 1366

It was held (contradicting *Re AR*) that a shared residence order was not 'the rule rather than the exception'. The paramount consideration is what is in the best interests of the child. Equal time with each parent, and cooperation and goodwill between the adults, is not a pre-requisite for shared residence.

....

If the parents live together continuously for six months, a residence order will lapse— **s 11(5)(b)**.

Contact order

This is an order requiring the person with whom a child lives, or is to live, to allow the child to visit or to stay with the person named in the order or for that person and the child otherwise to have contact with each other.

Contact may be:

- direct—the person in whose favour the order is made (usually, but not necessarily the non-residential parent) and the child meet face-to-face;
- staying—the child stays overnight at the home of the non-residential parent;
- indirect—where it is not in the child's interests for them to see the applicant directly, but it is decided that some contact will be beneficial, indirect contact may be ordered. Examples of this form of contact are letters, emails, and telephone calls.

....

Re L (Contact: Transsexual Applicant) [1995] 2 FLR 438

The father had a sex change, and his teenage sons found it very embarrassing to have direct contact with him. Indirect contact was ordered in the hope that, in time, they would come to terms with the situation.

....

The general approach of the courts to contact is:

1. Where possible a child should know his estranged parent unless there are good reasons for denying contact

In *Re F (Minors) (Denial of Contact)* (1993), a father was refused contact where the child had strong objections to it. The older the child, the greater the weight that will be given to their views.

2. The court should not deprive a child of contact unless it is wholly satisfied that it is in the interests of the child that contact should cease, a conclusion a court should be extremely slow to arrive at

This approach accords with **Article 9 of the UN Convention on The Rights of the Child**, which provides that children should not be separated from their parents unless to do so would be in the best interests of the child.

3. It is the normal assumption that a child would benefit from continued contact with a natural parent

However, where there is implacable opposition on the part of the resident parent, or extreme hostility between the parties, it may prove impossible to make a contact order that will be in the child's interests. Even if contact would otherwise be ordered, it may then be refused. This is more likely if it is unavoidable that the parties will have to meet or speak to each other in the course of arranging contact or putting arrangements into effect.

In *Re D (A Minor: Mother's Hostility)* (1993), there was extreme hostility on the part of the mother towards the father. Contact was refused.

4. Evidence of domestic violence will not necessarily preclude contact if it can be arranged safely

In *Re L, V M & H* (2001), the court established guidelines for cases where domestic violence is an issue. See 'Key Cases', p 120.

See Chapter 4, 'Other steps', p 57. See also *Practice Direction: Residence and Contact Orders: Domestic Violence and Harm* (2008), issued on 9 May 2008.

Contact activity directions and conditions

If a court makes or varies a contact order it can add contact activity conditions and directions to the order—**s 11C–s 11G**.

The activity directions or conditions would require a party to take part in activity to promote contact with the child, such as:

- programmes, classes, and counselling or guidance sessions to assist establishing, maintaining, or improving contact; or which may, by addressing a person's violent behaviour, enable or facilitate contact.

- sessions in which information or advice is given about making or operating arrangements for contact, including making arrangements by means of mediation.

Specific issue order

This is an order to determine a specific question which has arisen, or which may arise, in connection with any aspect of parental responsibility for a child.

It gives positive directions on the exercise of an aspect of parental responsibility other than contact or residence. Specific issue or prohibited steps orders cannot be made to achieve something which could be achieved by a contact or residence order—**s 9(5)**.

Where a residence order is in force in respect of a child, no person may cause the child to be known by a new surname; or remove the child from the UK without either the written consent of every person who has parental responsibility for the child or the leave of the court—**s 13**.

This does not prevent the person with a residence order taking the child abroad for less than one month, for example, for a holiday.

However, if that person wishes to leave the UK permanently with the child, this is unlikely to be agreed, so the court's permission (by way of specific issue order) will be required. Alternatively, if the non-resident parent learns of emigration plans they have not consented to, they may seek a prohibited steps order to prevent what amounts to child abduction.

Issues of changing a child's surname give rise to many applications. For example:

....

Re B (Change of Surname) [1996] 1 FLR 791

Three children, two of whom were teenagers, were not allowed to change their surname. The court felt that they should retain that link with their father.

....

....

Re S (Change of Surname) [1999] 1 FLR 672

A similar application was granted on the basis that careful consideration should be given to the views of a child who was competent in terms of *Gillick* to make the decision. This case differed from *Re B* in that the father had abused the child.

....

Prohibited steps order

This is an order that no step which could be taken by a parent in meeting their parental responsibility for a child is to be taken without the consent of the court.

These orders give negative directions, prohibitions, on the exercise of some aspect of parental responsibility (other than contact or residence). They are 'the other side of the coin' from specific issue orders.

✅ *Looking for extra marks?*

Consider whether there are good reasons to have separate orders for positive and negative directions—could specific issues and prohibited steps be dealt with by a single order, especially in the light of the proposed combination of residence and contact orders into child arrangements orders?

Note the different wordings in the definitions of residence and contact orders, and child arrangements orders. The new order will not be just a combination of the other two. Are these differences likely to be significant in practice?

Family assistance orders

Under **s 16(1)** the court can require **CAFCASS** or a local authority to 'advise, assist and befriend' a parent, guardian, special guardian, anyone else with whom the child lives or has a contact order, and the child. Orders last for 12 months, unless a shorter period is specified. Apart from **s 16(4A)**, which refers to the officer 'giving advice and assistance as regards establishing, improving and maintaining contact', the Act says nothing about the purpose of these orders.

Factors the court takes into account in making a s 8 order

In making a decision in relation to the child, the court must take the following into account:

- The welfare principle.
- The no delay principle.
- The welfare checklist.
- The no order principle.

The Children and Families Bill will add **s 1(2A)**, 'involvement of both parents in the child's life' principle—a presumption that involvement of the parents in the child's life in a way that does not put the child at risk of harm, will further the child's welfare.

The welfare principle—s 1(1)

The child's welfare is the court's paramount consideration.

The no delay principle—s 1(2)

The court must have regard to the general principle that any delay in the proceedings is likely to prejudice the welfare of the child.

Factors the court takes into account in making a s 8 order

✶✶✶✶✶✶✶✶✶✶

Section 11 requires a court to draw up a timetable and give directions to the parties to ensure that delay is avoided. The **Family Procedure Rules 2010** (which came into effect in April 2011) expand on the obligations of the court and the parties in this regard, as does the Practice Direction which issued the Revised Private Law Programme in April 2010.

C v Solihull MBC [1993] 1 FLR 290

Child C was removed from his parents following allegations of physical abuse. He spent two weeks with foster parents, but the magistrates then made a residence order in favour of the grandparents, with a view to C's prompt return to his parents under local authority supervision. The case was transferred to the County Court for rehearing, with the Court of Appeal stating that, although delay is ordinarily detrimental to a child's welfare, planned and purposeful delay (eg to obtain the results of an assessment) may be beneficial and should sometimes be encouraged.

This 'principle' of purposeful or constructive delay is often cited by lawyers in family proceedings almost as if it outweighs the clear words of **s 1(2)**.

The welfare checklist—s 1(3)

When proceedings are opposed, the court must have regard to:

- The ascertainable wishes and feelings of the child concerned (considered in the light of his age and understanding).
- His physical, emotional, and educational needs.
- The likely effect on him of any change of circumstances.
- His age, sex, background, and any characteristics of his which the court considers relevant.
- Any harm which he has suffered or is at risk of suffering.
- How capable each of his parents, and any other person in relation to whom the court considers the question to be relevant, is of meeting his needs.
- The range of powers available to the court under this Act in the proceedings in question.

Revision Tip

In spite of the limited circumstances where the welfare checklist *must* be considered, courts usually refer to the checklist in any proceedings relating to a child's upbringing.

The no order principle—s 1(5)

A court should not make an order unless it considers that doing so would be better for the child than making no order at all.

Factors the court takes into account in making a s 8 order

✳✳✳✳✳✳✳✳✳✳

Figure 6.4 Interpretation of the checklist

Case	Facts
Ascertainable wishes and feelings of the child in light of his age and understanding—**s 1(3)(a)**	How mature is the child? The court is unlikely to go against the wishes of a 16-year-old unless the issue is of major importance, eg life-saving medical treatment. The wishes of a younger child will be taken into account if they are *Gillick* competent. The court will wish to ensure that the views expressed are really those of the child, and not those of the parent in disguise. **Article 12 UN Convention on the Rights of the Child** allows those of sufficient age and maturity to express their views and be heard in legal proceedings.
His physical, emotional, and educational needs—**s 1(3)(b)**	*Physical*—are the children well cared for—fed, clothed, supervised, etc? Does the child have a disability which one parent could deal with more effectively than the other? *Emotional*—which parent can better support their emotional needs? There is no general presumption that one parent will be favoured over another—***Re S (A Minor) (Custody) (1991)*** Generally brothers and sisters should not be separated —***N (Children) (2006)*** *Educational*—can the child continue to live near their school? Is the parent supportive of their education?
Likely effect of any change in circumstances —**s 1(3)(c)**	The courts will maintain the status quo where possible, unless it is causing harm to the child.
Age, sex, background, and any other characteristics which the court considers relevant—**s 1(3)(d)**	A young baby *may* be better with the mother if she is breast-feeding. A teenager *may* be better with a parent of the same sex. Background may include factors such as race, religion, culture, language, etc.
Any harm which he has suffered or is at risk of suffering—**s 1(3)(e)**	Harm means ill-treatment or the impairment of health or development, including, for example, impairment suffered from seeing or hearing ill-treatment of another—**s 31(9)**. Has the child witnessed or been involved in domestic violence?
How capable each parent, and any relevant person, is of meeting his needs—**s 1(3)(f)**	Can this parent or some other person meet this child's needs—eg caring for a sick child? Is that person physically or mentally ill rendering them incapable of caring for the child? Extreme religious beliefs may be taken into account if they affect the child—eg refusal of blood transfusions. Sexual orientation of parent is irrelevant. It is unlawful to discriminate on such grounds in relation to contact or residence—***Da Silva v Portugal (2001)***. The natural parent will not necessarily be preferred. Each case will be examined on its merits—***Re G (Children) (Residence: Same Sex Partner) (2006)***. Also ***Re B (A Child) (2009)*** where it was held that in such cases the welfare of the child is paramount.

Who can apply?

✳✳✳✳✳✳✳✳✳✳✳

Case	Facts
The range of powers available to the court in the proceedings—**s 1(3)(g)**	The court will consider all options and remedies available, eg another person or relative, if willing, may be better suited to caring for the child. An alternative order (to the one applied for) may be more appropriate. In some circumstances this could be a care or supervision order.

Who can apply?

A range of people (as shown later) are entitled to apply for **s 8** orders; anyone else will require the leave of the court before they can make an application—**s 10**.

Further restrictions are imposed on local authority foster parents (or those who have been foster parents in the last six months), who need the local authority's consent before they can apply for leave unless they are a relative of the child or the child has been living with them for the last year.

Before the child can be granted leave, the court must be satisfied that they have sufficient understanding to make the application, that is to say, they are *Gillick* competent.

Entitled to apply for any s 8 order

- Parent.
- Guardian appointed under **s 5**.
- Special guardian appointed under **s 14A**.

Entitled to apply for residence and contact orders (but needs leave to seek other orders)

- Party to a marriage or civil partnership in relation to which the child is a child of the family.
- Anyone with whom the child has lived for at least three years.
- Anyone, who has the consent of
  - those who have a residence order in respect of the child; or
  - a local authority in whose care the child is; or
  - all those with parental responsibility.

Entitled to apply for residence orders (but needs leave to seek other orders)

- A relative of the child or a local authority foster parent with whom the child has lived during the year before applying.

Leave to apply for an order

Anyone not entitled to apply for an order must seek leave from the court to apply.
Under **s 10(9)**, when deciding whether to grant leave the court must consider:

- the nature of the application;
- the applicant's connection with the child;
- any risk that the proposed application would disrupt the child's life to an extent that he would be harmed by it;
- if the child is being cared for by the local authority, that authority's plans for the child's future and the wishes and feelings of the child's parents.

Section 10(9) will not apply if it is the child who is seeking leave to apply. However, the court must be sure the child is of sufficient age and understanding to make the application—**s 10(8)**. Leave will usually be granted if it is in the child's best interests to do so.

....

Re C (A Minor) (Leave to seek Section 8 Order) [1994] 1 FLR 2

The child was refused leave to apply for a specific issue order which she sought to be allowed to go on holiday to Bulgaria with the family she was living with. The court felt that the issue was not of sufficient importance to justify an application to the court.

....

✅ *Looking for extra marks?*

Section 8 orders deal with aspects of the child's upbringing. Parents, and some others, have an automatic right to apply, but children need to seek the leave of the court. Consider whether you think this can be justified.

Reports and investigations

The Child and Family Court Advisory and Support Service (CAFCASS or, in Wales, CAFCASS Cymru) or a local authority may be directed by the court to provide an oral or written report on any matter relating to the welfare of a child who is the subject of proceedings.

The court may take account of any statement made in the report; and any evidence given if it is relevant, whether or not it would otherwise be inadmissible in evidence—**s 7**.

Key cases

****

(✱) Key cases

Case	Facts	Principle
(Axon) v Secretary of State for Health [2006] EWHC Admin 37	A similar application by Mrs Axon in respect of the same advice that Mrs Gillick had objected to. Mrs Axon objected to sections in the leaflet about abortion. She asserted that the *Gillick* case should be decided differently in the light of the Human Rights Act and the court's duty to have regard to Article 8 of the ECHR.	The *Gillick* principle extends the minor's right to have an abortion. The advice might interfere with the parents' Article 8 right to respect for private and family life, but any such interference was necessary and proportionate; if confidentiality were not available, young people would be deterred from seeking advice and treatment 'with undesirable and troubled consequences'.
Re B (A Child) [2009] UKSC 5	A four-year-old boy had been raised by his grandmother. He had regular contact with his parents, who were separated. The father remarried and applied for a residence order. The magistrates refused this. There were no compelling reasons to disrupt the child's status quo. A residence order was made in favour of the grandmother (with a contact order in favour of both parents). The Supreme Court upheld this decision.	The natural parent presumption does not outweigh the welfare principle. The best interests of the child must be paramount, even though care given by the natural parent may be 'good enough'.
CW v NT and Another [2011] EWHC 33	A couple made an informal surrogacy agreement with the woman, who was inseminated by the father. The child was to be handed to the couple at birth but the mother changed her mind during pregnancy. The father sought a residence order. A residence order was granted to the mother, with contact to the father, because of the attachment between mother and daughter. The baby was thriving in the mother's care and removing the baby would cause the baby harm. The mother was better suited to meet the baby's needs, particularly emotional needs and she would promote contact, which seemed unlikely if the roles were reversed.	Sometimes a promise to give up a baby may indicate a lack of commitment and raise questions over the mother's capacity to care for the child, but this mother had a genuine change of mind. The test in cases like this (see **Re P (Surrogacy: Residence)** (2008) is: which home is most likely to enable the child to mature into a happy and balanced adult and achieve their fullest potential?
Gillick v West Norfolk & Wisbech Area Health Authority [1986] 1 AC 112	Mrs Gillick failed in her attempt to have declared unlawful government advice that doctors might prescribe contraception for girls under 16.	A girl under 16 can consent to treatment, including contraception, if they are of sufficient understanding and intelligence to comprehend advice given to them and sufficiently mature to appreciate the implications. Health providers are not required to notify parents nor seek their consent.

Case	Facts	Principle
Re L (1998)2 FLR 810	A 14-year-old Jehovah's Witness had been badly burned and required life-saving treatment, possibly involving blood transfusion. She refused to consent. It was held that although mature, she was not *Gillick* competent as she did not understand the potential consequences of her action. Treatment was ordered.	Where a seemingly mature child refuses to consent to medical treatment, a court will overrule their wishes if it is in their best interests to do so.
Re L, V M & H [2001] Fam 260	Four cases were heard together. In each of them fathers had been refused contact with their children as there had been issues of domestic violence between the parents. The court issued guidelines in such cases: • There is no presumption against contact. • The judiciary need a heightened awareness of the effect on children of being exposed to domestic violence. • Past and present conduct of both parties should be considered. • The effect on the child and the residential parent should be assessed. • The motivation of the parent seeking contact is relevant.	There is no presumption against contact in cases of domestic violence. Each case must be decided on its merits.
Leeds Teaching Hospital v A [2003] EWHC 259	The husband and wife underwent fertility treatment together. In error her eggs were fertilised with the sperm of another. Was the husband the legal father of the resulting twins? It was held that he was not, as he had consented to his own sperm being used and not the sperm of another. The genetic father was the legal father.	The husband or partner of a woman undergoing fertility treatment will be regarded as the legal father of a child born only if he consents to the actual treatment received.

⑨ Key debate

Topic:	Shared parenting
Academics:	Fehlberg, Smyth, Maclean, and Roberts
Viewpoint:	A legal presumption of shared parenting in not in the interests of the child.
Reading:	'Caring for children after parental separation: Would legislation for shared parenting time help children?' (May 2011) Family Policy briefing 7, Department of Social Policy and Intervention, University of Oxford.

(?) Exam questions

Problem Question

Tom and Dianne have three children, Angel aged 9, Biff aged 11, and Cherub aged 13. They have recently divorced. Tom is a film producer who spends a large part of his working life on location overseas. He has a new girlfriend, Tiffany, aged 23, who finds it difficult to get on with the three children.

Dianne is a University lecturer who has recently started a relationship with Daisy. They are hoping to set up home together. Daisy works part-time in a local charity shop and adores children. At present the children are living with their mother. However, both Tom and Dianne want the children to live with them.

Biff and Angel would like to live with their father as they think his way of life is more exciting. Cherub wants to stay with her mother.

Describe the factors that the court would take into account in deciding what should happen to the children.

An outline answer is included at the end of the book.

Essay Question

'So many people have lost contact with their children through the courts, it was inevitable something like Fathers 4 Justice was going to emerge' (Matt O'Connor, founder of F4J).

Are the courts' powers, and their decisions on ordering and enforcing contact, adequate to ensure that children have contact with their parents whenever it promotes their welfare to do so?

 Scan here

Scan this QR code image with your mobile device to see an outline answer to this question or log onto www.oxfordtextbooks.co.uk/orc/concentrate

#7

The Children Act—the public law

Key Facts

- Local authorities have a range of powers and duties to protect children in need. They must investigate if there is evidence that a child is suffering or is likely to suffer significant harm.

- The police have powers to protect a child if they have cause to believe that unless they act immediately the child is likely to suffer significant harm.

- The relevant law is in **Parts III, IV, and V of the Children Act 1989**.

- Where a child is in need of immediate protection, an **emergency protection order** may be granted.

- Interim orders are temporary orders used where there are *reasonable grounds* to believe that the threshold criteria have been satisfied.

- If parents object to their child being assessed, a child assessment order may be applied for.

- Under a care order, the local authority gains parental responsibility for the child (in addition to the parents) and the child may be removed from home.

- Under a supervision order the child remains at home and a supervisor is appointed who will advise, assist, and befriend.

- The court may make a care or supervision order if the 'threshold criteria' in **s 31(2) of the Children Act 1989** are satisfied.

Note: section numbers in this chapter refer to sections of the **1989 Act**, unless it is made clear that another Act is being referred to.

Introduction

Local authorities, through their Children's Services Departments, have duties imposed on them by the **1989 Act**. The main duties are to:

- safeguard children who are in need—**s 17**;
- provide accommodation—**s 20**; and
- investigate the welfare of the child in certain circumstances—**s 47**.

Social workers face an unenviable task when deciding if and when a child should be removed from their home. They are frequently criticised if they make the wrong decision. Failure to act may mean the child will be harmed or even lose their life at the hands of the parents or carer, as in the case of Baby P in 2007.

However, if a child is removed on evidence which is later discredited, as in the Cleveland child abuse cases in the 1980s, the family and the child suffer unnecessarily and social workers are criticised for interfering in family life. In the Cleveland case, 121 children were taken from their parents following disputed diagnoses of sexual abuse.

✅ Looking for extra marks?

Consider the case of *Re S (Minors)* (2010) where the Court of Appeal criticised a local authority for removing two children from their mother, without notice, two days before Christmas. There was no immediate fear for their safety.

An independent Children's Guardian, appointed through CAFCASS (the Children and Family Court Advisory and Support Service), will advise the family courts on what they consider to be in the best interests of the child in public (and private) law applications concerning children.

The Children Act 2004

Following the death of Victoria Climbié, who was seriously abused by her great-aunt, Lord Laming made recommendations for the reform of the child protection system. The Government accepted many of his proposals and issued a Green Paper, *Every Child Matters*. Legislation followed in the form of the **Children Act 2004**. Under the Act:

- a Children's Commissioner was appointed to promote awareness of the views and the interests of children;
- the various agencies that deal with children, for example the local authority, the police, the probation service, and the education authority are required to work together to improve children's welfare;
- local Safeguarding Boards have been created to coordinate the work of these agencies; and

- Children's Services authorities have to publish a Children and Young People's Plan (CYPP) to set out their strategy for services for children and relevant young people.

✅ Looking for extra marks?

The Norgrove Review made recommendations for the reform of the family justice system. Based upon this, the Children and Families Bill was introduced into Parliament in February 2013. For an analysis of the Norgrove Review and the Government's response to it see Anna Heenan and Susan Heenan, 'Norgrove and after: An overview of the Family Justice Review and the government's response' (2012) *Journal of Social Welfare and Family Law*, Vol 34(3), 381–394.

Care proceedings and human rights issues

The **Human Rights Act 1998** has had an impact on the law in relation to care proceedings. When making an order the courts must consider whether it is proportionate to the risk of harm to the child. For example:

....

P, C and S v United Kingdom [2002] 2 FLR 631

A child was taken from her parents at birth and placed into care before being freed for adoption. It was held that there must be a fair balance struck 'between the interests of the child remaining in care and those of the parent being reunited with the child'.

In this case the parents' **Article 8** rights (to respect for private and family life) had been breached.

....

Also in:

....

Re H (Care Plan: Human Rights) [2011] EWCA Civ 1009

The Court of Appeal endorsed a County Court judge's decision that the local authority's care plan to separate mother and daughter infringed the mother's Article 8 rights and was 'neither a necessary nor proportionate interference with her right to respect for her family life'.

....

The court should also consider whether a less intrusive order could be made. For example, would it be more proportionate to make a supervision order, where the child would remain at home, instead of a care order where the child may be removed from home?

Revision tip

Problem questions often ask you to advise Children's Services what action they should take in certain circumstances, or the range of orders that may be appropriate in relation to a child.

In an essay question you may be asked to discuss the risk of allowing the child to remain with the parents balanced against the rights of the parents to a family life.

The law is set out in Parts III, IV, and V of CA 1989:

Figure 7.1 Parts III to V Children Act 1989

Part	Sections	Subject Matter
III	17–30A	Local authority support for children and families
IV	31–42	Care and supervision
V	43–52	Protection of children

Local authority support for children and families

The main powers and duties of the local authority are as follows:

General duty to children in need—s 17(1)

The local authority has a duty to safeguard and promote the welfare of children in their area who are in need and where possible to promote their upbringing by their families.

Remember that the child's family is not restricted to the mother and father. It includes anyone with whom the child is living or who has parental responsibility for the child.

Section 17(1)

It shall be the general duty of every local authority (in addition to the other duties imposed on them by this Part)—

(a) to safeguard and promote the welfare of children within their area who are in need; and

(b) so far as is consistent with that duty, to promote the upbringing of such children by their families,

by providing a range and level of services appropriate to those children's needs.

You should note that the concept of parental responsibility is central to the **1989 Act**. The local authority must provide services which assist the parents in carrying out their obligations as a parent.

Who is a child in need?—s 17(10)

- One who is unlikely to achieve or maintain a reasonable standard of health or development without the provision of services by the local authority; *or*

- His health or development is likely to be significantly impaired or further impaired without these services; *or*

- He is disabled.

This definition covers a wide range of needs, for example those who are homeless, have suffered abuse, are living with domestic violence, or have a physical or mental disability or illness.

Duty to provide accommodation

The local authority has a duty to children in need who appear to require accommodation. It includes those who are orphans and those whose parents are unable to look after them.

Section 20(1)

Every local authority shall provide accommodation for any child in need within their area who appears to them to require accommodation as a result of—

(a) there being *no person who has parental responsibility for him*;

(b) his being *lost* or having been *abandoned*; or

(c) the person who has been caring for him being *prevented* (whether or not permanently, and for whatever reason) from *providing him with suitable accommodation or care*.

Wherever possible the child's wishes and feelings (in light of their age and understanding) must be taken into account in the choice of accommodation.

Revision tip

As the child is not in the care of the local authority but is being accommodated voluntarily, the child can be removed at any time by the person with parental responsibility. If the local authority has serious concerns about the care that will be given to the child if they are removed, it can apply for an emergency protection order or request that the police intervene using their emergency powers.

Duty to investigate—s 47

The local authority has a duty to investigate the welfare of the child if they are subject to an emergency protection order; in police protection; or there is cause to suspect they are suffering or likely to suffer **significant harm**.

Section 47 Local authority's duty to investigate

1. Where a local authority—

(a) are informed that a child who lives, or is found, in their area—

(i) is the subject of an emergency protection order; or

(ii) is in police protection;

(b)   have reasonable cause to suspect that a child who lives, or is found, in their area is suffering, or is likely to suffer, significant harm,

the authority shall make, or cause to be made, such enquiries as they consider necessary to enable them to decide whether they should take any action to safeguard or promote the child's welfare.

In carrying out its investigation, the local authority will work with others who may be involved with the child, such as teachers, doctors, and the police.

In any family proceedings where any question relating to the welfare of a child arises (for example, private law proceedings between parents) if it appears to the court that there may be a need for a care order or a supervision order to be made, it can direct the local authority to investigate the child's circumstances. If the local authority decides not to bring any proceedings, it must report its reasons to the court within eight weeks—**s 37**.

Orders available to protect children under the Children Act 1989

Court action to protect children falls into three stages:

* Emergency action—emergency protection orders (EPOs) and police protection.
* Interim orders—interim care/supervision orders, child assessment orders.
* Final orders—care orders, supervision orders.

You should note that although the police have emergency powers to protect children, they do not require a court order to exercise those powers.

Emergency protection of children

Police protection—s 46

The police have powers to protect children where a police officer has reasonable cause to believe that the child would otherwise be likely to suffer significant harm. For example, the police may act to retain a runaway child or to protect a child they discover living in poor conditions. The police can act immediately as they do not need to obtain a court order.

The child can be kept in police protection for up to 72 hours. The police do not acquire parental responsibility for the child, but a designated officer will safeguard and promote the child's welfare. During this time the police must make appropriate enquiries into the case. Afterwards the child must be released to a parent or person with parental responsibility unless there is cause to believe the child will suffer significant harm if released.

For longer-term protection, the police will liaise with the local authority with a view to applying for an EPO or a care order or supervision order.

Emergency protection order—s 44

EPOs are short-term orders which should only be made in cases of a genuine emergency. They allow the applicant, usually the local authority, to remove a child to safe accommodation or to prevent the child being removed from safe accommodation.

There are three categories of applicant—(i) the local authority; (ii) an authorised person (NSPCC); (iii) any other person—with differing grounds for an application:

Figure 7.2 Applicant and grounds for application

Local Authority **or** **Authorised Person** **or** **Any Applicant**	There is reasonable cause to believe the child is likely to suffer significant harm if 1. he is not moved to accommodation provided by or on behalf of the applicant; or 2. he does not remain in the place where he is being accommodated.
Local Authority	1. enquiries are being made under **s 47(1)(b)**; and 2. enquiries are being frustrated by access to child being unreasonably refused and there is reasonable cause to believe access is required as a matter of urgency.
Authorised Person **(NSPCC)**	1. the applicant has reasonable cause to suspect that a child is suffering, or is likely to suffer, significant harm; 2. the applicant is making enquiries with respect to the child's welfare; and 3. those enquiries are being frustrated by access to the child being unreasonably refused and there is reasonable cause to believe that access is required as a matter of urgency.

Effects of an EPO

1. The court can direct that the child must be *produced* to the applicant. Any person who is in a position to do so (for example, a parent) must produce the child to the applicant (usually the local authority).

2. The court can authorise the child to be *removed* at any time to accommodation provided by or on behalf of the applicant *or* it can *prevent* the child being removed from such accommodation. For example, the child may be removed from the place where they are at risk to a foster home or, if the child is safe in a foster home and a parent wants to remove the child, this can be prevented.

3. The applicant acquires *parental responsibility* for the child for the duration of the order.

4. The applicant may only *exercise such parental responsibility* as is reasonably required to safeguard and promote the welfare of the child. The applicant should not make major decisions about the child, for example in relation to medical treatment.

5. The court can make directions as to the people the child can have *contact* with. There is a presumption of reasonable contact between the child and the parents or those whom the child was living with.

6. Additional *directions* can be attached to the order, that the child undergoes medical or psychiatric examination or other assessment, though a child of sufficient understanding to make an informed decision can refuse to submit to such an examination or assessment.

An EPO lasts for a maximum of eight days. It can be extended once only, for up to seven days. Only the local authority or NSPCC can apply for an extension.

The child should be returned if it appears safe to do so.

Revision tip

EPOs may be challenged by the child; the parent; any other person with parental responsibility; or anybody the child was living with. The application cannot be heard until 72 hours after the order was made. There is no right of challenge if the person who wishes to challenge attended the original hearing, as they should have challenged it at that time.

Exclusion requirements in EPOs—s 44A

An exclusion requirement can be added to an EPO (**s 44A**) or an interim care order (**s 38A**). This allows an alleged abuser to be removed from the child's home rather than having to remove the child from home to safe accommodation.

The effect of the requirement is to:

- require the alleged abuser to leave the place where the child is living;
- prohibit them from entering that place;
- exclude them from a defined area around that place.

They will only be made when:

- there is reasonable cause to believe the exclusion will mean the child will cease to suffer (or be likely to suffer) significant harm; *and*
- another parent or person in the home:
  - is able and willing to give the child the care which it would be reasonable to expect a parent to give him; *and*
  - they consent to the exclusion requirement.

Revision tip

The difficulty with these orders is that the other parent may not wish to consent to their partner's exclusion from the home. However, their refusal to give consent may mean that their child will be removed into care.

Child assessment order

This type of order can be made under **s 43**, where the local authority suspects that the child may be at risk of significant harm, but there is no immediate risk, so the grounds for an EPO would not be made out. The local authority or the NSPCC can apply for an order.

These orders will only be made where:

- there is cause to believe the child is suffering or likely to suffer significant harm; *and*
- an assessment is required to determine whether or not the child is suffering or likely to suffer significant harm; *and*
- it is unlikely that such an assessment will be made without an order.

The court must consider the welfare principle, the no order principle, and the no delay principle.

The order requires that anybody who is able to do so must produce the child to the person named in the order. The child does not need to be taken away from their family for the duration of the order. Further orders may be necessary following the result of the assessment.

The maximum time allowed for a child assessment order is seven days from the date specified in the order.

Unless the court directs otherwise, if the child is of sufficient age and understanding they may refuse to undergo an assessment.

Revision tip

An order is not necessary if the parents consent to their child being assessed.
If they refuse to comply after an order has been made, then an emergency protection order may be necessary.

Care and supervision orders

These orders are used for protecting children when voluntary arrangements have failed. The local authority or an authorised person can apply for an order. At present the only authorised person is the NSPCC. An order can only be made in respect of a child who is under 17 years of age. An order cannot be made in respect of a child who is married except in the unusual case of one who is under 16 (for example, a person who has married abroad in a jurisdiction where marriage under 16 is allowed).

Revision tip

The local authority (or the NSPCC) initiates *care proceedings* when it wants to apply for a care *or* a supervision order. A care order places the child in the care of the local authority; a supervision order places the child under the supervision of the local authority.

Care and supervision orders

✱✱✱✱✱✱✱✱✱✱✱✱

Under a **care order** (but not under a supervision order), the local authority gains parental responsibility for the child in addition to the parents. However, it can determine the extent to which parental responsibility of the parents is exercised. The child may be removed from their home. When the local authority applies for a care order it must prepare a care plan for the child—**s 31A**.

✅ Looking for extra marks?

The Children and Families Bill 2013 provides for timescales to be prescribed for preparation of care plans, and requires a family court to consider only those parts of a care plan which relate to the long-term upbringing of the child and with whom the child is to live. This is to overcome the suggestion that delay is being caused by courts examining care plans in unnecessary detail.

While the child is in care, the local authority must allow reasonable contact with his parents, special guardians, those who have a residence order in their favour in respect of the child, and others who had care of the child—**s 34**.

If there is a dispute about contact **s 34** enables a family court to specify what contact is to be allowed, or to authorise the local authority to refuse contact with a particular person or persons. Clause 7 of the Children and Families Bill will insert **s 34(6A)** to provide that once a refusal of contact has been authorised, the local authority will no longer be under a duty to promote future contact between the child and that person.

A **supervision order** involves less control and intervention in the family's life and the child remains at home. The order may require that the child undergoes a medical, psychiatric, or other examination or treatment. It may require the child to attend certain activities. The role of the supervisor is to advise, assist, and befriend the child. The supervisor must ensure that the order is complied with and consider whether it is still necessary for it to remain in force.

The threshold criteria

The court can only make a care or a supervision order if it finds that the *threshold criteria* are met.

Figure 7.3 The threshold criteria

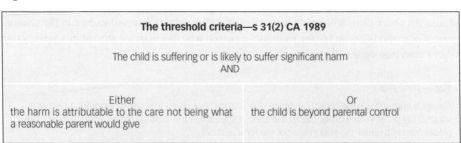

The threshold criteria—s 31(2) CA 1989	
The child is suffering or is likely to suffer significant harm AND	
Either the harm is attributable to the care not being what a reasonable parent would give	Or the child is beyond parental control

If the threshold criteria are met the court must also have regard to:

1. **welfare principle**—**s 1(1)**—*the welfare of the child is the paramount consideration*

   The court will have to balance the **Article 8** rights of parents and child; if that consideration does not point to a clear conclusion, this principle means that the child's rights will outweigh those of the parents

2. **no delay principle**—**s 1(2)**—*any delay is likely to prejudice the welfare of the child*

   Despite the clear words of this provision, and the anticipation that proceedings would normally be completed within 12 weeks, proceedings usually take considerably longer.

   The Children and Families Bill provides that the family court must timetable proceedings to dispose of the application within a maximum of 26 weeks, though a family court may extend that period if it is 'necessary to enable the court to resolve the proceedings justly'. The Bill also provides that expert evidence in family and proceedings concerning children should only be allowed where necessary.

Critics argue that the 26-week limit will be difficult to achieve and complex cases will require much longer to complete. It remains to be seen how the courts will interpret 'necessary'.

✔ *Looking for extra marks?*

The House of Commons Justice Committee's Pre-Legislative Scrutiny of the Bill (December 2012) states that there should be greater flexibility to identify cases requiring longer than 26 weeks early on, 'rather than requiring constant relisting and fruitless, taxpayer-funded, extension hearings'.

3. welfare checklist—s 1(3)—for more details see Chapter 6, 'The welfare checklist', p 115.

4. no order principle—s 1(5)—it must be better for the child to make an order than not to make one.

This recognises the need, in accordance with the **ECHR**, to ensure that any interference is proportionate.

Revision tip

Even if the threshold criteria are met, the court is under no obligation to make a care or supervision order. It must also be better for the child to make an order than not to make one. The court must consider whether a **s 8** order may be more appropriate.

A **s 8** order can be made if the threshold criteria are *not* met.

What is required to prove the threshold criteria under s 31(2)?

Figure 7.4 Proving the threshold criteria

The child is suffering	There must be proof on the balance of probabilities—***Re H (Minors) (Sexual Abuse: Standard of Proof)* (1996)**. Harm the child has suffered in the past will not count— ***Re M (A Minor) (Care Order: Threshold Conditions)* (1994)**.
The child is likely to suffer	There must be a real possibility that the child will suffer significant harm— ***Re H (Minors) (Sexual Abuse: Standard of Proof)* (1996)**.
Significant	It must be something unusual and more than commonplace— ***Re L (Care: Threshold Criteria)* (2007)**.
Harm	'ill-treatment or the impairment of health or development including, for example, impairment suffered from seeing or hearing the ill-treatment of another'—**s 31(9)**. A child may suffer harm from witnessing the domestic violence of her mother—***Re R (Care: Rehabilitation in Context of Domestic Violence)* (2006)** or her father—***Re M (A Minor)* (1994)**. • development—'physical, intellectual, emotional, social, or behavioural development' • health—'physical or mental health'; • ill-treatment—'includes sexual abuse and forms of ill-treatment which are not physical' Note: If harm relates to the child's health or development, then his health and development will be compared with what would be expected of a similar child who has not suffered harm.
Harm attributable to the care given to the child	The harm must be as a result of care given to the child (or the child being beyond parental control). If the child has more than one carer, the harm can be attributed to any of those carers—***Lancashire County Council v B* (2000)**.
The child is beyond parental control	May not be the fault of the parents. Parents may have intervened without success; for example, the child is anorexic, violent, or takes drugs.

Care order or supervision order?

***Re D (Care or Supervision Order)* (2000)** gives guidance on the factors that the court should consider when deciding between these two orders.

1. The court should only intervene to the extent necessary to protect the child, taking into account whether:

   (a) a care order is necessary;

(b) the risks could be met by a supervision order;

(c) there is a need for the speed of action that a care order gives;

(d) parental responsibility should be shared with the authority;

(e) parental cooperation could only be obtained through a care order;

(f) the child's needs could be met by advising, assisting, and befriending him rather than by sharing parental responsibility for him;

(g) cooperation and care of the child has improved during the proceedings.

2. Courts should not saddle local authorities with care orders, when they have so many demands on their resources, unless really necessary.

Note that **s 31(5)** allows a court to make a supervision order on an application for a care order, and vice versa.

Figure 7.5 Comparison of care and supervision orders

Care order	Supervision order
Threshold criteria must be satisfied.	Threshold criteria must be satisfied.
Local authority acquires parental responsibility for the child (in addition to the parents).	Local authority does not acquire parental responsibility.
Local authority can determine the extent to which parents can exercise their parental responsibility but the local authority cannot make major decisions about the child, for instance, agree to adoption, agree to change of religion, change child's surname.	Child is placed under the supervision of the local authority.
Child may be removed from home, but does not have to be.	Child remains with their family.
Local authority controls who has contact with the child.	Local authority has no control over who has contact with the child.
Order comes to an end when child reaches 18, unless discharged by the court or brought to an end earlier, for example, on adoption.	Lasts for up to one year. Can be extended to a maximum of three years.

Care proceedings and adoption

If care proceedings are in progress and the local authority decides that adoption is in the best interests of the child, to avoid future delay, it must consider making an application for a placement order. (See Chapter 8, 'Placement orders', p 146.)

Interim orders

It is possible for the court to make an interim order to protect the child in the short term if there is likely to be any delay caused by adjournments in proceedings for a care or a supervision order—**s 38**.

There must be *reasonable grounds* to believe that the threshold criteria in **s 31(2)** are met.

The effect of an interim order is the same as a full order in that the child is placed in the care or under the supervision of the local authority. An order can be granted for an initial period of up to eight weeks, and can be extended for periods of up to four weeks at a time. Even if an interim order is made it does not necessarily mean that a full order will be made.

The Children and Families Bill removes the limitations on the length of interim orders, so that, once granted, they will last until the proceedings are concluded.

Figure 7.6 Summary of Children Act public law orders

Type of Order	Who can apply	Relevant factors
Care Order— **s 33**	Local Authority/ Authorised Person	Local authority acquires parental responsibility. Local authority has power to remove the child from home. Threshold criteria—**s 31(2)** Welfare principle—**s 1(1)** No delay principle—**s 1(2)** Welfare checklist—**s 1(3)** No order principle—**s 1(5)**
Supervision Order—**s 35**	Local Authority/ Authorised Person	Local authority does not acquire parental responsibility Child cannot be removed from home. Threshold criteria—**s 31(2)** Welfare principle—**s 1(1)** No delay principle—**s 1(2)** Welfare checklist—**s 1(3)** No order principle—**s 1(5)**
Child Assessment Order—**s 43**	Local Authority/ Authorised Person	Cause to believe the child is suffering or likely to suffer significant harm, *and* Assessment is required to determine whether that is so, *and* Assessment is unlikely to be made without an order. Welfare principle—**s 1(1)** No delay principle—**s1(2)** No order principle—**s 1(5)**

Type of Order	Who can apply	Relevant factors
Emergency Protection Order—**s 44**	Any person	Reasonable cause to believe child is likely to suffer significant harm if either: He is not removed to accommodation provided by or on behalf of applicant *or* He does not remain in the place where he is being accommodated.
	Local Authority	As above or **s 47** enquiries are being made *and* Those enquiries are being frustrated by access to child being unreasonably refused *and* access is required as a matter of emergency.
	Authorised Person	As for any person *or* There is reasonable cause to believe child is suffering or likely to suffer significant harm; Inquiries are being made in respect of child's welfare; *and* Those inquiries are being frustrated by access to child being unreasonably refused and there is cause to believe access is required as a matter of urgency.
Police Protection— **s 46**	Police officer	Cause to believe that the child is likely to suffer significant harm (no court order needed).
Recovery Order—**s 50**	Those who have PR because they have an EPO or care order. If child in police protection—a police officer	There must be reason to believe: • the child has been taken away unlawfully or is being kept away unlawfully from whoever is responsible for them; or • the child has run away; or • the child is missing.

Wardship and the inherent jurisdiction of the court

Wardship is the process by which the High Court assumes responsibility for the child. No important decision relating to the child can be made without the consent of the court.

Schedule 10 to the Crime and Courts Bill (introduced into Parliament in February 2013) will create a new Family Court to have the existing family jurisdiction of the High Court, County Courts, and magistrates' Family Proceedings Courts, but would keep wardship and inherent jurisdiction matters in the High Court.

Any person can apply for a child to be made a ward of court.

Key cases

✳✳✳✳✳✳✳✳✳✳

The powers may be used in situations such as when there is fear that the child will be abducted by one parent against the wishes of the other (see Chapter 9, 'Court orders', p 165) or where there are issues in relation to consent to medical treatment (see Chapter 6, 'The rights of the child', p 102).

Wardship can be used only in relation to unmarried people under the age of 18.

The inherent jurisdiction of the court can be used to decide a particular issue in relation to a child even if they are not a ward of court.

The powers arise from the common law and not from statute, but **s 100 of the Children Act 1989** limits the use of wardship, so that it *cannot* be used to:

- put a child in the care, or under the supervision, of a local authority;
- require a child to be accommodated by a local authority;
- make a child who is subject to a care order a ward of court;
- confer on a local authority the power to determine any question about the exercise of parental responsibility.

A local authority can only apply to use wardship with the leave of the court, and leave can only be granted if the child is otherwise likely to suffer significant harm *and* what the local authority wants to achieve cannot be achieved by any other order.

✳ Key cases

Case	Facts	Principle
Re B (Care Proceedings: Standard of Proof) [2008] UKHL 35	A 16-year-old girl alleged that she had been sexually abused by her step-father. What was the standard of proof to be applied in considering the allegations for the purpose of a care order?	The standard of proof in relation to such abuse is the ordinary civil standard—it must be more probable than not. There is no sliding scale depending on the seriousness of the allegation and the consequences of the abuse.
Re H (Minors) (Sexual Abuse: Standard of Proof) [1996] AC 563 (HL)	The eldest of four sisters claimed her step-father had raped her. He was tried but acquitted. The girl went to live elsewhere but the other girls remained at home. The local authority applied for a care order in respect of them. This was dismissed as there was insufficient proof of the allegations.	A care order cannot be made without proof even if there is suspicion of abuse. There must be a real possibility of significant harm.

Case	Facts	Principle
Re M (A Minor) (Care Order: Threshold Conditions) [1994] 2 FLR 557	Four children witnessed their father murder their mother. He was imprisoned. Three of the children went to live with another relative. The youngest child initially went to foster parents but later joined the rest of his family. The local authority applied for a care order in case the child needed to be removed at a later date. The application was refused as the threshold criteria had not been satisfied. The child was no longer suffering from harm.	The date on which the child is judged to be suffering or likely to suffer significant harm is the date when the proceedings are initiated.
Re O (A Minor) (Care Order: Education: Procedure) [1992] 4 All ER 905	A care order was granted in respect of a 14-year-old persistent truant. On appeal it was argued that truancy was not a ground for a care order. It was held that the threshold criteria were satisfied. If she had not truanted her intellectual and social development would be improved.	When deciding whether a child is suffering significant harm the child should be compared with a child of equal intellectual and social development who had gone to school, not with an average child who might or might not have gone to school.
X Council v B and Others (Emergency Protection Orders) [2004] EWHC 2015 (Fam)	A local authority obtained an emergency protection order in respect of three brothers. The social worker's evidence to the court had been inaccurate. On appeal the judge gave guidance on the future use of such orders.	These orders are 'draconian' and should not be used if suitable alternatives are available. If made they should be for as short a time as necessary. Evidence given must be full and compelling and hearsay evidence must be identified. High regard must be given to the human rights of both parents and child.
R (A Child) [2011] EWHC 1715; *A County Council v M & F* [2011] EWHC 1804; *Islington LBC v Alas & Others* [2012] EWHC 865	Local authorities produced evidence, including that of experts, that the children involved in these cases had suffered non-accidental injuries (leading to death in one case), and sought care orders (in respect of a sibling in the one case).	Courts must ensure that the evidence meets the requisite standard of proof. Local authority evidence pointing to the possibility of non-accidental injury is not conclusive, even in the absence of an alternative explanation, if the standard of proof is not met. Scientific evidence cannot be judged in isolation, but must be weighed against an assessment of the credibility of witnesses and the probability (or improbability) that the events took place.

Key debate

Case	Facts	Principle
In the Matter of J (Children) [2013] UKSC 9	A local authority brought care proceedings in relation to three children. It relied on a finding in another case that it was a 'possibility' that the adult female in this household had been responsible for non-accidental injuries to another child, and submitted that this was sufficient as a matter of law to satisfy the s 31(2) threshold.	Significant harm can only be established by reference to past facts that are proved on the balance of probabilities. Mere possibility is insufficient.

⑨⑨ Key debate

Topic:	Children who are under suspicion of being abused cannot be made the subject of a care order without actual proof. How can they be protected?
Academic:	Andrew Bainham
Viewpoint:	A balance must be struck between protecting the child and removing a child unnecessarily. A solution would be to introduce a longer-term order whereby children thought to be at risk could be monitored in the home. Supervision orders in their present form are not appropriate, as they require the same threshold criteria to be satisfied as for care orders.
Reading:	'Striking the Balance in Child Protection' (2009) *Cambridge Law Journal*, Vol 68, 42–45.

⑦ Exam questions

Problem Question

Maud lives alone with her three children, Alison (aged 14), Brian (5), and Charlotte (3).

Richard (Maud's former partner) is Alison's father, while the father of the two younger children is Derek, with whom Alison was living until recently.

Children's Services received an anonymous telephone call saying that the children are being physically abused and are often left at home on their own. When a social worker visited, she found that the younger children were not at school. They looked dirty and were rather withdrawn. Brian had a large bruise on his leg. When questioned, he said that Derek had done it. Maud denies this and says that Brian fell off a swing.

Alison's teacher has expressed concerns about her behaviour and has also contacted Children's Services. She says that Alison frequently truants from school. She has heard that Alison is taking drugs and she pays for these by having sex with boys at school.

Advise the local authority on what action it may take to protect the children.

An outline answer is included at the end of the book.

Essay question

Does the **Children Act 1989** adequately balance the need for local authorities to investigate abuse and remove children from the risk of harm, against the rights of parents and children to respect for their private and family life under **Article 8 of the ECHR**?

 Scan here

Scan this QR code image with your mobile device to see an outline answer to this question or log onto www.oxfordtextbooks.co.uk/orc/concentrate

#8
Adoption

Key facts

- Adoption ends the legal relationship between a child and their birth parents. The child is treated in virtually all respects as the child of the adoptive parents.

- Adoption proceedings are governed by the **Adoption and Children Act 2002**.

- Adoption can be granted in respect of a person who has never married nor entered into a civil partnership. They must be under 19 years of age, although proceedings must start before their 18th birthday.

- Adopters must be over 21 years old, but need only be over 18 if they are a natural parent of the child.

- Adopters may be married couples, civil partners, unmarried couples, or a single person. One of a married couple can adopt in limited circumstances.

- A local authority can place a child for adoption with prospective adopters. If the child's parents or guardians do not consent to this, then a placement order is required which dispenses with parental consent.

- The welfare of the child throughout its life must be the paramount consideration when an adoption agency or a court makes any decision affecting the child.

- When dealing with an adoption application, the court must consider the available alternative orders—residence order; parental responsibility; special guardianship order; no order—and must consider making a contact order.

Chapter overview

The adoption process

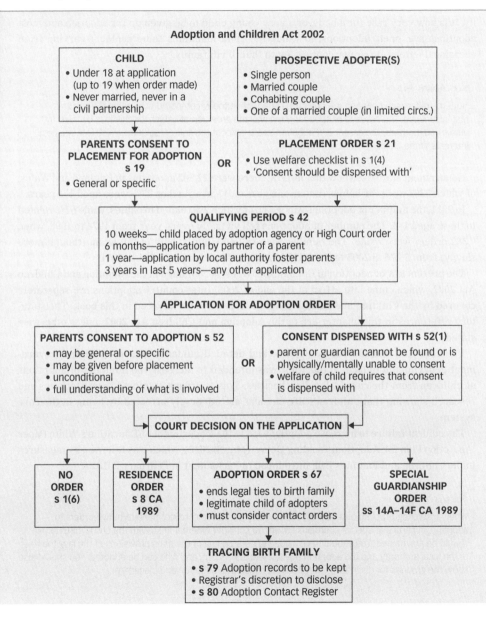

Adoption and Children Act 2002

CHILD	PROSPECTIVE ADOPTER(S)
• Under 18 at application (up to 19 when order made) • Never married, never in a civil partnership	• Single person • Married couple • Cohabiting couple • One of a married couple (in limited circs.)

PARENTS CONSENT TO PLACEMENT FOR ADOPTION s 19
• General or specific

OR

PLACEMENT ORDER s 21
• Use welfare checklist in s 1(4)
• 'Consent should be dispensed with'

QUALIFYING PERIOD s 42

10 weeks— child placed by adoption agency or High Court order
6 months—application by partner of a parent
1 year—application by local authority foster parents
3 years in last 5 years—any other application

APPLICATION FOR ADOPTION ORDER

PARENTS CONSENT TO ADOPTION s 52
• may be general or specific
• may be given before placement
• unconditional
• full understanding of what is involved

OR

CONSENT DISPENSED WITH s 52(1)
• parent or guardian cannot be found or is physically/mentally unable to consent
• welfare of child requires that consent is dispensed with

COURT DECISION ON THE APPLICATION

NO ORDER s 1(6)	RESIDENCE ORDER s 8 CA 1989	ADOPTION ORDER s 67 • ends legal ties to birth family • legitimate child of adopters • must consider contact orders	SPECIAL GUARDIANSHIP ORDER ss 14A–14F CA 1989

TRACING BIRTH FAMILY
• s 79 Adoption records to be kept
• Registrar's discretion to disclose
• s 80 Adoption Contact Register

Introduction

The nature of adoption has changed since the first adoption law, the **Adoption of Children Act**, was introduced in 1926. Virtually all adoptions were 'transplants' of a child into a new family. It is now very rare for a baby, or a very young child to be given up for adoption and most adoptions are 'open' adoptions, in which the child maintains some contact—varying from occasional letters to regular contact—with their birth family.

Revision Tip

Note the difference between the objectives of adoption today compared with when the law was first introduced. *The essence of adoption then* was the provision of babies for childless couples, by unmarried mothers. *The essence of adoption today* is about providing a solution which is in the best interests of the child.

Government statistics show that in 1974, there were 22,502 adoptions in England and Wales, of which 23% were for babies (under one year old) and a further 27% were aged 1–4 years.

In 2011, the number of adoptions was 4,734, of which 2% related to babies, while 62% related to those aged 1–4. The number of adoptions fell virtually every year from 1974 to 1998, when 4,382 orders were made. The number then rallied slightly, only to fall again (though more slowly) from 5,276 in 2005 to the 4,472 in 2010, before rising to 4,734 in 2011.

The present law of adoption in England and Wales is contained in the **Adoption and Children Act 2002**, which came into effect at the end of 2005. Inter-country adoptions are separately covered by the **Children and Adoption Act 2006**, and are not covered in this book. The statutory references in this chapter are to the **Adoption and Children Act 2002** unless otherwise stated.

The **2002 Act**, and the very extensive and detailed guidance issued by central government departments to local authorities, was intended to increase the numbers of adoptions of children from the care of local authorities. This approach stemmed from statistics and research showing that children's life chances are adversely affected by being in the care system.

The evident failure to increase adoptions led to the Department of Education's White Paper 'An Action Plan for Adoption: Tackling Delay' (March 2012), which was followed by measures in the Children and Families Bill, introduced to Parliament in February 2013.

Revision Tip

When answering problem or essay questions it is important to consider the alternative orders to adoption, in particular special guardianship, and to consider whether links with the child's birth family should be maintained. You should have a good understanding of the main provisions of the law, the role of the local authority and the adoption agency, who can adopt, and who can be adopted. You should also know the grounds for dispensing with parental consent to adoption and placement.

Adoption and human rights

Article 8 of the European Convention on Human Rights states that everyone has the right to respect for their private and family life. The court and the adoption agency must ensure that adoption is in the best interests of the child and that any interference in the **Article 8** rights of the child and the parents is necessary and proportionate.

....

Scott v UK [2000] 1 FLR 958, ECHR

The mother was a recovering alcoholic. An adoption order was made in relation to her child without the mother's consent and she complained that her **Article 8** rights had been infringed.

It was held that although there had been interference with her **Article 8** rights this was justified as adoption was in the best interests of the child.

....

Who can be adopted?

- Any person aged under 19 can be adopted, provided they were under 18 when the adoption application was made (ie submitted to the court).

- They must not have been married nor have entered into a civil partnership at any time.

- Unlike some other jurisdictions (where adoption can be used to ensure inheritance), an adoption application cannot be made to the courts in England and Wales in respect of an adult.

- No application can be made in relation to a child who is under six weeks old.

Who can adopt? Sections 49–51

- A single person.
- A person who is the partner of a parent of the person to be adopted.
- A married couple.
- A couple who have entered into a civil partnership.
- An unmarried couple (whether heterosexual or homosexual) who are living as partners in a stable and enduring family relationship.
- A prospective adopter must be at least 21 years old, except a natural parent of the child, who must be at least 18.
- They must have been habitually resident in the British Isles for at least a year.
- They (or one of them if it is a joint application) must be domiciled in the British Isles (ie they regard the British Isles as their permanent home).

You should remember that under **s 51(3)** a married person can only adopt on their own if they can show that their spouse cannot be found; or that they are permanently separated; or that their spouse's mental or physical condition is such that they are incapable of making an application.

Different types of adoption

Transplant (or traditional) adoption

'**Transplant adoption**' is the term often used to describe the more traditional form of adoption, where a child severs all links with their birth family. This may be a very suitable approach when a baby is adopted, but can give rise to difficulty when an older child, with memories of their birth relatives, is adopted. It may be especially awkward when it skews family roles, for instance when a grandmother or aunt adopts, causing the natural mother to become the child's sister or aunt.

Step-parent adoption

Until the **Children Act 1975** came into force, many adoption applications were made by a person who had brought up their child as a single parent (most often the mother) applying to adopt the child jointly with their new spouse after marriage. A further number of applications were made by remarried parents jointly with their new spouse.

The **1975 Act** introduced custodianship orders (the forerunner of special guardianship orders), and **s 37 of that Act** required courts to treat in-family adoption applications as if they were custodianship applications, if 'the child's welfare would not be better safeguarded and promoted by...adoption' than by custodianship. This was widely interpreted as a presumption against step-parent adoptions and the number of step-parent adoptions granted decreased from over 9,000 in 1975 to 4,000 in 1984.

Open adoption

'**Open adoption**' refers to an arrangement where the child retains contact with members of their birth family. It has become more common as the average age of children being adopted has risen, so that more and more adopted children retain a memory of their natural parents and their extended natural family.

The role of local authorities and adoption agencies

Local authorities have a duty under **s 2** of the Act to provide adoption services in their area to meet the needs of:

- children who may be adopted;

- their parents and guardians;
- those who wish to adopt;
- those who have been adopted; and
- their natural parents and former guardians.

Some of these services and facilities can be provided by voluntary organisations, provided they are registered with the Care Quality Commission.

An adoption agency may be either a local authority or a registered voluntary organisation—**s 2(1)**.

Adoption panels

These are set up by adoption agencies. They will consider plans for adoption, the suitability of prospective adopters, and they will match them with available children. They will make a recommendation to the adoption agency on whether the adoption should go ahead.

Avoiding delay

Section 1(3) requires any court or adoption agency to always bear in mind that, in general, any delay in coming to a decision is likely to prejudice the child's welfare—*the no delay principle*.

- The Department for Education's Adoption Guidance requires local authorities to consider a child's need for permanence and make a 'permanence plan'.
- They must consider whether or not adoption is an option at the child's four-month review after they have been received into care.
- The adoption panel should receive information within six weeks of the completion of the plan.
- The adoption panel should decide whether to recommend **placement for adoption** within two months of a review where adoption has been identified as the appropriate option.

Even if all the stages mentioned are all dealt with on time, the period of the court process must be added, so that an adoption necessarily takes a significant time. Government concerns at the length of time adoptions take led to the publication of the Children and Families Bill in February 2013. Two measures in the Bill are intended to help accelerate the adoption process.

Clause 1 would require a local authority which is considering adoption for a child in care to consider placing the child with foster parents who are already approved as adopters (rather than those still to undergo the approval process).

Clause 2 (which applies to England, but not Wales) would repeal the requirement to give consideration to a child's religion, race, culture, and language in placing the child for adoption.

Section 109 requires any court dealing with a placement or adoption application to draw up a timetable to ensure the matter is determined without delay, and to give directions to keep all parties to that timetable.

Dual planning

To avoid delay in the planning process, local authorities will sometimes consider 'dual planning'. This is where more than one option is considered for the child's future. For example, to widen the pool of potential carers in cases where a child has extensive needs, the local authority may look for foster carers as well as prospective adopters. See *Re P (A Child)* (2008) in 'Key Cases', p 157.

Placement for adoption

Before an application can be made for an adoption order, the child must have lived with the applicants for a trial period. The length of this period will vary depending on the relationship that the prospective adopter already has with the child. A child can only be placed with prospective adopters under the following circumstances:

- *either* the parents or guardians of the child consent to the placement; *or*
- a placement order is made by the court.

Parental responsibility following placement

The existing parental responsibility of the child's parents or guardians continues. However, parental responsibility for the child is also given to the adoption agency and, while the child is placed with prospective adopters, parental responsibility is given to them. The adoption agency can restrict the exercise of parental responsibility by any parent or guardian or the prospective adopters, to the extent it decides—**s 25**.

Parental consent to placement

Section 19 allows an adoption agency to place a child with prospective adopters if the parents or guardians have consented to the placement and consent has not been withdrawn.

Parental (or guardian) consent may be *specific*, which means that placement is with identified prospective adopters, or it can be *general*, permitting placement with any prospective adopters who may be chosen by the agency.

Placement orders

A placement order authorises a local authority to place a child for adoption with any prospective adopters who may be chosen by the local authority.

ONE or MORE of these must apply	AND ONE of these must apply
The child is subject to a care order	Each parent or guardian of the child has given a general consent to placement—which has not been withdrawn
The court is satisfied that the conditions for making a care order in s 31(2) of the Children Act 1989 are met	
The child has no parent or guardian	The consent of a parent or guardian should be dispensed with

Figure 8.1 Grounds for making a placement order

Under **s 21**, a court can only make a placement order if one or more of the three grounds in column 1 in Table 8.1 applies *and* one of the two items in column 2 also applies:

Dispensing with consent to placement

There are two grounds for dispensing with parental consent to placement—**s 52**.
These are:

- the parent or guardian cannot be found or is incapable of giving consent; *or*
- the welfare of the child requires the consent to be dispensed with.

The welfare checklist

In deciding placement order applications (as in other decisions relating to adoption) the court (and adoption agencies) must have regard to the 'welfare checklist' in **s 1(4)** which is largely similar to that in **s 1(3) of the Children Act 1989**.

The **Children Act 1989** checklist governs decisions relating to special guardianship orders, as those orders are made under that Act and not the **Adoption and Children Act 2002**. The **Children Act** also contains an additional heading (g), which requires a court dealing with an application under the **1989 Act** to consider the range of powers available to the court under the Act in the proceedings in question. This enables a court to make any order that it considers appropriate, if it is satisfied that, although not applied for, the order will promote the child's welfare.

Note: item (f) differs considerably between the two Acts.

Placement for adoption

****

Figure 8.2 The welfare checklist

The Adoption and Children Act 2002—s 1(4)	The Children Act 1989—s 1(3)
(a) the child's ascertainable wishes and feelings regarding the decision (considered in the light of the child's age and understanding)	(a) the ascertainable wishes and feelings of the child concerned (considered in the light of his age and understanding)
(b) the child's particular needs	(b) his physical, emotional, and educational needs
(c) the likely effect on the child (throughout his life) of having ceased to be a member of the original family and become an adopted person	(c) the likely effect on him of any change in his circumstances
(d) the child's age, sex, background, and any of the child's characteristics which the court or agency considers relevant	(d) his age, sex, background, and any characteristics of his which the court considers relevant
(e) any harm which the child has suffered or is at risk of suffering	(e) any harm which he has suffered or is at risk of suffering
(f) the relationship which the child has with relatives, and with any other person in relation to whom the court or agency considers the relationship to be relevant, including: (i) the likelihood of any such relationship continuing and the value to the child of its doing so; (ii) the ability and willingness of any of the child's relatives, or of any such person, to provide the child with a secure environment in which the child can develop, and otherwise to meet the child's needs; (iii) the wishes and feelings of any of the child's relatives, or of any such person, regarding the child.	(f) how capable each of his parents, and any other person in relation to whom the court considers the question to be relevant, is of meeting his needs

✅ *Looking for extra marks?*

Consider whether the different wordings of **s 1(4)(b) and (c) of the Adoption and Children Act 2002** and **s 1(3)(b) and (c) of the Children Act 1989** might cause difficulty in a case where a court is deciding between adoption or special guardianship, and would thus have to have regard to both checklists.

Matching the child to prospective adopters

Once consent to placement is given or a placement order is made, the adoption agency can place the child with adopters who are able to provide the most suitable upbringing for the particular child. In many cases, this will be existing foster parents, and the reality will be that the child continues to reside with them with an altered status.

Before the placement starts, the local authority must provide the adopters with a full report about the child's health, needs, and history. A local authority may be negligent if it does not disclose information which would have persuaded the adopters not to proceed.

....

A and B v Essex County Council [2002] EWHC 2709 (Fam)

Two prospective adopters successfully sued the local authority in negligence claiming damage to their health, their home, and their family life, as they had not been told about the extent of the behavioural problems of two children who had been placed with them for adoption.

....

Since 2004, a national adoption register has been maintained by the British Association for Adoption & Fostering (BAAF) on behalf of the Government to provide details of prospective adopters and children seeking adoptive parents, to enable adoption agencies to have the widest possible range of potential matches.

Clause 6 of the Children and Families Bill will require local authorities to add details of children for whom they are considering adoption to the Adoption and Children Register, and allow prospective adopters to search that part of that Register to assist them to identify a child for whom they would be appropriate adopters.

Section 1(5) provides that, in placing the child for adoption, an adoption agency must give due consideration to the child's religious persuasion, racial origin, and cultural and linguistic background.

✅ Looking for extra marks?

The subsection requires that the agency 'must give due consideration to…'. It does not require that those factors are matched perfectly. The Department for Education's revised Adoption Guidance, issued in February 2011, states (at p 85): 'A prospective adopter can be matched with a child with whom they do not share the same ethnicity, provided they can meet the child's other identified needs'.

The adoption agency must also carry out a full investigation into the suitability of the prospective adopters to adopt the child. **Section 45** provides for there to be regard to 'the need for stability and permanence in their relationship'.

As previously mentioned, Clause 2 of the Children and Families Bill would repeal **s 1(5)** in England.

Application for an adoption order

Section 42 requires that the child must have lived with the prospective adopters for one of the periods shown in the table below before an application can be made. The residence must have been throughout the period, except in the case of an application by relatives, where there may be gaps in the period.

Note that the Act does not specify when an application is 'made', but it is implicit in **s 49(4) and (5)**, which distinguish between making an application and when the proceedings are concluded, that an application is 'made' when the written application is first submitted to the court.

Figure 8.3 Applicant and qualifying period

Application made by	Qualifying period
Any person, provided the adoption was arranged by an adoption agency	10 weeks
A parent of the child	10 weeks
A partner of a parent	6 months
A local authority foster parent	12 months
A relative	A total of 3 years during the last 5 years

Consent to adoption

Whose consent is required?

Section 52 requires the same consents to adoption (from each parent or guardian of the child), or a court decision to dispense with consent, as for a placement order.

Parent means a parent with parental responsibility, but does not include a step-parent even if they have parental responsibility.

An unmarried father without parental responsibility is not required to give consent; however, he can be made a party to the proceedings.

....

Re H: Re G (Adoption: Consultation of Unmarried Fathers) [2001] 1 FLR 646

In *Re H*, the father had lived with the mother for some time and had a continuing commitment to the child, and **Article 8 of the Human Rights Convention** (right to respect for family life) was engaged.

In *Re G*, the parents had not cohabited and the father had no constant relationship with the child. **Article 8** was not engaged. It was held that in *Re H* the father should be informed and in *Re G* the father need not be informed.

In both cases it was held that although the consent of a birth father without parental responsibility is not required, they should be informed of adoption proceedings unless there is a good reason not to do so.

In a rare case where a child is adopted for a second time, a parent would include the existing adoptive parents, but not the birth parents.

Although **s 1(4)(a)** requires that the child's ascertainable wishes and feelings regarding the decision are taken into account, there is no requirement to obtain the child's consent, even if they are of sufficient age and understanding within the *Gillick* principles.

A mother cannot give effective consent to adoption until the child is at least six weeks old (**s 52(3)**), but she can give consent to placement for adoption during that time.

Dispensing with consent to adoption

The test is the same as for dispensing with consent in relation to placement orders.

Adoption orders

Effect of an adoption order

Section 67 provides that an adopted person is to be treated in law as if born as the child of the adopters or adopter, and is their legitimate child. Their adoptive parents' family becomes the child's family in virtually all respects.

The only limitation to this total immersion is that the child may not inherit a peerage or property arising via a peerage through his adoptive family—**s 71**.

The parental responsibility of all other persons and agencies comes to an end, and only the adoptive parents have parental responsibility.

All existing contact orders come to an end, though the court granting the adoption order has power to make fresh contact orders, and must consider using that power—**s 46(6)**.

Clause 8 of the Children and Families Bill provides for contact orders to be made subsequently to an adoption order, and allows a court to prohibit contact. Such a contact order may be made on application by the adopters or the child, or anyone else with the court's leave.

The adopted person retains one connection to their birth family—they remain within the prohibited degrees of affinity to their birth relatives for marriage or civil partnership purposes. So, for example, the marriage or civil partnership between an adopted child and their brother or sister by birth would be void, even if they have not been brought up together.

Alternative orders

There are a number of alternatives to adoption:

Residence order—s 8 of the Children Act 1989

If a residence order is made, the carers will share parental responsibility with the parents. The advantage is that the child maintains a link with their birth family. However, there may be concerns about interference by the parents in the child's upbringing which may be distressing for the carers and the child. There is also the continuing possibility that the parents will apply for a residence order themselves.

Special guardianship order—s 14A of the Children Act 1989

This type of order gives the special guardian enhanced parental responsibility for the child, but it does not sever the ties with the child's birth family. It is appropriate where the child needs a stable home but where adoption may not be a suitable option.

A special guardian can exercise parental responsibility to the exclusion of everyone else who has parental responsibility (apart from any other special guardian)—**s 14C(1) of the Children Act 1989**.

Making an order does not affect the position of natural parents in relation to consent to adoption or placement for adoption—**s 14C(2) of the Children Act 1989**.

Section 14C(3) of the Children Act 1989 provides that no person (including a special guardian) can change the child's surname or take the child abroad without either the consent of everyone who has parental responsibility for the child, or in accordance with a court order (either one made under **s 14B(2)** or a specific issue order). However, this is subject to **s 14C(4)** which allows a special guardian to take a child abroad for a period of less than three months without any consents.

Who can be a special guardian?

A special guardian must be aged 18 or over; and must not be a parent of the child. Applications may be made jointly or individually. Joint applicants do not have to be married. Applications may be made by:

- a (non-special) guardian of the child;
- anyone who has a residence order in respect of the child;
- anyone who has consent of all those with parental responsibility;

- a local authority foster parent (if the child has lived with them for the last one year);

- a relative (if the child has lived with them for the last one year); and

- any other person with the leave of the court.

When making a special guardianship order, the court must consider whether an order for contact should be made, and whether or not to discharge any existing **s 8** orders—**s 14B(1) of the Children Act 1989**.

✅ *Looking for extra marks?*

Consider when special guardianship may be appropriate. When special guardianship was first proposed in a 2000 White Paper, 'Adoption: A New Approach' (December 2000), it was considered that it might be suitable for:

- older children wishing to keep ties with their birth parents but who need greater security;

- children being cared for on a permanent basis by other family members; and

- children from minority ethnic communities where adoption is not recognised.

However the cases of *Re S* **(2007)**, *Re AJ* **(2007)**, and *Re M-J* **(2007)** (see 'Key Cases', p 157) make it clear that nothing limits special guardianship or adoption to any given set of circumstances.

The no order principle

The *no order* principle applies to the **2002 Act**, as it does to the **Children Act 1989**. If no order is made it will leave matters as they were before the adoption application was made. However, generally, if the court wishes to maintain the status quo, it will simply refuse the adoption application. 'No order' may be appropriate once the court has considered ordering contact with an adoption order. The court appears reluctant to order contact. If contact can be agreed, the voluntary arrangement is left to operate; if the adoptive parents oppose any contact, the court will not often force it upon them.

In *A Local Authority v Y, Z and Others* **(2006)** the court reviewed the various alternative orders. The parties all agreed that the children involved should remain with their aunt and uncle. Making no order 'would provide no security at all' and would leave the children vulnerable to a change of mind by the mother. A residence order would not cement the relationship between the aunt and uncle and the children as successfully as a special guardianship order. A care order would continue restrictions on the lives of the children and necessitate regular reviews by the local authority. Adoption would 'be harsh on the mother' and would skew the family relationships—the mother would become an aunt, and vice versa. It was emphasised that, on the particular facts of the case, a special guardianship order would best promote the children's welfare.

Alternative orders

✳✳✳✳✳✳✳✳✳✳

Figure 8.4 Comparison of alternative orders

	Adoption Order	Special Guardianship Order	Residence Order
Parental Responsibility	Adopter has parental responsibility (PR) to the exclusion of all others.	Special guardian acquires PR. Natural parents (and local authority if there is a care order) retain PR. However, special guardian can exercise it to the exclusion of the others. Special guardian cannot consent to adoption, change of surname, or consent to serious medical treatment without the agreement of all others with PR.	Carers would acquire PR, shared with the natural parents (and local authority if there is a care order). Day-to-day exercise would have to be by agreement, or in accordance with specific issue and/or prohibited steps orders.
Take child abroad	Adopter may take the child abroad without consulting with anyone else.	Special guardian may take the child abroad for less than 3 months without consulting others.	Carer could take child abroad for up to a month without consent of others with PR. This can be longer with written agreement.
Change child's name	Adopter is free to change the child's given names and/or surname.	Special guardian could only change child's name with consent of all with PR.	Carers could only change child's name with the consent of all with PR.
Nationality	The child takes the nationality of the adopter.	Unaffected	Unaffected
Financial support	All financial orders for the child cease. Some local authority support may be available.	Local authority support may be available if the child was previously looked after. Parents still have maintenance obligation.	Any local authority support would be unaffected. Parents still have maintenance obligation.
Contact with others	Existing contact orders cease, but the court must consider whether contact should be ordered.	Court must consider whether to end existing orders and whether fresh contact should be ordered.	Existing contact orders continue unless revoked or replaced.

	Adoption Order	Special Guardianship Order	Residence Order
Duration of order	Permanent	Lasts until the child reaches 18 unless discharged earlier by the court.	Lasts until the child reaches 18 unless discharged earlier by the court.

Note: No column is shown in Figure 8.4 for 'No Order'—the status quo would continue unaltered in all respects.

✅ Looking for extra marks?

Consider whether the changed nature of adoptions (more 'open' adoptions: fewer 'transplants'), and the availability of alternative orders, means that there is no longer any need for adoption orders.

Setting aside

An adoption order cannot be set aside unless there are highly exceptional circumstances.

Re B (Adoption: Setting Aside) [1995] 2 FLR 1

A child of an unmarried English Catholic mother and Kuwaiti Muslim father was adopted as a baby by a Jewish couple. He later emigrated to Israel, but was suspected of being an Arab spy and deported. He discovered his origins, and sought to have the adoption set aside to allow him to take his Arab identity. His application was refused.

A similar approach was adopted in *Webster v Norfolk County Council & Others* (2009).

However, in *Re W (Adoption Order: Set Aside and Leave to Oppose)* (2010), an adoption order was set aside in the County Court, only to be reinstated by the Court of Appeal.

Tracing birth family

The Registrar-General of Births, Marriages and Deaths is required by **s 79** to keep records of adoptions that can be referenced to birth records. Adopted persons can look for their original birth certificate, though the Registrar-General has discretion to refuse disclosure.

R v Registrar General, ex p Smith [1991] 1FLR 255 CA

Smith, who had been adopted, had killed his prison cellmate under the delusion that he was killing his mother. The court upheld the Registrar-General's refusal of access to his birth certificate, as it was clear that he would be likely to harm his natural mother if he could trace her.

Revised adoption guidance
✱✱✱✱✱✱✱✱✱✱✱

An Adoption Contact Register is maintained by virtue of **s 80**.

Part 1 contains details of adopted persons who are now adults and who have recorded their wish to be (or not to be) contacted by their natural relatives.

Part 2 contains similar details of natural relatives of adopted persons. This enables either party to ascertain whether contact is likely to be possible. Although details of a considerable number of persons are included in each Part of the Register, relatively few 'matches' are made.

Revised adoption guidance

In February 2011, the Government announced its view that fewer children for whom adoption is the right plan were currently being found new families. This was based on a fall in the number of children placed for adoption between March 2009 and 2010, while the number of children in the care of local authorities rose. It was said that black children take on average over 50% longer to be placed for adoption than children from other ethnic groups, and children over five were four times less likely to be adopted compared to children under five in the previous year.

Certain measures to 'improve the situation' were put forward, including considering a stronger inspection regime for local authority adoption services; examining whether enough is being done to support approved adopters who are not matched with a child; and issuing revised adoption guidance for local authorities in England.

This new guidance specifies that:

- local authorities must not refuse to place a child with prospective adoptive parents on the basis of their different ethnic or cultural background (further emphasised, in England (only) by the provision for repeal of **s 1(5)** by Clause 1 of the Children and Families Bill);

- adoption should be considered for children who may have been overlooked in the past—such as older children or those with disabilities;

- local authorities should welcome enquiries from those wanting to adopt and no person should be turned away on the grounds of race, age, or social background;

- local authorities should make better use of the Adoption Register to match adoptive parents with children; and

- local authorities should use the specialist expertise of voluntary adoption agencies in finding families for difficult to place children—particularly older children, children with disabilities, sibling groups, and BME children.

However, the announcement contained no mention of the success or otherwise of the alternatives to adoption (such as residence or special guardianship orders), and made no reference to the differences between 'transplant' and 'open' adoptions.

The Adoption Statistics 2010, published by the Office for National Statistics, do not entirely support the Government contentions—60% of adoptions related to children under five and 40% to those over five (a proportion very similar to 2008 and 2009).

Revision tip

In your examination you may be asked to consider whether adoption or special guardianship is a more appropriate option. You could also be asked a question in relation to the range of people who are now permitted to adopt.

✳ Key cases

Case	Facts	Principle
Re P (A Child) [2008] EWCA Civ 535	A local authority applied for a placement order in respect of two children. To widen the range of potential carers they simultaneously looked for foster parents (dual planning). It was unlikely that the children could be placed together. The mother objected to the placement as she believed it would affect her contact with the children. Her consent to placement was dispensed with. She appealed on the grounds that the court had not considered her Article 8 rights. Her appeal was dismissed.	The judgment gives guidance on three main issues in relation to adoption: 1. In dispensing with parental consent the paramount consideration is the child's welfare throughout his life. 2. Dual planning is an appropriate approach as it widens the range of carers and shortens the period of time that the child 'remains in limbo'. 3. Although it is unusual for a contact order with the birth family to be made if the prospective adopters object it is ultimately a matter for the court to decide.
Re: P (A Child) (Adoption Order: Leave to Oppose Making of Adoption Order) [2007] EWCA Civ 616	The child was placed for adoption because of the parents' problems with violence, alcohol, and drugs. They overcame their problems and sought leave under **s 47** to defend the adoption proceedings. Their application was refused and their subsequent appeal was dismissed.	When granting leave to oppose adoption proceedings a two-stage test must be satisfied: • There must have been a change in circumstances—**s 47(7)**. If this is satisfied, then: • The paramount consideration must be the welfare of the child throughout his life—**s 1**.
Re R (Adoption: Contact) [2005] EWCA Civ 1128	A girl aged four in foster care, had weekly contact with her 17-year-old half sister. When she was placed for adoption, the older girl sought leave to apply for a contact order. The prospective adopters were concerned about the disruption to the child and the issue of confidentiality as the older girl was still in touch with the mother. The application was refused.	'The imposition on prospective adopters of orders for contact with which they are not in agreement is extremely, and remains extremely, unusual.'—Wall LJ A similar approach was taken in ***Oxfordshire County Council v X and Others*** [2010] EWCA Civ 581.

Key debate

✶✶✶✶✶✶✶✶✶✶

Case	Facts	Principle
Re S (A Child) (Adoption Order or Special Guardianship Order) [2007] EWCA Civ 54; *Re AJ (A Child)* [2007] EWCA Civ 55; *Re M-J (A Child)* [2007] EWCA Civ 56	Adoption orders were applied for in each case, but the local authorities recommended special guardianship.	The situations in the White Paper, where special guardianship may apply, are merely examples. Nothing limits special guardianship or adoption to any given set of circumstances. The Human Rights Act requires intervention in family life be only such as is necessary and proportionate so, if the welfare objective can be equally met by special guardianship, that should be preferred to adoption.
Webster v Norfolk County Council & Ors [2009] EWCA 59	A couple had three children, one of whom had suffered injuries which were believed to be non-accidental and caused by the parents. All three children were taken into care and were subsequently adopted. In proceedings in relation to a fourth child, medical evidence was submitted that the injuries were a result of iron and vitamin C deficiency. The parents applied for the adoption orders in respect of their other children to be set aside. This was refused.	Once adoption orders have been made they can only be set aside in highly exceptional and very particular circumstances.

⑨⑨ Key debate

Topic:	**Adoption by gay and lesbian couples**
Academic:	Zimran Samuel
Viewpoint:	The 2002 Act allows gay and lesbian couples to adopt. In spite of this they are still encountering prejudice when attempting to do so.
Reading:	'In Practice: Adoption for Gay and Lesbian Couples' (2010) *Fam Law* 1220

⑦ Exam questions

Problem Question

A married couple, Dave and Jane, wish to adopt Cindy, aged six. Cindy was placed with them for adoption two years ago because her mother Candice is serving a life sentence for murder. Candice has had no contact with Cindy for the past two years, but she opposes adoption because she is sure that her conviction will be overturned. Cindy still sees her grandmother Dora and sometimes stays overnight with her. However Dora feels unable to care for Cindy on a full-time basis. Candice was not married to Cindy's father, Jim, and she split up from him before Cindy was born. He has never met his daughter.

Advise Dave and Jane whether they will be allowed to adopt Cindy.

An outline answer is included at the end of the book.

Essay question

Is the welfare of some children best provided for by way of an adoption order under the **Adoption and Children Act 2002**, or do other orders provide adequately for all cases, so that adoption is now an outdated concept?

Scan here

Scan this QR code image with your mobile device to see an outline answer to this question or log onto www.oxfordtextbooks.co.uk/orc/concentrate

#9

International parent–child abduction

Key facts

- **Section 1(2) of the Child Abduction Act 1984** (CAA 1984) makes it an offence for a person connected with the child to remove a child under 16 from the UK without consent from certain specified people.

- Child abduction may be by way of taking a child abroad without consent (removal), or by keeping a child abroad beyond a period for which consent was given (retention).

- Recovery of an abducted child may be effected through the International Child Abduction and Contact Unit (ICACU), if the child is in a country which has ratified the **Hague Convention 1980 (HC 1980)**, the **Hague Convention 1996 (HC 1996)** or the **European Convention**. The Conventions have legal force by virtue of the **Child Abduction and Custody Act 1985** (CACA 1985).

- Defences to Hague Convention recovery proceedings may be raised by asserting that the court lacks jurisdiction to deal with the application.

- The defences provided in **Articles 12 and 13 HC 1980** may be used (though these rarely succeed).

- If the child is in a country which is not a party to any of the Conventions, it may be necessary to take civil proceedings through the courts in that country. The UK has Protocols with Pakistan and Egypt dealing with the approach to be taken in dealing with abduction cases.

- If a child is brought into England and Wales from another country, recovery may be achieved by the use of orders under **s 8 of the Children Act 1989** or by making the child a ward of court.

Chapter overview

Routes to enforce rights of custody in respect of an abducted child

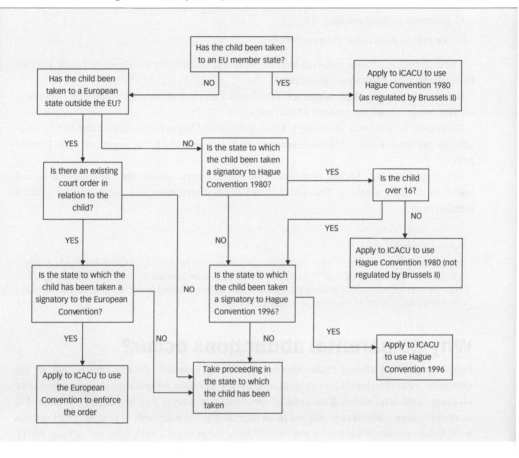

Introduction

The phrase '**child abduction**' can cover a wide range of scenarios, for example, the taking or kidnapping of a child by a stranger (or, at least, a non-family member) for sexual abuse, for ransom, or to keep as their own child.

This chapter deals only with abduction by a parent where a child is taken out of England and Wales. This is an increasing problem and recent research by the Foreign and Commonwealth

Office indicates that the number of parent child abductions has almost doubled in the last decade. A summary of that research can be found at www.familylawweek.co.uk/site. aspx?i=ed106422.

Parent–child abduction can take two forms:

- Removal without consent.

- Retention once consent has expired.

The difference between removal and retention was clarified by the House of Lords in *Re H; Re S (Abduction: Custody Rights)* **(1991)**.

Removal is 'when a child, which has previously been in the state of its habitual residence, is taken away across the frontier of that state'.

Retention is 'where a child, which has previously been for a limited period of time outside the state of its habitual residence, is not returned on the expiry of such limited period'.

For example, the child is *removed* from the country where they normally live and taken to another country. The child is *retained* where they are not returned after a contact visit.

Revision tip

The removal or retention must be in breach of rights of custody for it to be wrongful. 'Rights of custody' is defined below. You should note that it is a wider concept than 'residence' under the **Children Act 1989** and can extend to, for instance, the right to make decisions about a ward of court which the High Court acquires as soon as wardship proceedings start.

Why do parental abductions occur?

People may move abroad from their home country because of wars, oppression, or for economic reasons (long-term migration), or for holiday, education, or work (short- or medium-term migration). This type of movement of people has increased considerably in recent years. This in turn has led to an increase in the numbers of family relationships established across what might previously have been racial, religious, or cultural barriers. If such a relationship founders, it is not uncommon for the parent who previously migrated to want to return to the perceived safety of their original country, taking their children with them. The growth of cheaper and easier air travel has made this easier.

✅ *Looking for extra marks?*

Agopian suggests in 'The Impact on Children of Abduction by Parents' (1984) *Child Welfare* 63(6), 511–519, four reasons why a parent may abduct their child:

- a belief that the other parent will harm or neglect the child;

- a wish by the abductor to keep a full-time parenting role;
- a wish to punish the other parent for failure of the relationship;
- a wish to force a reconciliation, using the child as a means of exerting pressure on the other parent.

In cases where the abductor takes the child into another jurisdiction, there may be added:

- a real or perceived belief that courts locally will favour the other parent;
- moving to another jurisdiction with a new partner, with a wish to include the child in the new family relationship they have established.

The Child Abduction Act 1984

The Act creates a range of criminal offences to deal with the full range of potential child abductions. **Section 1(1)** deals with international parent/child abduction:

Section1(1) CAA

A person connected with a child under the age of 16 commits an offence if he takes or sends the child out of the United Kingdom without the appropriate consent.

A person is 'connected with a child' if they are a parent or guardian of the child; anyone in whose favour a residence order is in force with respect to the child or who has custody of the child and, if a child's parents were not married to each other at the time of his birth, there are reasonable grounds for believing that he is the father of the child—s 1(2).

Section 1(3) defines 'the appropriate consent' in relation to a child as:

- the consent of each of the child's mother; father (if he has parental responsibility for him); a guardian; anyone with a residence order in their favour; or anyone who has custody of the child; or
- the leave of the court granted under or by virtue of any provision of **Part II of the Children Act 1989**; or the leave of any court which has awarded the custody of the child to anyone.

Section 1(4) and **s 1(5)** provide for defences to a **s 1(1)** charge:

A person does not commit an offence if he has a residence order in his favour *and* he takes or sends the child out of UK for less than a month, unless he does so in breach of an order under **Part II of the Children Act 1989—s 1(4)**.

Methods of preventing abduction

✳✳✳✳✳✳✳✳✳✳✳

Section 1(5) provides that a person does not commit an offence by doing anything without the consent of another person whose consent is required, if:

Section 1(5)

(a) he believes that the other person has consented or would consent if he was aware of all the relevant circumstances; or

(b) he has taken all reasonable steps to communicate with the other person but has been unable to communicate with him; or

(c) the other person has unreasonably refused to consent, unless that person is someone with a residence order in their favour in respect of the child; or who has custody of the child; or the person taking or sending the child out of the UK does so in breach of an order made by a court in the UK.

If the defence raises one of the issues in **s 1(5)**, the onus then shifts to the prosecution to prove that subsection does *not* apply—**s 1(6)**.

Note that abduction may also amount to other offences—the common law offences of kidnapping or false imprisonment. Kidnapping is to take someone, by force or fraud, without their consent and without lawful excuse. This may include a parent who takes a child away without the child's consent.

However, in *R v D* **(1984)**, the House of Lords held that parents should only be prosecuted for the crime 'in exceptional cases, where the conduct of the parent concerned is so bad that an ordinary right-thinking person would immediately and without hesitation regard it as criminal in nature'.

False imprisonment is the intentional or reckless restraint of someone's freedom of movement from a particular place without lawful excuse. A restraint on a child by a parent will be unlawful if it is 'outside the realm of reasonable parental discipline'.

In *Rahman* **(1985)**, the Court of Appeal upheld the conviction of a father who had been trying to take his 15-year-old daughter back to her country of origin against her will. His car was stopped by police officers as the daughter was screaming for help out of the car window.

Methods of preventing abduction

Port alerts

If there are real grounds for believing that there is an immediate risk of a child being taken out of the UK, the police can be notified, which can lead to an all ports warning. This puts Border Agency staff and police officers at ports and airports on alert to prevent the removal of the child. Once instigated, the alert lasts for 28 days.

As well as police powers to arrest, a designated immigration officer can detain anyone he suspects of committing an offence for up to three hours, and must arrange for a constable to attend as soon as practicable—**s 2 of the Borders Act 2007**.

Between 2008 and 2014, the UK is reintroducing embarkation controls for those travelling into and out of the UK. These controls are administered by the UK Border Agency (UKBA) under the e-Borders process, which requires travellers to provide Advance Passenger Information (basically, passport details and travel plans) either directly or indirectly to UKBA, which can be checked by immigration officers and police.

The Official Solicitor (who administers ICACU in England and Wales) has indicated the type of information that will assist the police to make an all ports warning more effective:

- on the child—full name, date and place of birth, passport number, date and place of issue, photographs or a physical description, any entitlement to a passport other than a British passport;

- on the person who has taken the child—full name (including any prior or maiden name and any aliases if applicable), date and place of birth, passport number, date and place of issue, photograph or a physical description, occupation, probable date of departure, departure information (ie flight, train, ferry), details of ties to a foreign country, such as the names, addresses, and telephone numbers of relatives, friends, and business contacts;

- copies of documents—any agreements or court orders which relate to the child, child's birth certificate, marriage certificate.

Reunite (a UK-based charity specialising in international parent–child abductions) suggests that a range of information should be collated in advance in any case where there is a possibility of abduction, and adds other items to the list, such as the child's fingerprints, and provides a checklist of relevant items.

Court orders

If it is anticipated that a child may be taken abroad without consent, various proceedings can be taken to prevent it:

- a prohibited steps order under **s 8 of the Children Act 1989** can forbid taking a child out of the UK;

- a residence order made in favour of the other parent;

- wardship proceedings under the High Court's inherent jurisdiction. As soon as proceedings are commenced to make a child a ward of court, it is a contempt of court to remove the child from the court's jurisdiction;

- mirror orders—an order dealing with residence and/or contact with a child may be applied for in the same terms as an order in this country, but in the country to which it is anticipated the child may be abducted. In the event of abduction actually taking place, action can be taken to enforce the foreign 'mirror' order in that country;

- order for bond against the child's return.

Recovery following abduction

The European Convention

Thirty-five of the 47 members of the Council of Europe have joined the **European Convention on Recognition and Enforcement of Decisions concerning Custody of Children** signed in Luxembourg on 20 May 1980 (sometimes referred to as the Luxembourg Convention).

From March 2005, this Convention has been largely superseded by Brussels II, and its operation is largely confined to countries outside the European Union or in relation to orders made before 2005.

The Convention provides for mutual recognition and enforcement of orders made in contracting states (that is, states which are parties to the Convention). There must be an order in force, duly made in a Convention country which can be recognised and enforced in the receiving state.

Even before Brussels II, the European Convention was not often used in abduction cases where a child's return was sought because it is limited to cases where an order already exists. It is more usually applied to enforce access or contact orders.

Revision tip

Be aware that the Council of Europe has no direct connection with the European Union. It is an organisation covering 47 European nations which 'seeks to develop common and democratic principles based on the European Convention on Human Rights and other reference texts on the protection of individuals'. Unlike the European Union, it has no elements of political or economic union.

Also, be careful not to confuse the European Convention of 1980 with the European Convention on Human Rights.

The Hague Convention 1980

The **Hague Convention on the Civil Aspects of International Child Abduction** (HC 1980) was concluded on 25 October 1980. **Article 1** contains the objects of the Convention:

- to secure the prompt return of children wrongfully removed to or retained in any contracting state; and

- to ensure that rights of custody and of access under the law of one contracting state are effectively respected in the other contracting states.

HC 1980 can be used where:

- a child under the age of 16,

- was habitually resident in a contracting state immediately before his removal from it, and
- has been removed to or retained in another contracting state,
- in breach of rights of custody or in breach of access rights relating to the child.

Certain phrases used in and in connection with the Convention may need to be clarified:

- *child under 16 years of age*—the Convention ceases to apply as soon as the child in question becomes 16 years of age (even if proceedings have started). Anyone seeking the return of the child would then have to bring proceedings under **HC 1996** (discussed further later in the chapter) or, if **HC 1996** did not apply, proceed as if the child was in a non-Convention country.
- *habitual residence*—this differs from domicile. It denotes residence in a state with a fixed intention to remain there. Habitual residence can be lost fairly immediately simply by moving elsewhere with an intention of changing permanent residence. However, it is much less easily acquired.

A child will normally have the same habitual residence as the parents; where parents are separated, the habitual residence of the child will be that of the usual carer-parent.

✅ Looking for extra marks?

The meaning of habitual residence in relation to child abduction cases was considered in the case of **Mercredi v Chaffe** (2011), where it was considered to be the place which reflects some degree of integration by the child in a social and family environment.

- *contracting state*—any one of the 89 states (as at December 2012) which have ratified the Convention.
- *removed to or retained in*—the Convention can apply to a child who has been taken from one state to another without the appropriate consent, or a child who was so taken with appropriate consent but who is later kept for longer or in a way not covered by the consent.
- *rights of custody*—these are the custody rights of the person or body who cares for the child which have been determined by the laws in their home country.
- *access rights*—has approximately the same meaning as contact.
- *central authority*—the Convention requires each state to establish a central authority to deal with applications to return abducted children. It has a duty to:
  - receive applications from persons resident in the state and transmit them to the relevant central authority in another contracting state; and
  - accept applications from central authorities in other contracting states and appoint solicitors to represent the claimant and commence court proceedings under the Convention.
- The Lord Chancellor is designated as the Central Authority for England and Wales under both Conventions, but his functions are discharged by the ICACU.

Opposing Hague Convention applications

If the child has been wrongfully removed or retained and an application for their return is made within 12 months of the abduction, the court will order their return unless one of the following defences is successfully raised.

- It may be shown that the court does not have jurisdiction to hear the application, because the child is not habitually resident in a Convention country or that the person seeking return of the child has no rights of custody in respect of the child.
- **Articles 12 and 13 of the Convention** itself provide defences on which a court may refuse to order return of a child to the state from which they were abducted.

Even if a defence under **Article 12 or 13** is successfully raised, the court retains a discretion to order the return of the child if that is in the child's best interests.

Article 12 defence
The child is settled in their new environment

Under **Article 12**, the court must return the child unless it is demonstrated that the child has settled in their new environment. It is for the abducting parent to prove that the child is settled. Even if the child is settled, the court still has a discretion to return the child—*Re M (Abduction: Zimbabwe)* **(2007)** (see 'Key Cases', p 173).

Being settled involves a physical and an emotional element, for example being established in a community and feeling secure and stable—*Re N (Minors) (Abduction)* **(1991)**.

In *Re L (Abduction: Pending Criminal Proceedings)* **(1999)**, the mother was living in hiding with the children in England to prevent the father finding them and the family had no previous connection with the country. The children were not settled in their new environment.

In determining whether the child is settled, each case will be considered on its own facts—*Cannon v Cannon* **(2004)**.

Article 13 defences
Custody right, consent, or acquiescence

The person, institution, or other body having the care of the person of the child was not actually exercising the custody rights at the time of removal or retention, or had consented to or subsequently acquiesced in the removal or retention—**Article 13a**.

Custody rights

The abduction must be in breach of custody rights in the state where the child is normally habitually resident. In this country those who have parental responsibility for the child would have rights of custody.

Consent

The meaning of consent was considered in the following case:

....

P-J (Children) [2009] EWCA Civ 588

The family lived in Spain. When the marriage broke down the mother took the children to live in Wales. There was a dispute over whether the father had consented to their removal. When determining this, the following factors are relevant:

- Consent must be clear and unequivocal.
- Consent can relate to future removal provided it is still in force at the time of removal and has not been withdrawn.
- Consent must be viewed in the context of family life.
- The burden of proof is on the person who asserts consent.
- Each case will depend upon its facts.

....

The meaning of consent was also considered more recently in the case of *A v T (Abduction: Consent)* (2012) which also considered the defence of acquiescence.

Acquiescence

This is when the wronged parent appears not to object to the abduction. Delay in taking proceedings is often cited as evidence of acquiescence, as in:

....

Re S (Minors) (Acquiescence) [1994] 1 FLR 819 CA

The mother brought her three sons to England from Australia when her relationship with the father ended. Although he consulted lawyers straight away, incorrect legal advice resulted in a delay of eight months in the start of proceedings for their return. It was held that under the circumstances this did not amount to acquiescence.

....

The key case on the meaning of acquiescence is *Re H (Abduction: Acquiescence)* (1998). See 'Key Cases', p 173.

Grave risk of physical or psychological harm

There is a grave risk that his or her return would expose the child to physical or psychological harm or otherwise place the child in an intolerable situation—**Article 13b**. The risk of harm must be substantial and not trivial.

Figure 9.1 Examples where **Article 13b** has been used

Case	Risk of harm alleged	Outcome
Re S (Abduction: Custody Rights) [2002] EWCA Civ 908	Return to Israel would cause harm due to terrorist attacks.	Rejected. Risk of terrorism was not great enough to justify refusal to return.
Re F (Child Abduction: Risk of Return) [1995] 2 FLR 31	The child witnessed violence by his father against his mother and grandmother. He had also been abused and was in substantial fear of his father.	Accepted. Return refused.
Re H (Children) (Abduction) [2003] EWCA Civ 355	Father's violence towards the children if returned to Belgium.	Rejected. They would not be living with the father. The authorities in Belgium could take any necessary action in relation to the violence.
Re E (Children) [2011] UKSC 27	Father's psychological abuse would cause mother's psychiatric condition to worsen thus affecting children.	Rejected. Measures could be put in place to protect mother.

✅ Looking for extra marks?

Recent case law has considered the nature of the court's enquiry into the **Article 13b** defence. In **Neulinger and Shuruk v Switzerland (2011)** the European Court of Human Rights suggested that the parties' **Article 8** rights required an in-depth examination of the issues. However, in *Re E* **(2011)** (see 'Key Cases', p 173), the Supreme Court held that a full-blown examination of the child's future was not required. In *X v Latvia* **(2012)**, the European Court of Human Rights again suggested that an in-depth examination of the issues was required but the later Supreme Court case of *Re S* **(2012)** (see 'Key Cases', p 173) reinforced the approach taken in *Re E*.

Objection by the child

Under **Article 13**, the return of the child may also be refused if the child objects to being returned and has attained an age and degree of maturity at which it is appropriate to take account of its views. This defence was considered in the case of *Re D (Abduction: Child's Objections)* (2011) (see 'Key Cases', p 173).

The Hague Convention 1996

The Hague Convention on Jurisdiction, Applicable Law, Recognition, Enforcement and Co-operation in Respect of Parental Responsibility and Measures for the Protection of

Children (HC 1996) came into force in the UK on 1 November 2012. As its full title suggests, **HC 1996** does not only deal with child abduction.

HC 1996 can be used where a child is under the age of 18. This contrasts with the position under **HC 1980** where the child must be under 16 years of age. The definitions of removal and retention are the same under both instruments.

Relationship between HC 1980 and HC 1996

It is important to distinguish between two different situations:

1. Cases in which both **HC 1980** and **HC 1996** apply. In these cases, **HC 1996** may be used to complement **HC 1980**; and

2. Cases in which **HC 1980** does not apply but **HC 1996** does apply. In these cases, **HC 1996** may provide a remedy in its own right.

Cases in which HC 1980 and HC 1996 both apply

HC 1996 may complement **HC 1980** in a number of ways. For example, in some cases under **HC 1980** the court may only wish to order the return of the child if interim protective measures are put in place to ensure the child continues to be protected in the state to which the child is returned. **HC 1996** increases the strength of these protective measures by providing that any interim measures must be recognised and enforceable by the state to which the child is returned. **HC 1996** may also allow the courts to deal with questions of interim access where proceedings are pending under **HC 1980** for the return of the child.

As with the Brussels II Regulation (discussed further later in the chapter), if a decision is made not to return the child then the left-behind parent can take proceedings in their own country (they effectively get a second attempt). If they then obtain an order requiring the return of the child that order must be enforced in the country in which the child is located despite the earlier non-return order.

Cases in which only HC 1996 applies

Where **HC 1980** is not in force between two **HC 1996** contracting states, **HC 1996** may assist in child abduction cases. This would apply, for example, where a child was abducted from England and taken to Morocco. Another use of **HC 1996** would be in a case where the two countries are both members of **HC 1980** but the child is over 16.

If there is an existing order in force in the home state and the abduction breaches that order then the left-behind parent could enforce that order under **HC 1996** in the state that the child has been taken to.

Whilst the home state retains jurisdiction, the left-behind parent could also bring an application for an order that the child should be returned. However, **HC 1996** does not emphasise the swift return of the child in the same way as **Article 12 HC 1980**.

✱✱✱✱✱✱✱✱✱✱

✅ *Looking for extra marks?*

For a more detailed consideration of the interplay between **HC 1980** and **HC 1996**, you may find it helpful to consider the Handbook on the operation of **HC 1996** (www.hcch.net/upload/wop/abduct-2011pd04e.pdf) and 'The 1996 Hague Convention: The Fourth Dimension' by Eleri Jones, Anne-Marie Hutchinson and Richard Kwan (http://www.familylawweek.co.uk/site.aspx?i=ed105739).

Brussels II Regulation

For applications between countries within the European Union (except Denmark), the working of the **HC 1980** is modified by **European Council Regulation 2201/2003**, often referred to as the 'Brussels II Regulation' or 'Brussels II Revised' (as they replaced Regulations made in 2000), or sometimes even 'B II R'.

Where the Regulations apply, the **HC 1980** is modified as follows:

- applications must be concluded within six weeks unless this is impossible;

- the court should hear the views of the child if appropriate to their age and maturity;

- the left-behind parent must be given an opportunity to be heard before making any decision not to return a child;

- if **Article 13(b) of the HC 1980** is invoked, the court cannot refuse to return the child if adequate arrangements have been made to protect the child when they are returned;

- if a decision is made not to return the child under the Convention, the left-behind parent can take proceedings for a residence/custody order in their own country. If they obtain an order that requires the return of the child, that order must then be enforced in the country in which the child is located despite the earlier non-return order.

✅ *Looking for extra marks?*

To find out more about the relationship between the **HC 1980** and the **Brussels II Regulation** see Andrea Schulz, 'Guidance from Luxembourg: First ECJ Judgment Clarifying the Relationship between the 1980 Hague Convention and Brussels II Revised' (2008) *International Family Law* 221.

Extradition

If proceedings are started to prosecute the abducting parent under **s 1(1) of the Child Abduction Act 1984**, this could form the basis of a request for extradition of that parent to the UK, provided a comparable offence exists in the country to which the child has been abducted *and* there is an extradition treaty between the UK and the country in question.

If extradition succeeds, it *may* secure the return of the child with the parent. However, it risks compounding the trauma for the child if the abducting parent is extradited but the child remains abroad in the care of that parent's relatives or friends, who may have been unknown to the child prior to the abduction.

Non-Convention countries

If a child is abducted to a country which is not party to either of the Conventions, nor in the European Union, a parent seeking return of the child will not be able to rely on any governmental agency to assist in any court proceedings, though the British Embassy in the country in question can offer advice on the local approach to such proceedings and lawyers who are experienced in the field.

Note that, although Pakistan and Egypt are both non-Convention countries, proceedings to deal with applications to return abducted children are covered by Protocols between the UK and each of those countries. The Protocols each include a presumption in favour of return of the child.

In a non-Convention country, taking proceedings for the return of the child, and funding the cost of those proceedings, falls on the parent seeking return.

Leave to remove from the jurisdiction

If one parent wants to move abroad with the child, and the consent of the other parent is refused, they may apply to court for permission to remove the child from the jurisdiction.

Three cases are important in relation to these applications, *Payne v Payne* **(2001)**, *Re Y* **(2004)**, and *MK v CK* **(2011)**:

....

Payne v Payne [2001] EWCA Civ 166

The British father and New Zealand mother met and married in England and subsequently had a daughter. When the marriage broke down, the mother, who was extremely unhappy living in England, applied to take the child to live in New Zealand permanently. She was successful in her application and the father's application for a residence order was rejected. The father's appeal failed. The court held that it would look at the effect of the removal on all parties, but the reasonable proposal of the parent with residence to take the child abroad would carry great weight. Opportunities for future contact are important. However the paramount consideration is the welfare of the child.

....

Payne v Payne has been much criticised over the years. In *Re D (Children)* **(2010)**, Sir Nicolas Wall commented that the case placed 'too great an emphasis on the wishes and feelings of the relocating parent, and ignores or relegates the harm done to children by a permanent breach of the relationship which children have with the left behind parent'.

In *Re Y (2004)*, the parents shared the care of the child and the result was different:

Re Y [2004] 2 FLR 330

The parents lived in Wales. When the relationship broke down, the mother sought leave to return to the USA with the child. Leave was refused. The case differed from *Payne v Payne* in that the parents had a shared residence order. In such cases the welfare checklist under the **Children Act 1989** should be considered.

The next case concerns shared care where the Court of Appeal held that *Re Y* should be followed rather than *Payne* in such cases:

MK v CK [2011] EWCA Civ 793

The Canadian mother and Polish father lived in England with their two daughters. Upon their divorce, the mother applied for leave to take the children back to Canada. At first instance, the judge, following *Payne v Payne*, granted leave. The father's appeal was allowed on the grounds that the judge should have considered the recommendations from the CAFCASS officer and the arguments put forward by the father as well as the mother. Also, *Re Y* should have been followed rather than *Payne* as this was a shared care case.

✅ Looking for extra marks?

In *MK v CK*, Moore-Bick LJ held that *Payne* established the principle that the welfare of the child was paramount and the rest of the judgment amounted to guidance only. Consider what impact the ruling in *MK v CK* may have on future decisions in relation to removal from the jurisdiction.

International parent–child abduction is a problem which is on the increase. In a problem question you may be asked to advise how abduction can be prevented or to advise one parent when their child has been abducted by the other. You need to be familiar with the remedies and the defences available.

Essay questions will often ask you to consider whether the courts have been too ready to give permission to the resident parent (usually the mother) to remove a child from the jurisdiction when the relationship with the other parent breaks down. You may also be asked whether the **Hague Conventions** are at odds with human rights laws.

(✱) **Key cases**

Case	Facts	Principle
Re E (Children) [2011] UKSC 27	A British mother brought her daughters (aged 4 and 7) from Norway to England against the wishes of her Norwegian husband. When he applied under the **Hague Convention 1980** for the children's return, the wife asserted that **Article 8** of the European Human Rights Convention and **Article 3.1** of the **United Nations Convention on the Rights of the Child** required the English court to examine fully whether it was in the best interests of the children to order their return to Norway.	The **Hague Convention 1980** had been designed with the best interests of children generally, and the individual child concerned, as a primary consideration. It was thus compatible with the **ECHR** and the UN Convention. The national court did not order return of the child automatically and mechanically, but examined the particular circumstances of the child to ascertain whether a return accorded with the Convention. That was not the same as a full-blown examination of the child's future.
Re S (Children) [2012] UKSC 10	A British mother brought her two-year-old son from Australia to England without the consent of the Australian father. The mother relied on the **Article 13b** defence against the father's application to return the child. The father had serious drug and alcohol problems and the mother alleged that he was violent. The mother was suffering from Battered Women's Syndrome (a form of post-traumatic stress disorder) and the evidence suggested that a return to Australia would trigger clinical depression in the mother, which would impact on the child.	In *Re E* (see earlier) the Supreme Court had held that the terms of **Article 13b** were plain, did not need elaboration or gloss; and that they demonstrated the defence was not widely available. Where there were disputed allegations of domestic violence the court should ask whether, if they were true, there would be a grave risk that the child would placed in an intolerable situation. If there was a grave risk, then the court must ask how the child could be protected against the risk. If the child could not be protected, then the court should consider whether the disputed allegations were true. At first instance, the judge had concluded that the protective measures suggested by the father would not protect the mother (and thus the child).The allegations made by the mother could not reasonably be disputed. The defence was successful. (Note that *Re E* allows the defence to be used where the anxieties of a parent are not objectively reasonable if those anxieties are so serious that they would destabilise that parent so much that the child would be placed in an intolerable situation.)

Key cases

✳✳✳✳✳✳✳✳✳✳✳✳

Case	Facts	Principle
Re H (Abduction: Acquiescence) [1998] AC 72	The parents were Jewish, living in Israel. Without the father's consent, the wife took the children to live in England. The father initially took the case to a religious court but it was six months after the abduction before he invoked proceedings under the Hague Convention in London. Did this amount to acquiescence? The Court of Appeal held that it did. The House of Lords thought otherwise and overturned the decision. It was ordered that the children be returned.	The test for acquiescence is subjective, and depends on the state of mind of that particular wronged parent • All the facts of the case must be considered. • The burden of proof is on the abductor. • If the wronged parent, by their words or actions, clearly led the abducting parent to believe they would not take action to seek the child's return, this will amount to acquiescence.
Re M (Abduction: Zimbabwe) [2007] UKHL 55	The parents were from and lived in Zimbabwe. When they separated, the two children remained in Zimbabwe with the father. On a contact visit, the mother brought the children to the UK and claimed asylum. The father found out six months later but did nothing until a year had passed. The trial judge and Court of Appeal ordered the return of the children. However the House of Lords ruled that the children could remain in the UK.	Where a child is settled into their new environment, a judge still has discretion under the Hague Convention to return the child. But the child's rights and welfare must take priority.
Re D (Abduction: Child's Objections) [2011] EWCA Civ 1294	The two children, who were French, had been living with their father in France. The mother took them to England on holiday and wrongfully retained them. The father applied for their return under **HC 1980**. The CAFCASS officer in the case gave evidence that the older child held mature views and did not want to return to France as he had been racially bullied. However, the CAFCASS officer had had very little time with the children and was unaware that the boy had changed schools before the trip to England and that he was settled there. The judge did not order the return of the children.	The Court of Appeal held that there were two stages to the **Article 13** defence: first, the judge had to be satisfied that the child had a mature objection and second, the judge had to exercise his or her discretion as to whether or not to return the child. Here it was clear that the child was mature and objected to being returned. However, the judge's decision not to return the children was tainted by the misunderstanding of the facts.

⟨⟩⟩ Key debate

Topic:	Is the Hague Convention and its application at odds with the UN Convention on the Rights of the Child?
Academic:	Eran Sthoeger
Viewpoint:	The article discusses arguments for and against this premise but concludes that it is not.
Reading:	'International Child Abduction and Children's Rights: Two Means to the Same End' (2011) *Michigan Journal of International Law*, vol 32(3), 511–552.

⟨?⟩ Exam questions

Problem Question

Inge and Nigel married 12 years ago, and have two children, Niel aged 10 and Annelise aged 4. Eight months ago, without any warning to Nigel, Inge left their home in England with the children and returned with them to her parents' home in Denmark. Nigel contacted Inge for the first time last week to ask when she is going to return. She told him that she and the children are now settled in Canada and she has no intention of coming back. He now seeks your advice on how to have the children returned to England. Inge alleges that Nigel has been violent towards her over a considerable period of time, and that the children have witnessed several incidents. She asserts that Niel is so afraid of his father that he cries whenever he is mentioned.

Advise Nigel.

An outline answer is included at the end of the book.

Essay question

Does the case law in England and Wales indicate that the courts have found a proper balance between the interests of the child and the Hague Convention objective 'to secure the prompt return of children wrongfully removed to or retained in any contracting state'?

 Scan here
Scan this QR code image with your mobile device to see an outline answer to this question or log onto www.oxfordtextbooks.co.uk/orc/concentrate

Exam essentials

Plan your revision timetable

The key to exam success is to start early and to plan your revision well. This sounds obvious, but do not underestimate the value of this. Your exam timetable should guide how you plan your revision timetable. If your exams are very spread out you may find it easier to revise for one exam at a time and begin working for each exam in turn. If you have a large number of exams in a short space of time, then you may find it helpful to have a rolling revision timetable so that you spend a few days on each subject to begin with and, once you have been through everything once, start again.

Gear your revision to the exam

It is important to know what sort of questions you will have to answer. If your university runs revision lectures or seminars, then make sure you go along to them. You may get an indication of the style of answers expected of you, you may be told about new cases, or you may even get some hints about what will appear in the exam!

Get hold of as many past exam papers as you can and have a go at the questions. If you have the time to do some of these under exam conditions, then do so: this is the best way to find out what you don't know. Even if you can't do full answers to all questions then it is worth doing answer plans. This will force you to gear what you know to the questions and make you think about the different types of question you could be asked.

Subject areas

The best way to know what you will face in an exam is to look at past papers, as every course is different.

A good way to boost your marks is to consider the links between different subjects. This will improve your understanding of the subject and will also impress an examiner. Some examples of the links to consider are as follows:

1. Consider how the idea of no-fault divorce fits with the idea of conduct as a factor in determining a financial settlement. How does this impact on your ideas about whether the law of divorce should be reformed?

2. Consider the differences between the welfare checklist in the **Children Act 1989** and the **Adoption and Children Act 2002**. Do you think the differences are significant? Is there a reason for the differences or should the two checklists be combined?

3. Consider the differences between married couples or civil partners and people who are cohabiting. This will involve considering the matters in Chapter 1, domestic violence provisions, and children matters.

4. Consider whether the law should favour certainty or discretion. In financial provision on divorce the law is highly discretionary whereas child support through the CSA is based upon a rigid calculation. Consider the approach of the courts in other areas, for example, in making decisions under the **Children Act** or the **Adoption and Children Act** and the approach taken by the courts.

Mistakes to avoid

1. **Don't be too strategic!**
   If you know that you will have to answer four questions, then don't just learn enough material to answer four questions. All it takes is one topic to be left off the paper that year or a really horrible question in one of your four areas and you will struggle to complete the paper. We have seen students who answer three questions very well and don't attempt a fourth one. It is very difficult to get high marks if you only answer three questions, however well you have answered those three.

2. **Read through the whole paper before you begin**
   You may find that you are able to answer more questions than you need to. Taking the time to consider the questions will help you to make the right choice about which ones to answer. There is nothing worse than beginning to answer one question and realising you could have produced a far better answer to an alternative question.

3. **Make sure you answer the question**
   This sounds obvious, but gearing your knowledge to the question asked is crucial. Students who learn and reproduce a standard answer that doesn't quite fit the question will not do as well as those who produce a targeted answer.

4. **Spend the same amount of time on every answer**
   It is very easy to get caught up in an answer that you feel confident about and lose track of time. One thing that may help is to work out timings at the beginning of the exam and write down the times at which you should be starting the next question.

5. **Make sure your handwriting is legible**
   It is very difficult for the examiner to give you marks if they cannot read your writing!

Outline answers

Chapter 1

Problem answer

- Robert and Jane are unmarried. There is no such thing as 'common law marriage' so Jane has limited claims against Robert.

- Divorcing spouses could make claims under s 25 **Matrimonial Causes Act** for periodical payments lump sums, property adjustment orders, pension sharing orders, and pension attachment orders.

- Jane has given up work to care for Ben so she has no income. She cannot claim maintenance for herself from Robert. If they were married, Jane could claim for periodical payments under s 25 MCA. Contrast the idea of compensation in *Miller v Miller; McFarlane v McFarlane*. If married, would there be an argument that Jane should be compensated for her lost career? Compensation is only relevant where the assets exceed the needs.

- Jane may have a claim in respect of Ben. As Robert is Ben's father he will be liable under the **Child Support Act**. In addition, Jane may be able to bring a claim under **Schedule 1 of the Children Act**.

- Jane is not working so she may have limited pension provision. Contrast her position with that of a divorcing spouse.

- Consider whether Jane has any claim against the house. She is not the legal owner so needs to claim beneficial ownership. There is no evidence of an express trust and Jane has not contributed to the purchase price or the mortgage so she cannot claim under a resulting trust.

- Can Jane show an interest under a constructive trust or proprietary estoppel? A constructive trust requires a common intention that she should have a beneficial interest and that Jane has acted to her detriment on the basis of that common intention. For proprietary estoppel Jane must show that Robert promised her an interest in the property, she relied on that promise to her detriment, and it would be unconscionable to deny her relief. Do you think that Jane has established these elements?

- Discuss the issues of quantifying an interest. Under a constructive trust *Stack v Dowden* (2007) provides guidance. In proprietary estoppel cases the award is the minimum required to do justice as between the parties (*Crabb v Arun District Council* (1976)).

Chapter 2

Problem answer

- Sarah and Guy cannot petition for divorce as they have not been married one year.

- Sarah could petition because the marriage has not been consummated. Failure must be due to incapacity (s 12(a) MCA) or wilful refusal (s 12(b) MCA). On the facts this looks like wilful refusal. Outline the test in *Horton v Horton* (1947): 'a settled and definite decision come to without just excuse'.

- Discuss the meaning of 'settled and definite intention' and 'just excuse' (*Potter v Potter* (1975) and *Kaur v Singh* (1972).

- Did Sarah validly consent in accordance with s 12(c) MCA? If not, this would make the marriage voidable. Discuss the test of duress in *Szechter v Szechter* (1971) and whether Sarah satisfies it. In *Hirani v Hirani* (1983) the test was relaxed to 'whether the threat or pressure is such as to overbear the will of the individual petitioner so as to destroy the reality of consent'. This is a subjective test—does Sarah satisfy it? If so, she must petition within three years.

- Guy could petition because Sarah was pregnant by someone else at the time of the marriage (s 12(f) MCA). Guy did not know this at the time of the marriage (s 13(3) MCA). Guy must petition within three years.

- Although Guy thought he would be elected if he got married, this does not make his consent invalid under s 12(c). The only mistakes that make a marriage voidable are as to the nature of the ceremony or the identity of the person.

- The s 13(1) bars do not apply.

- Sarah and Guy's marriage is voidable, not void, so they need to apply for a decree. Mention

Outline answers

✱✱✱✱✱✱✱✱✱✱✱

the consequences of annulment: the marriage is treated as if it had never occurred and the parties can apply for financial provision.

Chapter 3

Problem answer

• There is one ground for dissolution: that the civil partnership has broken down irretrievably (s 44(1) Civil Partnership Act 2004). Tom must show that his civil partnership has broken down irretrievably.

• Before he can apply for a dissolution order, he must wait for one year from the date of the formation of the civil partnership (s 41(1)).

• Irretrievable breakdown is evidenced by one of four facts which are set out in s 44(5).

• Adultery is not a fact that can be used to prove a civil partnership has broken down irretrievably.

• On the facts it does not appear that Tom can rely on either two years' or five years' separation and there is no evidence that Fred has deserted Tom. This means Tom must prove irretrievable breakdown on the basis of Fred's behaviour. Remember that Tom cannot rely on his own behaviour.

• Behaviour has objective and subjective elements (*Livingstone-Stallard v Livingstone-Stallard* (1974)). Behaviour includes a wide range of conduct, for example an association short of adultery (*Wachtel v Wachtel (No 1)*(1973)).

• Do you think Fred's affair probably counts as behaviour? The facts state that Tom was 'devastated'. Does this satisfy the test in *Livingstone-Stallard*?

• Might Tom be unable to rely on Fred's behaviour because of his own affair in light of *Ash v Ash* (1972)?

• Consider whether to ask Tom for any other examples of behaviour he might be able to rely on.

• If you think that Tom is able to petition on the basis of Fred's behaviour you should advise him that if he and Fred live (or have lived) together for a period or periods totalling six months or more the court will consider whether Tom has

proven that that it is not reasonable to expect him to live with Fred.

Chapter 4

Problem answer

• The government definition of domestic violence includes psychological, emotional, or sexual abuse.

• Susan wants to leave Adam but has nowhere to live if she does.

• Criminal remedies are inappropriate. There has not been physical violence so no offence under the **Offences Against the Person Act** and the **Protection from Harassment Act** is not really appropriate on the facts.

• The most useful civil remedy for Susan would be an occupation order. These orders regulate occupation of property and it might be possible for Susan and Amy to occupy the flat and to exclude Adam.

• It does not appear that Susan has any interest in the flat. She is not the legal owner, she did not contribute to the purchase price or the mortgage, and there does not seem to be any evidence of a constructive trust or proprietary estoppel. This means Susan must apply under **s 36 Family Law Act 1996** as she is a cohabitant and Adam is entitled to occupy the property.

• The property is a dwelling house and it was Susan and Adam's home. Consider each of the factors in **s 36(6)** and how they apply to the facts. For example, Susan does not work but Adam does, so her financial resources are less. Susan and Adam have been together for five years, they live together (although it is unclear for how long they have cohabited), and have a child together.

• An order can be granted under **s 36** for six months and can be extended once by up to six months.

• If Susan does actually have an interest in the property then she would be able to apply under **s 33 FLA**.

• Briefly consider non-molestation orders. Susan is scared of Adam so this may be appropriate but her primary concern is that she has nowhere to live.

Chapter 5

Problem answer

- Consider which orders might be appropriate. Rufus earns more, so perhaps periodical payments to Geraldine for her benefit? Remember, Rufus wants a clean break, so even if this might be appropriate, you should try and offer him alternatives too.

- We do not know about assets other than the properties but there is lots of capital and income, so lump sum payments by either party might be possible. Whether either should make a lump sum payment is likely to depend on the property situation.

- Both parties have a property. As the boys live with Geraldine it's unlikely the Manor House would be transferred to Rufus or the flat to Geraldine.

- We don't have any details of the parties' pensions so can't really consider pension orders. Perhaps Geraldine will have a better pension as her job is more stable?

- First consideration is the welfare of any child under 18. Sebastian is 16, so this is relevant.

- Consider income, earning capacity, property, and other financial resources. Rufus seems to have a greater income and earning capacity but is this as stable as Geraldine's? Geraldine's property is much more valuable.

- Geraldine's financial needs, obligations, and responsibilities are greater as the boys live with her.

- The parties had a high standard of living.

- The five years pre-marital cohabitation is likely to be taken into account (*CO v CO* (2004)).

- Geraldine has arguments about inherited property. Might these be weakened because she and Rufus have lived in it (*K v L* (2010) and *Miller v Miller; McFarlane v McFarlane* (2006))?

- Geraldine's affair is not conduct (*Miller; McFarlane*).

- The assets are likely to meet the parties' needs. There are no obvious arguments for compensation, but sharing is appropriate (*Miller; McFarlane*).

- Third party assets won't be taken into account directly but a court may conclude the partner's contribution to household expenses would reduce the needs of the spouse. Rufus is likely to live with Emmeline. Geraldine has no plans to live with Max but the pregnancy may change things.

- The court has a duty to consider a clean break. It may be appropriate as the parties are reasonably financially independent and there is a lot of capital. Remember, that you are advising Rufus, who wants a clean break, so think about whether and how this could be achieved.

- Under the CSA regime Rufus will have to pay child maintenance for Henry and Sebastian. Max would be liable for any new child.

- The Law Commission is reviewing the law in this area to consider how 'needs' should be defined and how far one party should be required to meet the financial needs of the other on dissolution or divorce. It is also considering whether the law should treat inherited property differently from other property.

Chapter 6

Problem answer

- Tom and Dianne were married—both have parental responsibility.

- Tom could apply for a residence order (**s 8(1) Children Act 1989**). Dianne does not need to as the children live with her. (Consider whether shared residence might be appropriate.)

- Biff and Angel could also apply for a residence order with leave of the court. The test is 'sufficient understanding' (**s 10(8)**).

- The court will consider the welfare principle (**s 1(1)**), the no delay principle, (**s 1(2)**), and the no order principle (**s 1(5)**).

- The court will also consider the welfare checklist:

(a) The ascertainable wishes and feelings of the child concerned (considered in the light of his age and understanding)

The children are 9, 11, and 13. The court will consider whether they are *Gillick* competent. Angel and Biff want to live with their father because his life is more exciting—might the court question their understanding?

Outline answers

✱✱✱✱✱✱✱✱✱✱

(b) His physical, emotional, and educational needs

Both parents could meet physical needs.

Dianne might be better able to meet emotional needs: Tom works on location, so Tiffany might end up looking after the children, which she finds difficult. Generally brothers and sisters should not be separated—*N (Children)* (2006).

Dianne might better meet emotional needs as Tom moves around a lot.

(c) The likely effect on him of any change of circumstances

The courts will maintain the status quo where possible (living with Dianne).

(d) His age, sex, background, and any characteristics of his which the court considers relevant

Cherub is a teenager and may be better off with her mother?

(e) Any harm which he has suffered or is at risk of suffering

(f) How capable each of his parents, and any other person in relation to whom the court considers the question to be relevant, is of meeting his needs

Tiffany finds the children difficult. Dianne living with Daisy is irrelevant. It is unlawful to discriminate on grounds of sexual orientation in relation to contact or residence—*Da Silva v Portugal* (2001).

(g) The range of powers available to the court under this Act in the proceedings in question.

Conclude with what you think the court might do.

Chapter 7

Problem answer

- Explain the context. For example, the duties on the local authority. It can be difficult for local authorities who may be criticised for failing to intervene or for intervening wrongly.

- Emergency protection orders (EPO) are short-term orders used in genuine emergencies so probably not justified.

- A child assessment order is appropriate (**s 43 Children Act 1989**) where the local authority suspects that the child may be at risk of significant harm, but there is no immediate risk, so the grounds for an EPO would not be made out.

- Run through the conditions for a child assessment order. It would not be needed if Maud would consent to an examination of the children.

- If an order is needed the court must consider the welfare principle, the no order principle, and the no delay principle.

- Outline the effect of a child assessment order and its duration.

- Unless the court directs otherwise, a child of sufficient age and understanding may refuse to undergo an assessment. Alison is 14, so may be considered of sufficient age and understanding. It is unlikely that Brian would be.

- Outline the effects of a care order and a supervision order.

- Care or supervision orders can only be made if the threshold criteria are satisfied: that the child is suffering significant harm and the harm is attributable to the care not being what a reasonable parent would give or the child is beyond parental control (**s 31(2)**).

- There must be proof on the balance of probabilities that the child is suffering or there must be a real possibility that the child will suffer significant harm (**Re H (Minors) (Sexual Abuse: Standard of Proof)** (1996). Is this satisfied?

- Discuss the definitions of 'significant' (**Re L (Care: Threshold Criteria)** (2007)) and 'harm' (**s 31(9)**). Are these satisfied?

- If Brian is suffering significant harm and Derek caused this, the harm is attributable to one of the carers (either Derek for causing it or Maud for allowing it to happen).

- If Alison's teacher is correct then she may be considered beyond parental control.

- The court will consider the welfare principle (**s 1(1)**), the no delay principle (**s 1(2)**), the welfare checklist (**s 1(3)**), and the no order principle (**s 1(5)**).

- Is a care order or a supervision order more appropriate? Consider **Re D (Care or Supervision Order)** (2000) and the human rights angle: a court must consider whether a less intrusive order could be made.

Chapter 8

Problem answer

• Cindy is under 18 and Dave and Jane are married so, assuming they live in the UK and are both over 21, adoption is an option if the criteria are met and it is considered that the placement has been successful.

• As Candice doesn't consent to Cindy's adoption her consent must be dispensed with.

• Unless Jim has parental responsibility for Cindy he will not be required to give his consent. It is unlikely the court would make him a party to the proceedings as he has had no relationship with Cindy.

• Candice's consent may be dispensed with if the welfare of the child requires it (**s 52**). Is Cindy's welfare in question?

• Cindy's welfare throughout her life will be the paramount consideration.

• The court will take into account the checklist in **s 1(4) of the Adoption and Children Act 2002**.

• Run through each of the factors in turn and consider how they apply to the facts. The court will also consider Cindy's relationship with her birth parents and whether any other relatives could look after her.

• Open adoption may be a possibility.

• Other orders would have to be considered, for example a residence order or special guardianship order.

• In view of the relationship that Cindy has with her grandmother, special guardianship would be a strong possibility.

Chapter 9

Problem answer

• The **Hague Convention 1980** is relevant as both the UK and Canada are signatories.

• The children are both aged under 16 and were habitually resident in the UK.

• Consider whether they have been wrongfully removed or retained.

• Nigel needs to apply through the central authority—the ICACU.

• As less than a year has elapsed, the courts must order their return unless the court does not have jurisdiction to hear the case or **Article 12 or 13** applies.

• Under **Article 12** the children's return will not be ordered if Inge can show they are 'settled in their new environment'—**Article 12**.

• Under **Article 13a** the court may refuse return of the child if whoever has care of the child was not actually exercising the custody rights at the time of removal or retention, or had consented to or subsequently acquiesced in the removal or retention.

• It is relevant to consider whether Nigel has consented to their removal or has subsequently acquiesced. See *Re H (Abduction: Acquiescence)* **(1998)**.

• In relation to consent consider *P-J (Children)* **(2009)**.

• Has Nigel acquiesced because he has done nothing for eight months?

• Under **Article 13b** the children will not be returned if there is a grave risk that his or her return would expose the child to physical or psychological harm or otherwise place the child in an intolerable situation. Consider this and the cases of *Re E* **(2011)** and *Re S* **(2012)** in the context of Niel's alleged fear of his father.

• Under **Article 13**, the return of the child may also be refused if the child objects to being returned and has attained an age and degree of maturity at which it is appropriate to take account of its views. There is no evidence of this.

• Even if **Article 12 or 13** applies the court retains a discretion to consider what is in the best interests of the child. See *Re M (Abduction: Zimbabwe)* **(2007)**.

Glossary

Adultery: a voluntary act of sexual intercourse between one spouse and a third party of the opposite sex.

Annulled: a marriage or civil partnership that is ended under the nullity provisions.

Arranged marriage: a marriage in which the parties' families have a role in choosing their spouse but in which both spouses validly consent.

Beneficial ownership (property): equitable ownership of a property which may be established, for example, through an express trust, a resulting trust, a constructive trust, or proprietary estoppel.

CAFCASS: the Children and Family Court Advisory and Support Service. Looks after the welfare of the child and advises the court what is in the best interests of the child in private and public law cases.

Care order: a local authority gains parental responsibility for the child (in addition to the parents) and the child may be removed from home.

Child abduction: may be by way of taking a child abroad without consent (removal), or by keeping a child abroad beyond a period for which consent was given (retention).

Civil partnership: a relationship between two people of the same sex which is formed when they register as civil partners of each other in accordance with the **Civil Partnership Act 2004**.

Clean break: a 'once and for all' order that ends continuing financial obligations between the parties. It is not possible to have a clean break relating to obligations to children.

Cohabitation: there is no clear legal definition but in the context of family law it generally means two people who live together as if they were husband and wife or civil partners but who are not in a marriage or civil partnership.

Conditional dissolution order: the first decree in the dissolution process showing that the parties are entitled to dissolution of their civil partnership.

Constructive trust: established where there is common intention that a party should have a beneficial interest and the claimant has acted to his detriment on the basis of that common intention.

Consummation: vaginal intercourse between a man and a woman, which must take place after the marriage to prevent the marriage being voidable.

Decree *nisi*: the first decree in the divorce process showing that the parties are entitled to a divorce.

Desertion: established where the parties have not lived in the same household for two years, there is no good reason for them living apart, the respondent intends to stay permanently separated, and the parties do not consent to the separation.

Dissolution: the legal end of a valid civil partnership on the ground that it has broken down irretrievably.

Divorce: the legal end of a valid marriage on the ground that it has broken down irretrievably.

Domestic violence: psychological, physical, sexual, or emotional abuse between adults in various different types of relationship or between parents and children.

Domicile: the place where someone has their permanent home. A person can only have one domicile at a time.

Duress: a subjective test concerned with threat or pressure such as to overbear a person's will and destroy the reality of consent.

Emergency protection order: short-term orders made in emergencies that allow the applicant, usually the local authority, to remove a child to safe accommodation or to prevent the child being removed from safe accommodation.

Express trust: created where the parties make an express agreement about how they intend to share the property.

Financial order: a court order dealing with any of the financial remedies available to parties who are applying for divorce, dissolution, or judicial separation.

Forced marriage: takes place without the valid consent of both parties and involves duress.

Habitual residence: a place where someone lives on a fairly fixed basis. It may be possible to have more than one habitual residence and it can be lost by moving with the intention to change permanent residence.

Irretrievable breakdown: the only ground for divorce or dissolution which, in the case of divorce, can be proved by one of five facts: adultery, behaviour, two years' separation with consent, desertion, or five years' separation. Adultery cannot be used to prove a civil partnership has broken down irretrievably but the other four facts can be used.

Judicial separation: a decree that allows the court to make orders relating to finances and children but which does not bring the marriage or civil partnership to an end.

Legal ownership (property): in registered land, this is the person whose name is on the register. In unregistered land this is the person to whom the land is conveyed.

Lump sum order: one party must pay a specified sum of money to the other.

Martin order: a variation on a *Mesher* order allowing one party to occupy the house until death, remarriage, or voluntarily moving out.

Mediation: an alternative to the court process in which the parties try and reach an agreement between themselves.

Mesher order: allows one party to occupy the house until various events occur, such as that party's death or the parties' children finishing in education, bring the order to an end.

Molestation: includes violence, pestering, and harassment. There is some uncertainty about whether conduct must be deliberate.

No delay principle: any delay in proceedings is likely to prejudice the welfare of the child.

No order principle: a court should not make an order unless it considers that doing so would be better for the child than making no order at all.

Non-marriage: does not resemble a marriage and has no legal consequences.

Non-molestation order: an order preventing someone molesting a person they are associated with or a relevant child (see **s 62 FLA 1996** for definitions of 'associated person' or 'relevant child').

Nullity: a way of ending a marriage or civil partnership on the basis that it is not valid.

Nuptial agreement: any agreement between the parties about their finances entered into before or during their marriage.

Occupation order: an order declaring that a person has an interest in property or regulating who lives in that property.

Open adoption: an arrangement where the child retains contact with members of their birth family.

Parental responsibility: all the rights, duties, powers, responsibilities, and authority which by law a parent of a child has in relation to that child and his property.

Periodical payments: payments of a specified amount for a specified time.

Placement for adoption: before an application can be made for an adoption order the child must have lived with the applicants for a trial period.

Polygamous marriage: a marriage where one party has more than one husband or wife, which is not permitted under the law of England and Wales.

Pre-Nups: see 'Nuptial agreement'.

Prohibited degrees: people who cannot be married or enter into a civil partnership because they are too closely related, whether by blood or otherwise.

Proprietary estoppel: established where the claimant can show the defendant promised him an interest in the property, the claimant relied on that promise to his detriment, and it would be unconscionable to deny the claimant relief.

Glossary

Resulting trust: presumed where a party has made a direct contribution to the purchase price.

Secured periodical payments: periodical payments which are tied to property so there is something to enforce against if the payer defaults.

Sham marriage: a couple marry or enter into a civil partnership intending that union to be valid but they do not intend to live together as husband and wife or civil partners afterwards.

Significant harm test: a two-stage test considering whether the applicant or a relevant child will suffer significant harm if an order is not made and then balancing that harm against the harm the respondent or a relevant child will suffer if that order is made.

Special guardianship order: gives the special guardian enhanced parental responsibility for the child but it does not sever the ties with the child's birth family. Such orders are used where the child needs a stable home but where adoption may not be a suitable option.

Supervision order: the child remains at home and a supervisor is appointed who will advise, assist, and befriend.

Transplant adoption: the more traditional form of adoption where a child severs all links with their birth family.

Undertaking: a formal promise to the court that can be enforced in the same way as a court order.

Void marriage or civil partnership: the marriage/partnership was never a valid one so no decree of nullity is required unless the parties wish to seek financial provision.

Voidable marriage or civil partnership: the marriage/partnership remains a valid one until the parties obtain a decree to annul it.

Wardship: the process by which the High Court assumes responsibility for the child which means the court's consent is required for any significant decision relating to the child.

Welfare principle: the child's welfare is the court's paramount consideration.

Index

abduction of children
'appropriate consent' 165
Brussels II Regulation 168,
174
Child Abduction Act 1984
165–6
'connected with child' 165
court orders 167
defences 170–2
acquiescence 171
child settled in new
environment 170
consent 171
grave risk of physical
or psychological
harm 171–2
non-exercise of custody
rights 170
objection by child 172
enforcement of custody
rights 163
European Convention 168
exam questions 179
extradition 174–5
'habitual residence' 169
Hague Convention 168–70,
172–4
key cases 177–8
key debates 179
key facts 162
leave to remove from
jurisdiction 175–6
meaning 163
methods of preventing
166–8
mirror order 167–8
non-Convention
countries 175
offences 165–6
port alerts 166–7
prohibited steps order 167
reasons for 164–5
recovery following 168–9
removal 164
residence order 167
retention 164
wardship 138, 167

adoption
adoption order
application 152
duration 157
effect 153
setting aside 157
adoption panels 147
agencies 147, 151
alternatives 154–7
care proceedings and 135
child's name 156
choice of adopters 151
consent 152–3
contact orders and 156
dispensing with
consent 153
dual planning 148
exam questions 160–1
financial support 156
human rights 145
key cases 159–60
key debates 160
key facts 142
legal parents 105
legislation 144
local authority role 146–7
national adoption
register 151
nationality of child 156
no delay principle 147–8
no order principle 155
open 146
overview 143
parental responsibility 109,
110, 148, 155
persons who can adopt 145–
6
persons who can be
adopted 145
placement for 148–50
dispensing with
consent 149
parental consent 148, 149
parental
responsibility 148
placement order 135, 148–9
process 143

qualifying period 152
revised guidance 158
statistics 144, 158
step-parent adoption 146
tracing birth family 157–8
traditional adoption 146
transplant adoption 146
travel abroad 156
types 146
welfare checklist 149–50
adultery
civil partnership 39
continued cohabitation 39
marriage breakdown 39
arranged marriage 2
arrest
power of 62, 69, 167
warrant of 62

behaviour
continued cohabitation 40–1
marriage breakdown 40–1
bigamy 4, 24
Brussels II Regulation 168, 174

care order 131–2
exclusion requirements 130
parental responsibility 108,
109
summary 136
supervision order
compared 134–5
threshold criteria 132–4
care proceedings 131
adoption 135
human rights 125
child assessment order
131, 136
**Child and Family Court
Advisory and
Support Service
(CAFCASS)** 119, 124
**Child Support Agency
(CSA)** 94
children
abduction *see* **abduction of
children**

Index

****

children (*cont.*)
  adoption *see* **adoption**
  capability of parents 116,
    117, 150
  care order 131–2
    exclusion
      requirements 130
    parental
      responsibility 108, 109
    summary 136
    supervision order
      compared 134–5
    threshold criteria 132–4
  change in
    circumstances 116,
      117, 150
  changing name 114, 154,
    156
  characteristics of
    child 116, 117, 150
  child assessment order 131,
    136
  Children Act 1989 101–3,
    128–35
  Children Act 2004 124–5,
    126
  contact order 112–13, 118,
    156
  definition 103
  divorce 44–5
  dual planning 148
  emergency protection
    order 128–30, 137
  exam questions 122
  family assistance order 115
  financial maintenance *see*
    **financial provision, for
    children**
  Gillick competence 104, 118
  guardianship 109, 110–11,
    154–5
  harm suffered or at
    risk 116, 117, 127–8,
    131, 134, 150
  human rights 104, 125
  interim orders 136
  key cases 120–1
  key debates 121
  leave to remove from
    jurisdiction 175–6

legal parents 104–6
local authority duties 124
  accommodation 127
  children in need 126–7
  general duty 126
  investigation of
    welfare 119, 127–8
nationality 156
need, in 126–7
no delay principle 115, 131,
  133, 147–8
no order principle 116, 131,
  133, 155
Norgrove Review 125
parental responsibility *see*
  parental responsibility
parents 104–6
physical, emotional and
  educational needs 116,
  117, 150
placement order 135,
  148–9
  see also **adoption**
police protection 127, 128,
  137
recovery order 137
relationship with
  relatives 150
reports and
  investigations 119
rights of 103–4
s 8 orders
  applicants 118–19
  care/supervision order
    not made 133
  contact order 112–13,
    118, 156
  court's powers 118
  factors taken into
    account 115–18
  leave to apply 119
  no delay principle 115
  no order principle 116
  prohibited steps
    order 114, 167
  residence order *see*
    residence order
  specific issue order
    113–14
  welfare checklist 116–18

  welfare principle 115
special guardianship 109,
  110–11, 150, 154–5,
  156–7
supervision order 131–2
  care order
    compared 134–5
  summary 136
  threshold criteria 132–4
travel abroad 114, 154, 156
  see also **abduction of
    children**
wardship 137–8, 167
welfare *see* **welfare of child**
wishes and feelings 116,
  117, 150
Children Act 1989
  exam questions 140–1
  key cases 120–1, 138–40
  key debates 140
  key facts 101–2, 123
  orders 128–35
  overview 102
  private law 101–22
  public law 123–41
Children Act 2004 124–5,
  126
civil partnership
  cohabitation
    distinguished 9–14
  definition 5–6
  dissolution *see* **dissolution
    of civil partnership**
  family home 9
  finances *see* **financial
    provision, divorce/
    dissolution**
  formalities 6–7
  formation 6
  inheritance 14
  key cases 15–16
  key facts 1
  marriage compared 7
  nullity *see* **nullity**
  termination 6
    see also **dissolution
      of civil partnership;
      nullity**
  void 24–5
  voidable 31

Index

clean break 91, 92
  advantages and
    disadvantages 93
  appropriateness 93
cohabitation
  children 9
  common law marriage 7
  domestic violence 9
  exam questions 16–17
  family home 9
  inheritance 14
  key cases 15–16
  key debates 16
  key facts 1
  Law Commission
    proposals 15
  maintenance 10
  marriage/civil partnership
    distinguished 9–14
  meaning 7–8
  occupation order 9, 66–8
  pre-marital 91
  property redistribution
    10–14
  reform of law 14–15
  termination 8–9
common law marriage 7
consent
  adoption 152–3
    placement for 148, 149
  child abduction 165, 171
  marriage voidable for lack
    of 27–9
  separation and 42–3
constructive trusts 11
contact order 112–13, 156
  activity conditions and
    directions 113
  applicants 118
  direct contact 112
  effect of other orders 156
  indirect contact 112
  staying 112
contempt of court
  domestic violence
    protection 62, 69
Council of Europe 168

desertion
  continued cohabitation 42

marriage breakdown 41–2
dissolution of civil
    partnership 37–8
  behaviour 40–1
  conditional dissolution
    order 37
  desertion 41–2
  exam questions 53
  financial provision see
    financial provision,
    divorce/dissolution
  five facts 37, 38–43
  ground 37, 38
  irretrievable breakdown 38
  key debates 52–3
  key facts 36
  mediation 48–50
  nullity distinguished 20
  separation
    five years 43
    separation order 50
    two years with
      consent 42–3
divorce 3, 37–8
  adultery 39
  bars to 38, 44–5
  behaviour 40–1
  children 44–5
  clean break 91, 92–3
  decree absolute 37
  decree nisi 37
  defence 43–4
  desertion 41–2
  exam questions 53
  Family Law Act 1996 47–8
  financial provision see
    financial provision,
    divorce/dissolution
  five facts 37, 38–43
  ground 37, 38
  irretrievable breakdown
    38
  judicial separation see
    judicial separation
  key cases 51–2
  key debates 52–3
  key facts 36
  mediation 48–50
  no-fault 46–8
  nullity distinguished 20

problems with current
    law 45–6
  religious marriages 44
  separation
    five years 43
    two years with
      consent 42–3
domestic violence
  associated persons 59–61
  causes 56–7
  civil law remedies 57, 58
  cohabitation 9
  contact order 113
  contempt of court 62
  criminal law remedies 57
  criminal offences 71–2
  dealing with 57–8
  definition 55–6
  domestic violence
    protection notice
    (DVPN) 72
  domestic violence
    protection order
    (DVPO) 72
  enforcement of orders
    contempt of court 62, 69
    non-molestation order 62
    occupation order 69
    power of arrest 62, 69
    undertakings 70
    warrant of arrest 62
  ex parte orders 69–70
  exam questions 75–6
  harassment 70–2
  key cases 73–5
  key debates 75
  key facts 54
  non-molestation order 54,
    58–9
    applicants 59–61
    associated persons 59–61
    child applicant 61
    contempt of court 62
    duration 61
    effect of breach 62
    enforcement 62
    ex parte orders 69–70
    molestation defined 59
    overview 55
    power of arrest 62

Index

✱✱✱✱✱✱✱✱✱✱✱✱

domestic violence (*cont.*)
relevant child 61
warrant of arrest 62
when made 61
occupation order 54, 62
applicants 63
cohabitant or former
cohabitant 9, 66-8
entitled to occupy 65-6
former spouse or former
civil partner 66
no right to occupy 67-8
applications 64-9
breach of order 69
duration 69
enforcement 69
ex parte orders 69-70
factors considered 64-5
power of arrest 69
process 68
provisions 69
significant harm test 63-4
summary 68-9
power of arrest 61, 69
relevant child 61
remedies 57, 58
statistics 56
undertakings 70
warrant of arrest 62
**domestic violence protection
notice (DVPN)** 72
**domestic violence protection
order (DVPO)** 72
duress
marriage voidable for 27-8

e-Borders process 167
**emergency protection
order** 127, 128
applicants 129
duration 130
effects 129-30
exclusion requirements 130
grounds 129
summary 137
enforcement of orders
child abduction 163
contempt of court 62, 69
non-molestation order 62
occupation order 69

power of arrest 62, 69
undertakings 70
warrant of arrest 62
**European Convention
on Recognition
and Enforcement
of Decisions
concerning Custody of
Children** 168
extradition 174-5

false imprisonment 166
see also **abduction of
children**
family assistance order 115
family home
cohabitation 9
intention to share 10-11
parties' shares 11-13
termination, on 10-14
family asset, as 90
right to occupy 9
sale of property order 82
settlement of property 81-2
transfer of property 81
see also **property**
Family Law Act 1996
no-fault divorce 47-8
reasons for failure 47
**Family Procedure Rules
2010** 79, 116
**financial provision, for
children**
adoption 156
child maintenance
applicability 94-5
Child Support Agency 94
meaning 94
non-resident parent 95
periodical payments
and 96
qualifying child 94-5
reform 95
shared care 95
Child Support Act 1991
94-5
Children Act 1989 96
Civil Partnership Act 2004
96
cohabitation 9

key facts 77
lump sum order 96
Matrimonial Causes
Act 1973 96
periodical payments 80, 96
residence order 156
settlement of property
order 96
special guardianship 156
transfer of property
order 96
**financial provision, divorce/
dissolution**
age of parties 91
appeal 94
bar to divorce 44
challenging orders 94
circumstances of case 87-9
clean break 91, 92-3
cohabitation 10
compensation 86, 87
conduct of parties 92
contributions 92
duration of marriage 91
exam questions 99-100
factors taken into
account 85
age of parties 91
circumstances of
case 87-9
conduct of parties 92
contributions 91
disabilities 91
duration of marriage 91
income and resources
of parties 89-90
of third party 90
mental disability 91
needs, obligations and
responsibilities 90
pensions 82, 92
physical disability 91
pre-marital
cohabitation 91
relevant case law 85-6
standard of living 91
statutory factors 85,
87-92
value of benefit lost 92
welfare of child 85, 89

fairness 86–7
family assets 90
Family Procedure
    Rules 2010 79
financial needs 86
income and resources
    of parties 89–90
    of third party 90
inherited property 89
interim relief 79
key cases 97–8
key debates 98–9
key facts 77–8
lump sums 80, 83–4
maintenance pending
    suit 79
marital property 89–90
Martin order 81
mediation 48–50
Mesher order 81
money orders 79–80, 83–4
needs, obligations and
    responsibilities 90
nuptial agreements 77,
    87–9
pensions 92
    attachment order 82,
        83–4
    sharing order 82, 83–4
periodical payments
    order 80, 83–4
physical or mental
    disability 91
pre-marital cohabitation 91
property orders 81–2, 83–4
sale of property 82
secured periodical
    payments 80, 83–4
settlement of property
    81–2, 83–4
standard of living 91
summary 83–4
transfer of property 81,
    83–4
variation of orders 84, 93–4
welfare of child 85, 89
'yardstick of equality' 87
forced marriage 2–3, 72–3
foster parents
    s 8 orders 118

gender reassignment
    marriage 3–4, 24
    voidable marriages 30–1
guardianship
    parental responsibility 109,
        110–11, 154
    special 109, 110–11, 150,
        154–5, 156–7

Hague Convention 172–4
    child abduction 168–9
    opposing applications 170
harassment
    civil proceedings 72
    offences 72
    Protection from
        Harassment Act 1997
        70–2
    restraining order 71
harm
    children
        abduction cases 171–2
        harm suffered or at
            risk 116, 117, 127–8,
            131, 134, 150
        significant harm 127–8,
            131, 134
        significant harm test 63–4
human rights
    adoption 145
    children 104, 125
    marriage 2

inheritance
    cohabitation 14
    property 89

judicial separation 36,
    38, 50
    civil partnership 50
    reasons for 50–1

kidnapping 166
    see also **abduction of**
        children

local authorities, children
    adoption 146–7
    care order 131–2
        exclusion criteria 130

parental
    responsibility 108, 109
    summary 136
    supervision order
        compared 134–5
    threshold criteria 132–4
care proceedings 131
child assessment order 131,
    136
dual planning 148
duties 124
    accommodation 127
    children in need 126–7
    general duty 126
    investigation of
        welfare 119, 127–8
    emergency protection
        order 128–30, 137
    interim order 136
    parental responsibility 108,
        109, 132
    placement order 135, 148–9
    recovery order 137
    supervision order 131–2
        care order
            compared 134–5
        summary 136
        threshold criteria 132–4
    wardship 137–8
lump sum order 80, 83–4
    for children 96

maintenance pending suit 79
marriage
    arranged 2
    bigamy 4, 24
    civil partnership
        compared 7
    cohabitation
        distinguished 9–14
    common law 7
    definition 2–5
    exam questions 16–17
    exclusion of all others 4–5
    family home 9
    finances *see* **financial**
        provision, divorce/
        dissolution
    forced 2–3, 72–3
    formalities 6–7

Index

****

marriage (*cont.*)
 formation 6
 gender reassignment 3–4, 24
 inheritance 14
 key cases 15–16
 key debates 16
 key facts 1
 life, for 3
 man and woman 3–4
 non-marriage 20
 nullity *see* **nullity**
 polygamous 4–5, 24
 presumption of death of
  spouse 24
 prohibited degrees 6, 22–3
 religious marriages 44
 same-sex 4
 sham 21
 termination 3
  see also **divorce; nullity**
 void *see* **void marriages**
 voidable *see* **voidable**
  marriages
 voluntary nature 2–3
Martin **order** 81
mediation
 advantages 49
 meaning 48–9
 problems 49–50
Mesher **order** 81
mirror order 167–8
mistake
 marriage voidable for 28–9

no delay principle
 adoption 147–8
 child protection 131, 132
 s 8 orders 115
no order principle
 adoption 155
 child protection 131, 133
 s 8 orders 116
no-fault divorce 46–8
 Family Law Act 1996 47–8
non-molestation order 54,
  58–9
 applicants 59–61
 associated persons 59–61
 child applicant 61
 contempt of court 62

 duration 61
 effect of breach 62
 enforcement 62
 ex parte orders 69–70
 molestation defined 59
 overview 55
 power of arrest 62
 relevant child 61
 warrant of arrest 62
 when made 61
Norgrove Review 125
nullity 3
 bars to grant 20, 31–2
 divorce distinguished 20
 exam questions 34–5
 future of 32
 key cases 33–4
 key debates 34
 key facts 18
 legislation 19–20
 see also **voidable marriages**
nuptial agreements 77, 87–9

occupation of family home
 cohabitation 9
 right to 9
occupation order 54, 62
 applicants 63
  cohabitant or former
   cohabitant 9, 66–8
  entitled to occupy 65–6
  former spouse or former
   civil partner 66
  no right to occupy 67–8
 applications 64–9
 breach of order 69
 declaratory order 62, 65
 duration 69
 enforcement 69
 ex parte orders 69–70
 factors considered 64–5
 power of arrest 69
 provisions 69
 regulatory order 62, 65–6
 significant harm test 63–4
 summary 68–9

parental order 105
parental responsibility
 acquisition 108–10

 adoption 109, 110, 148, 156
 agreement 108
 care order 108, 109
 court order 107–8
 definition 106
 delegated 109–10
 elements 107
 guardianship 109, 110–11,
  154, 156
 key facts 101
 local authority 108, 109,
  132
 loss of 110–15
 overview 102
 persons having 108
 regulation 107
 residence order 109, 110,
  111–12, 156
 revocation 110
 s 8 orders 111–15
 shared 109
 special guardianship 109,
  110–11, 154, 156
 step-parents 108
 unmarried fathers 108
parents
 capability 116, 117, 150
 consent to adoption 152–3
 father 105, 108
 foster parents 118
 IVF 105, 106, 108, 109
 legal 104–6
 lesbian couples 106, 108
 mother 104–5, 108
 other parent 106, 108
 parental order 105
 step-parents 108, 146
 surrogacy 104
 unmarried fathers 108
pensions
 attachment order 82, 83–4
 marriage breakdown 82,
  92
 sharing order 82, 83–4
periodical payments 80, 83–4
 beneficiaries 80, 83
 child support and 96
 for children 80, 96
 secured 80, 83–4
placement order 135, 148–9

police
  child abduction 166
  child protection 127, 128, 137
polygamous marriage 4–5, 24
port alerts 166–7
powers of arrest
  child abduction 167
  domestic violence
      protection 62, 69
  warrant of arrest 62
pre-nuptial agreements *see*
    nuptial agreements
prohibited steps order 114,
    167
property
  beneficial interests 10–11
    constructive trusts 11
    express trusts 10–11
    proprietary estoppel 11
    resulting trusts 11
  inherited 89
  joint ownership 10
  legal ownership 10
  marital 89–90
  ownership by one party
      10–11
  see also **family home**
proprietary estoppel 11

recovery order 137
religious marriages 44
residence order 154
  abduction 167
  applicants 118–19
  child's name 156
  contact orders and 156
  duration 157
  financial support 156
  nationality 156
  parental responsibility 109,
      110, 111–12, 156
  revocation 110
  shared residence 111–12
  travel abroad 114, 156
restraining order 71

s 8 orders
  applicants 118–19
  care/supervision order not
      made 133

contact order 112–13, 118,
    156
  court's powers 118
  factors taken into
      account 115–18
  leave to apply 119
  no delay principle 115
  no order principle 116
  parental responsibility
      and 111–15
  prohibited steps order 114,
      167
  residence order *see*
      residence order
  specific issue order 113–14
  welfare checklist 116–18
  welfare principle 115
sale of property order 82
same-sex marriage 4
separation
  continued cohabitation 43
  five years 43
  judicial 36, 38, 50–1
  mental element 42
  physical element 42–3
  two years with
      consent 42–3
settlement of property
    order 81, 83–4
  beneficiaries 82, 83
  for children 96
  variation 82, 84
sham marriages 21
significant harm test
  occupation order 63–4
special guardianship 109,
    150
  child's name 156
  contact orders and 156
  duration 157
  financial support 156
  nationality of child 156
  order 154–5
  parental responsibility 109,
      110–11, 154, 156
  persons eligible 154–5
  travel abroad 156
specific issue order 113–14
step-parents 108
  adoption 146

supervision order 131–2
  care order compared
      134–5
  summary 136
  threshold criteria 132–4

time limits
  voidable marriages 32
transfer of property
    order 81, 83–4
  for children 96
trusts
  constructive 11
  express 10–11
  resulting 11

UK Border Agency 166–7
undertakings
  domestic violence
      protection 70

void marriages
  already married 24
  disregard of
      requirements 23
  either party under 16 23
  grounds 19, 21–4
  meaning 18
  non-marriage
      distinguished 20
  parties not male and
      female 24
  polygamy 24
  prohibited degrees 22–3
  voidable marriages
      distinguished 20, 21
voidable marriages
  bars to nullity 31–2
  duress 27–8
  gender reassignment 30–1
  grounds 19, 25–31
  incapacity 26–7
  knowledge of facts 32
  lack of consent 27–9
  meaning 18
  mental disorder 29
  mistake 28–9
  non-consummation 26
  pregnancy by another
      30

Index

voidable marriages (*cont.*)
time limits 32
unsoundness of mind
29
venereal disease 30
void marriages
distinguished 20, 21

wilful refusal to
consummate 27

wardship 137–8, 167
welfare of child
delay 115, 131, 133, 147–8
marriage breakdown 85, 89

reports and
investigations 119,
127–8
welfare checklist 116–18,
133, 149–50
welfare principle 115, 131,
133